Decentralization and Democracy in Latin America

RECENT TITLES FROM THE HELEN KELLOGG INSTITUTE
FOR INTERNATIONAL STUDIES

Scott Mainwaring, *general editor*

The University of Notre Dame Press gratefully thanks the Hellen Kellogg Institute
for International Studies for its support in the publication of titles in this series.

Juan E. Méndez, Guillermo O'Donnell, and Paulo Sérgio Pinheiro, eds.
The (Un)Rule of Law and the Underprivileged in Latin America (1999)

Guillermo O'Donnell
Counterpoints: Selected Essays on Authoritarianism and Democratization (1999)

Howard Handelman and Mark Tessler, eds.
*Democracy and Its Limits: Lessons from Asia, Latin America,
and the Middle East* (1999)

Larissa Adler Lomnitz and Ana Melnick
Chile's Political Culture and Parties: An Anthropological Explanation (2000)

Kevin Healy
*Llamas, Weavings, and Organic Chocolate: Multicultural Grassroots
Development in the Andes and Amazon of Bolivia* (2000)

Ernest J. Bartell, C.S.C., and Alejandro O'Donnell
The Child in Latin America: Health, Development, and Rights (2000)

Vikram K. Chand
Mexico's Political Awakening (2001)

Ruth Berins Collier and David Collier
Shaping the Political Arena (2002)

Glen Biglaiser
Guardians of the Nation? (2002)

Alberto Spektorowski
The Origins of Argentina's Revolution of the Right (2003)

Caroline C. Beer
Electoral Competition and Institutional Change in Mexico (2003)

Yemile Mizrahi
From Martyrdom to Power (2003)

Charles D. Kenney
Fujimori's Coup and the Breakdown of Democracy in Latin America (2003)

For a complete list of titles from the Helen Kellogg Institute for International
Studies, see http://www.undpress.nd.edu

Decentralization
AND
Democracy
IN
LATIN AMERICA

Alfred P. Montero & David J. Samuels
EDITORS

UNIVERSITY OF NOTRE DAME PRESS
Notre Dame, Indiana

Manufactured in the United States of America

Library of Congress Cataloging-in-Publication Data
Decentralization and democracy in Latin America /
Alfred P. Montero and David J. Samuels, editors.
p. cm.
"Recent titles from the Helen Kellogg Institute for International Studies."
Includes bibliographical references and index.
ISBN 0-268-02558-4 (cloth : alk. paper)
ISBN 0-268-02559-2 (pbk. : alk. paper)
1. Decentralization in government—Latin America.
I. Montero, Alfred P., 1969– .   II. Samuels, David, 1967– .
III. Helen Kellogg Institute for International Studies.
JL959.5.D42D458   2004
320.8'098—dc22
2003024940

∞ *This book is printed on acid-free paper.*

Contents

PART III
CONSEQUENCES FOR ECONOMIC REFORM

Tables and Figures

FIGURES

Acknowledgments

We thank the institutions that financed the conference held at the University of Minnesota on February 11–12, 2000, that launched this book project: the Latin American Studies Program at Carleton College, and the College of Liberal Arts and the Department of Political Science at the University of Minnesota.

Numerous scholars commented on drafts of the chapters. In addition to the contributors who participated at the initial meeting, we thank Tulia Falleti, Jonathan Rodden, and Eliza Willis, who joined us during that wintry February in Minnesota and provided their ideas. We thank Scott Mainwaring for taking a strong interest in the book manuscript and Jeff Gainey, associate director of the University of Notre Dame Press, for shepherding the project to publication. Finally, we wish to thank the press's two anonymous reviewers who provided useful comments on an earlier draft of the entire manuscript.

PART I
Introduction

CHAPTER I

The Political Determinants of Decentralization in Latin America

Causes and Consequences

ALFRED P. MONTERO & DAVID J. SAMUELS

Among the major political changes that have shaped Latin America since independence, decentralization of the state—the assignment of political, fiscal, and administrative duties to subnational governments—has been one of the most overlooked. Instead, scholars of the region have tended to focus more attention on what Claudio Véliz (1980) called the "centralist tradition" of Latin American politics, which asserts that highly centralized colonial-era political institutions generated a political culture that exerted a strong path-dependent effect on subsequent political evolution. Thus, political science research has focused on the evolution of the organs of the central government, in particular given the state-centered model of economic development in the twentieth century along with the emergence of state "corporatist" institutions and norms that affect state-society relations (e.g., Stepan, 1978; Wiarda, 1986; Collier and Collier, 1991; Cavarozzi, 1992). Yet, as is so often the case, the reality of Latin American politics has escaped the purview of the

3

"centralist tradition" in scholarship. Subnational governments and politicians have played and continue to play a major role in policy making, economic development, and democratization in the region. More recently, decentralization has been a key element of the major political transformations that Latin American states have experienced over the last two decades or so, along with regime change and the collapse of the developmentalist state. This development poses a puzzle for the centralist tradition, which assumes that the political, social, and economic forces that might favor decentralization are absent in Latin America. Yet the emerging empirical importance of decentralization suggests that scholars should focus their theoretical lenses on the phenomenon. Thus the major question that drives this collection: What explains decentralization in Latin America?

Subnational officials across Latin America—governors, state legislators, mayors, and city council members—now possess a historically unprecedented level of political authority and fiscal autonomy. For example, from 1980 to 1995 the number of countries in the region allowing the direct election of mayors increased from three to seventeen. In many countries, intermediate tiers of government have also emerged *de novo* or reemerged as autonomous units. In addition, keeping pace with these political developments, subnational governments' share of total public spending expanded impressively during the 1980s and 1990s (Stein, 1999). Democratization and neoliberal reforms have tended to reduce the role of the central government in politics as well as the market, and the growing importance of subnational governments and local or regional economies demands that scholars of Latin America turn their attention to the politics of subnational government (Ames, 1999: 232–33).

Of course, decentralization has not taken the same form or degree throughout the region or even within countries. Some public policies have been decentralized, while others remain largely in the hands of the central government; some countries remain highly centralized, while others have moved in the opposite direction; subnational governments in some regions within some countries have taken control of numerous policies, while governments in other regions remain deeply dependent on their central government for both resources and policy administration. We believe that these differences are not simply a matter of different local demands for services, different local capacities to raise revenue or administer programs, or varying technocratic views of which "correct formula" for decentralization will maximize welfare, macroeconomic stability, or growth. The purpose of this book is to demonstrate that political choices and political institutions have played a major role in explaining the variation in the form, degree, and success of decentralization in Latin America.

Little research has concentrated on the political causes of decentralization. Although a number of studies have examined institutional and policy variations among countries that have decentralized (e.g., Nickson, 1995; Bird and Vaillancourt, 1998; Burki, Perry, and Dillinger, 2000), research has tended not to *explain* the patterns of decentralization, but rather to focus on policy design ("getting the rules right") and fiscal issues. This book concentrates on the *political determinants* of variation in the patterns of decentralization in Latin America, and we hope that it sparks further research.[1]

The following chapters cover six significant cases of decentralization in Latin America: Argentina, Bolivia, Brazil, Chile, Mexico, and Venezuela. Additionally, some contributors include shorter analyses of Uruguay and Peru. This selection includes cases of two-tier subnational government (Argentina, Brazil, Mexico, and Venezuela) as well as one-tier cases (Bolivia and Chile). The former cases are also the major federal states of the region while the latter two are unitary. Table 1.1 summarizes the major characteristics of our case studies.

DEFINITIONAL ISSUES

Let us first address the question of identifying our object of study. Decentralization is, like many social science concepts, not easily and precisely defined. We view decentralization as a multidimensional process: it may have political, fiscal, and administrative dynamics. We examine these aspects of decentralization before exploring the causes and consequences of this process in Latin America. *Political* decentralization refers to direct elections of state/provincial[2] and/or local political offices. This dimension of decentralization addresses the arena that Stepan (1988) calls "political society": executive and legislative offices that politicians occupy as opposed to those held by executives, bureaucrats, and other civil servants. The extent and timing of political decentralization in Latin America—a move toward expanded formal electoral competition at the subnational level—has varied. For example, our survey includes polities that have had direct elections for governor and state legislatures and/or mayor and city councils since the nineteenth century. Yet other nations

Table 1.1. Structure, Degree, and Timing of Decentralization in the Country Cases

	Intermediate Level	Local Level	Subnational Share of Total Spending[a] (%)	Timing of Subnational Elections
Argentina	23 provinces	~1,100 municipalities	49	Since 1912 for provinces and since 1950s for municipalities. No provincial elections in 1930–46 and 1955–58. No provincial or municipal elections in 1962–63, 1966–73, and 1976–83.
Bolivia	9 departments[b]	308 municipalities	27	Since 1985 for municipalities.
Brazil	26 states, 1 federal district	~5,500 municipalities	46	Since 1891 for states and municipalities except 1930–46 and 1964–82 for states, and 1937–46 for municipalities.
Chile	13 regions[b]	335 municipalities	14	Since 1891, but limited from 1925 to 1973 and abolished from 1973 to 1992. Autonomous contests since 1992 for all municipalities.
Mexico	31 states, 1 federal district	2,397 municipalities	25	Since 1979 (de jure), 1982 in municipalities (de facto), and 1989 in states (de facto).
Venezuela	22 states, 1 federal district, federal dependencies	282 municipalities	20	Since 1989 for governors and municipalities (de facto).

a Source of subnational share is Stein (1999).
b These entities have little autonomy.

such as Bolivia, Mexico, and Venezuela have only more recently moved toward direct democratic election of subnational officials.

Political decentralization implies that subnational elections gain importance for both political actors and citizens. However, this book finds a corollary to the democratization literature's rejection of the "electoralist fallacy," which supposes that elections constitute democracy.[3] That is, the direct election of subnational officials does not necessarily mean that the country in question is highly decentralized, politically or otherwise. Political decentralization is only one significant dimension of the broader process of decentralization. If subnational government controls few resources and has no policy autonomy, subnational elections might be fairly meaningless. Thus, decentralization of fiscal resources and policy authorities are also necessary to empower subnational government.

Fiscal decentralization has two main dimensions: revenue decentralization and expenditure decentralization.[4] Revenue decentralization is the relative degree to which subnational governments come to control the sources of their revenues, usually taxes and/or national government transfers. Expenditure decentralization refers to the degree to which subnational governments may autonomously decide how to spend their revenues, and how much of their revenues to spend, independently of central-government guidelines or earmarking. In practice, fiscal decentralization may occur in both of these dimensions and to distinct degrees in the same country and over time.

Fiscal decentralization is, for obvious reasons, intimately related to the third dimension of decentralization, *administrative* or *policy* decentralization. Policy decentralization is the relative authority or responsibility that state/provincial and local governments have to set goals, muster resources, and administer and implement public policy. It may result from either an actual transfer of policy responsibility from one level of government to another or from the assumption of responsibility for public policy in an area where central-government coverage is lacking by an "entrepreneurial" public official. Thus, this kind of subnational autonomy has both de jure and de facto dimensions. Subnational policy autonomy varies de jure in terms of the categories of policies that are assigned (constitutionally or through legislation) to subnational governments and also in terms of the conditions (earmarking or mandates) that national governments place on the use of fiscal resources or on the range of policy choice. Policy autonomy varies de facto by the capacity that subnational governments have to be "policy entrepreneurs," which requires not only fiscal resources but also a capable subnational bureaucracy.

By noting the differences between political, fiscal, and policy decentralization, we hope to draw attention to the fact that decentralization is a *multidimensional* process that has a variety of combinations that may or may not occur simultaneously. For example, policy decentralization may occur along some dimensions but not others. Or, policy decentralization can occur without direct elections for subnational office. Policy responsibilities can also be decentralized (as they were in Carlos Menem's Argentina) in the absence of sufficient financing ("unfunded mandates" or "centralization via decentralization," as Wibbels [this volume] calls it). Finally, fiscal resources may be "decentralized" to subnational governments but be distributed according to central government priorities. The chapters in this volume attest to these multiple combinations. Research must pay careful attention to the particulars of each country's laws and political processes in order to reveal how and to what extent decentralization results in greater or reduced political autonomy for different levels of government.

The multidimensionality of the decentralization process has led some scholars to refer to certain aspects of decentralization with other terms: "deconcentration," "devolution," "delegation," and so on.[5] The number of empirical combinations exceeds the availability of distinct monikers. Rather than confuse the research program with a proliferation of terms, we prefer to speak of these as different dimensions of one decentralizing dynamic, and we therefore focus on the political logic that explains why certain policies are relatively more or less decentralized both across and within countries. This approach obviates the necessity to invent terms.

By claiming that decentralization is a political *process,* we mean three things. First, that the concept encompasses relatively long historical periods. Second, that decentralization involves political choices and is not inevitable. And third, that decentralization is not irreversible. These points are particularly important to keep in mind: although the degree of decentralization in Latin America has recently become unprecedented, countries across the region have all experienced swings along the centralization/decentralization continuum. For example, Getúlio Vargas's corporatist *Estado Novo* in Brazil and the centralized party regime of Chile between 1935 and 1970 period are early examples of centralization of previously less centralized regimes (see Eaton, this volume). These two examples also imply (and some of our contributors confirm) that there is no necessary link between democracy and decentralization (see below). Thus, a process definition leaves open the possibility that decentralization can be reversed. The advent of recentralizing reforms along some dimensions of policy in Argentina, Brazil, Venezuela, and Chile in the 1990s already constitutes empirical evidence for that outcome. Of course, these recentralized cases may one day decentralize again.

It may be too soon to claim that decentralization may have a "pendular" or even "regular" symmetry that can be mapped out according to general trends in Latin American history. But given the fact that some recentralization has already occurred within a broader process of political decentralization, we ought to accept decentralization as a *process* without a clear *telos* lying at either end of the recentralization/decentralization spectrum. With these definitional issues and caveats in mind, in the next section we consider some of the major hypotheses that seek to explain the political determinants of decentralization.

Assessing the Political Determinants of Decentralization in Latin America

We ought not to limit the consideration of the causal dynamics of decentralization to inductively compiling a set of independent variables and weighing their importance in country case studies. It is also not enough to understand how decentralization occurred in any one country or time period. Following much of the comparative scholarship on economic reform and democratization in Latin America, we seek to discover general patterns and to offer generalizable hypotheses concerning decentralization. Before discussing the hypotheses we have identified in the debates surrounding decentralization, we describe three methodological issues that appear in the literature and that serve to indicate the approaches that the contributors to this volume take to the causes of decentralization.

Methodological Issues

Scholars often characterize their arguments as either a "top-down" or a "bottom-up" approach. Of course, one is often tempted to comment that both matter. When are top-down decisions more important than bottom-up pressures, and vice versa? For our purposes, "top-down" arguments refer to *national* (elected and/or appointed) *policy-makers'* decision calculus, particularly why they might possess incentives to decentralize. For example, democratically elected presidents and legislators may favor decentralization under conditions that enhance their continued political survival (e.g., when decentralization increases the probability of reelection or the persistence of their partisan majority). In newly democratized regimes, national political elites might also advocate decentralization to extirpate authoritarian enclaves. These actors may also cultivate the support of subnational constituencies and local politicians by decentralizing. On the other hand, other national-level political actors may resist decentralization because it would constrict their future control over policymaking.

The top-down logic applies in authoritarian regimes as well. Authoritarian executives and bureaucrats at the national level may embrace decentralization after appointing subnational executives and bureaucrats, as a means of further tightening their control over the apparatus of government at all levels. Or, in authoritarian regimes that retain at least some direct elections for subnational offices, decentralization may also favor those who control the national government by strengthening the political elites who provide the regime with its base of support at the local level. On the other hand, "decentralization under dictatorship" might spin out of a regime's control and hinder its plans for political consolidation.

In short, central-government actors face a trade-off in that decentralization may advance some political goals but impede others. The cost of decentralization may vary according to the degree of power that central-government authorities retain over the collection and spending of tax revenues and the extent to which the control of subnational offices strengthens government leaders at the national level (whether democratic or not).

In contrast to top-down approaches, for our purposes "bottom-up" analyses highlight the importance of *subnational policy-makers'* incentives, goals, and decisions for an explanation of decentralization. For example, in democracies and authoritarian regimes with local elections, subnational elites might embrace decentralization of responsibilities and resources to enhance their own autonomy from the central government and to build up political capital through policy-making accomplishments and/or patronage. Under democracy, subnational political elites may possess tremendous leverage over national elites, as some of our case studies show. In these cases, the incentives for decentralization to proceed in particular ways are relatively greater. Under authoritarian rule, subnational political elites possess relatively less leverage over national policy-makers, but their ability to command a reservoir of democratic legitimacy might still make them formidable constituencies that authoritarian leaders must satisfy.

Subnational political elites also face a series of trade-offs in terms of decentralization. For example, decentralization may advance a goal of limiting the central government's authority, but it also means tremendous responsibility for newly empowered subnational officials. If voters are aware of decentralization, they will consequently demand much more of subnational officials. The strategies of subnational elites, therefore, are a function of their evaluation of decentralization's potential political risks and gains.

In cross-national perspective, we believe that neither top-down nor bottom-up approaches alone suffice.[6] Instead, it is the *interaction* between national and subnational political elites in both democratic and authoritarian regimes that is critical to understanding the incentives for decentralization. We return to this point below regarding the particular role of democratization.

It is useful to ask here whether the identity of the relevant decision-makers may be broader than we have just suggested, in particular for the bottom-up approach. Actors outside the government such as economic classes, nongovernmental organizations, labor unions, firms, and associations may exert important bottom-up pressures for decentralization. Or, less organized but forceful voter pressure could even be important. For example, in the Bolivian case, regional civic committees of businessmen campaigned for decentralization during the early 1990s (see O'Neill, this volume). However, a fuller examination of the cases indicates that these extra-governmental actors have only rarely played a prominent role in the promotion and implementation of decentralization and have instead tended to rely on politicians and their parties as interlocutors. Thus, excepting some policy-specific areas (Murillo, 1999), we suggest that actors in political society and the state have played the primary role in initiating, implementing, and shaping decentralization (Manor, 1999; Willis, Garman, and Haggard, 1999). Why this is the case is a question beyond the scope of this volume, but it points to the importance of positing an explicitly *political* logic of decentralization.

Another methodological issue to consider is the connection between "distal" and "proximal" causes. The prominent study by Willis et al. (1999) as well as the vast majority of the policy-oriented literature on decentralization has focused almost exclusively on the most recent period of decentralization, i.e., on proximal causes of decentralization. Yet there are no necessary reasons for limiting the research program to recent times, and in fact we see a danger in doing so. Such a time-bound approach focuses attention only on more recent potential causes of decentralization such as the debt crisis, the latest wave of neoliberal reforms, and democratization. Not only does this neglect the role of important distal factors such as patterns of urbanization, economic change, and persistent path-dependent institutional and social legacies, it also constrains the testing of general hypotheses to those based on potentially time-bound proximal causes. For example, it is highly possible that evidence allegedly demonstrating a close correlation between democratization and decentralization during the 1980s and 1990s is just that: a correlation. We cannot move from correlation to a discussion of causation if we cannot control for variables endemic to the most recent time period. A focus on recent times implicitly and arbitrarily rejects distal factors. Several of the contributions to this volume considerably broaden the research program on decentralization by pursuing longitudinal comparisons and by considering both distal and proximal factors.

A final methodological issue is the link between "macro" and "micro" factors. By favoring recent events, the "presentist" bias in some of the literature focuses too much on elite decision making, to the exclusion of sociostructural factors.[7] We believe that scholars ought to understand how demographic and economic changes shape the range of elite choices, and how existing social and economic structures shape the possible limits of decentralization both across and within countries. In addition, although institutional configurations—electoral rules, bureaucratic structures, fiscal patterns, and so forth—constrain elite choice at the time the decision to decentralize occurs, these rules are themselves the product of broader socioeconomic and institutional legacies. Therefore, analyses that employ a "micro" logic to understand decisions to decentralize should couple their explanation to a macro logic: the broader contextual factors that "set up" the micro logics that explain politicians' actual decisions. Indeed, decentralization in several of the countries in this study would not have been possible but for macro processes such as demographic, institutional, and economic change that determined the range of choices at the time that national and/or subnational elites opted for decentralization.[8]

In short, the contributors to this volume are not wedded to one particular methodological approach. The analyses here adopt neither a broad macrofoundational approach, nor do they rely on a purely microfoundational approach to politics. Research on decentralization could hardly adopt a traditional state-centered approach, since the object of study is not "the State" but the evolving dynamic between the states, the central government, and municipalities. On the other hand, although decentralization focuses attention on the actions of elected national and subnational politicians and thus on the micro incentives that such politicians face, we believe that path-dependent economic and political legacies are too important to ignore.

With the methodological issues in mind, we can now assess the major hypotheses regarding the political determinants of decentralization in Latin America. To be sure, our list is not exhaustive and each category needs further unpacking. Still, this list addresses the major economic, ideational, political-institutional, and macro factors present in the literature on decentralization.

Decentralization as a Neoliberal Reform

Arguments under this rubric hold that decentralization follows a particular political-economic logic, and that it emerges primarily in countries undergoing a weakening of state-led development models and the emergence of more market-oriented strategies. Several observers have connected the most recent wave of decentralization reforms in Latin America to the crisis and erosion of what Marcelo Cavarozzi (1992) has called the "state-centered matrix": a model of development based on import-substitution and extensive state intervention and regulation of markets. According to this view, the constraints produced by structural adjustments in response to the macroeconomic disequilibria produced, in turn, by the debt crisis of the 1980s compelled national authorities to decentralize the provision of major public goods and services to subnational government (e.g., Rondinelli, 1989).

Before considering this line of argument further, it is useful to ask if decentralization has historically been uniformly associated with any particular political-economic framework. The answer is clearly that it has not. Quite simply, both developmentalist and neoliberal governments have historically decentralized *and* recentralized. The developmentalist regimes of Juan Perón in Argentina and Juscelino Kubitschek in Brazil utilized decentralization, as did their neoliberal successors decades later during the 1980s and 1990s. Vargas's *Estado Novo* and the *Processo* governments of Argentina recentralized, but their economic policies were mirror opposites. While these examples do not eliminate "decentralization as neoliberal reform" from consideration, they sharply delimit the scope of this approach in explaining decentralization.

It is plausible that decentralization in the recent neoliberal period in Latin America is a specific response to pervasive fiscal deficits. Bresser Pereira (1993) and others have argued that the fiscal crisis of Latin American economies was the most salient factor strengthening the "Washington Consensus" reforms that swept the region in the 1980s and 1990s. Decentralization fits into that logic since devolution of policy responsibilities may free up resources at the national level (Bird and Vaillancourt, 1998: 4). Decentralization also reduces the costs of government by tapping into "allocative efficiencies" produced through a more rational division of labor among government levels. By following the "subsidiarity principle," a concept central to the study of fiscal federalism, decentralization may minimize the information asymmetries that commonly afflict centralized micromanagement of policies in areas such as education, health care, and housing, which require specific local knowledge (Oates, 1972; Musgrave, 1983). Moreover, interjurisdictional competition in service delivery may enhance the provision of government services by providing incentives for policy-makers to attract consumer-voters and businesses across subnational boundaries (Dye, 1990).[9] Fiscal federalism, therefore, enhances the efficiency of both national and subnational governments. That it emerges now throughout a region suffering from fiscal crisis should thus not be surprising.

As much as the fiscal federalist logic appeals to the international financial agencies (e.g., IDB, 1997; Campbell, Peterson, and Brakarz, 1991), we find little evidence that promoting efficiency in public policy in response to fiscal constraints has been a primary motive behind decentralization efforts in Latin America. Some cases decentralized under conditions of fiscal stability (Bolivia) while others recentralized in the face of fiscal crisis (Argentina; Brazil in the late 1990s). In fact, Wibbels (this volume) finds that the "economic efficiency" logic for decentralization often conflicts with decentralizers' political motives; as the Menem administration attempted to stabilize the economy, the expansive fiscal policy of many provincial governments foiled repeated attempts to consolidate reform at the national level (Remmer and Wibbels, 2000). The consequent intergovernmental conflict compelled Menem to recentralize fiscal authority and resources in ways that ultimately undercut the theorized economic and political advantages of decentralization. Increasingly, as they have become more concerned with the effects of decentralization on macroeconomic reform and structural adjustment, both international financial institutions (IFIs) and scholars have paid attention to this conflict between the economic and political logics for decentralization (Dillinger, Perry, and Webb, 1999; Prud'homme, 1995; Ter-Minassian, 1997; Tanzi, 1995; Treisman, 1999; Wibbels, 2001). In short, although we agree that the principles of efficiency, equity, and stability that inspire the policy literature are important, these ideas are not the chief motivating factors behind decentralization as it is conceived and practiced in Latin America.

Decentralization as the Result of International Factors

While neoliberal reforms have not made decentralization necessary, a number of the international factors that have accompanied the shift to market-oriented policies in the region might be more directly responsible for decentralization. The most prominent that we consider include the increased openness of Latin America's markets to foreign investors, the transnationalization of production, and the advice of international financial institutions on macroeconomic reform and structural adjustment.

The liberalization of Latin America's financial markets during the 1990s created new opportunities for state and local governments to finance their expenditures and attract investors. State and even some municipal governments have sold notes and cajoled investors with catchy advertisements in newspapers and international magazines such as the *Economist*. The privatization wave during the 1990s added to the trend by creating incentives for state and municipal managers of subnational public firms and regions dependent upon the national public sector to form ties to interested investors. While these changes have, in some places, involved subnational governments in their national and local economies in new ways, the proposition that these trends are a primary cause of decentralization in the region is untenable. Financial liberalization did not clearly accompany pre-1990 episodes of decentralization and in some cases, such as Argentina and Brazil, deregulation *followed* political and fiscal decentralization.

By contrast, foreign direct investors enjoy a longer history in the region. Globalization of production has created new opportunities for subnational governments to attract major components of expanding "commodity chains" by offering tax abatements, skilled labor, and infrastructure (Willis, 1996). Interjurisdictional competition for foreign investment has added to the pressure on subnational governments to implement so-called industrial policies. The case of new automotive investments in Brazil, where competing tax abatement schemes have produced a fiscal war among the states, illustrates this trend.[10] This dynamic, however, has not taken the same form in all countries. Mexico, which faces even greater pressures than Brazil to integrate production globally and especially across the border with the United States, has relied largely on federal policies such as the regulations governing the *maquiladora* or in-bond manufacturing sector. Moreover, there is little evidence that the incentives created by more dynamic export sectors and foreign investment to develop subnational forms of public goods provision explain decentralization. Beer (this volume) tests the importance of the growth of the *maquiladora* sector in Mexico but finds that this factor is statistically insignificant, although the incentives for states to develop their own revenue sources are stronger than the incentives to simply spend on public goods.

As liberalization of financial and production markets has become the chief constraint on both macroeconomic and structural adjustment policies in the region, the advice and public support of the international financial institutions, and particularly the International Monetary Fund, have emerged as valuable resources for signaling investors and enhancing domestic business confidence. This advice has included recommendations for decentralization that, as some scholars see it, are part of a neoliberal global discourse (Schuurman, 1998; Nickson, 1995: 24–25). Yet in her insightful survey of IMF, World Bank, and Inter-American Development Bank (IDB) discourse, Falleti (1999) found little evidence that the IFIs recommended fiscal decentralization as part of the slate of structural reforms that composed the initial formulation of the "Washington Consensus." Decentralization emerged as a major theme in the IFI discourse in the region only *after* 1988, and it did not mature until the middle of the 1990s, well after political, fiscal, and administration decentralization were under way in the cases under study here.[11] In other words, IFIs have joined the pro-decentralization chorus quite late, and we can discount their role as primary causal agents or forces that initially promoted decentralization.

Decentralization as a Result of Democratization

Scholars moved quickly to associate democratization, which swept across Latin America in the 1980s and 1990s, with decentralization. The "democratization promotes decentralization" hypothesis is intimately linked to the claim that democratization opens up "bottom-up" pressures for decentralization by creating new political spaces and providing for direct elections at the subnational level (e.g., Beer, this volume). By being "closer to the people," subnational governments are said to be more accountable to their constituencies. Thus, several scholars have suggested that as democratization progressed, pressures for decentralization followed close behind as citizens expressed a demand for more responsive government (Bird and Vaillancourt, 1998; World Bank, 1997; IDB, 1997; Nickson, 1995: 20–21; Souza, 1997).

Yet correlation is insufficient to establish causation, and in many cases there is little evidence that democratization *caused* decentralization. Moreover, in these studies the causal mechanism is never clearly elaborated, and several of our contributors present evidence that actually confounds this hypothesis. For example, O'Neill's study of Bolivia (chapter 2) finds little support for the democratization hypothesis. Although Bolivia had been holding democratic elections for some years, local leaders did not demand autonomy or resources prior to the 1994 Popular Participation Law (*Ley de Participación Popular,* or LPP), which was enacted not *because* Bolivia was democratizing but rather as part of a broader political-partisan dynamic.

A longitudinal, cross-national case comparison also provides only mixed support for the democratization hypothesis. In his four-country comparison of Argentina, Brazil, Chile, and Uruguay, Eaton's study in this volume tests the hypothesis that local elections generate pressures to decentralize fiscal resources. He finds some support for the proposition in Argentina and Brazil but contradictory evidence in Chile and Uruguay. For example, the Chilean Municipal Law that followed the civil war between Congress and the presidency in 1891 decentralized political authority and fiscal resources to municipalities *in the absence of* significant subnational (i.e., bottom-up) pressures to do so. Decentralization at that time served the interests of congressional elites who sought to limit the powers of the presidency. Moreover, in the more recent transition to democracy in Chile, Bland (this volume) finds that decentralization to municipalities was conceived "top-down" through agreements involving right and center-left political forces. Yet he also argues that decentralization was an integral part of elite-based negotiations for democratic transition and consolidation. Bland's treatment of the Chilean case and Beer's work on the role of more competitive subnational elections in Mexico in driving the decentralization process there provide the most compelling evidence in this volume for the decentralization-democratization link. However, systemic evidence for the proposition across the Latin American cases is hard to find.

For example, further consideration of the Argentine and Brazilian cases weakens the democratization-decentralization hypothesis. The Argentine experience suggests that scholars should not assume that decentralization is solely the product of democratic actors or pressures. Eaton notes that Alejandro Lanusse's outgoing military regime in 1973 decentralized revenue shares in favor of the provinces to constrain the incoming Peronist administration. That is, motivated by knowledge of their inevitable defeat, authoritarian elites have incentives to make institutional changes that preempt and constrain democratic elites and in some circumstances institutionalize authoritarian prerogatives (Boylan, 1998; Snyder, 1999). Decentralization may be shaped in ways that produce these same effects, making it a useful tool for antidemocrats. Building on earlier research on the Brazilian case, Samuels' chapter in this volume confirms that a similar process worked in Brazil, where military leaders implemented decentralizing reforms as part of their effort to bolster their support base. That is, decentralization was associated with the *abertura* of the regime, but it did not *follow* from democratization itself. It is important to note that these studies do not deny that democratization matters for the form and degree to which policy authorities and resources are decentralized. Rather they suggest that we require more nuanced hypotheses to tease out the complex linkages between regime change and decentralization.

Sociostructural Causes of Decentralization

Scholars have often associated sociostructural (distal and macro) factors with decentralization. The most important of these variables has been political-economic development itself. On average, the Latin American states (and developing countries in general) are not as decentralized as the more advanced capitalist states. The average subnational share of total government spending in the latter is more than twice the size of the Latin American average (Stein, 1999: 117). Bahl and Linn (1986) have found that this gap has held from the 1960s to the 1990s. Their studies also demonstrate that per capita GNP and urbanization are associated with subnational shares of total public expenditures. To be sure, other factors such as country size influence their findings, but these studies confirm what several authors in this text observe, namely, that urbanization and socioeconomic development strengthen the tendency to decentralize over time.

In particular, high urbanization rates since the 1960s help explain the most recent explosion of decentralizing reforms in the region, which greatly strengthened municipal governments. Diamond (1999: 120) notes that the growth of urban centers has increased the costs of centralized provision of services. The growth of urban populations in less-developed countries from 22 to 52 percent between 1960 and 1990 helps us understand the subsequent process of decentralization. Nevertheless, we currently lack a clear understanding of precisely how these factors affected decentralization in Latin America because most studies have focused upon micro factors such as elite decision making and ignored how longer-term structural changes might have affected these micro considerations. Thus, in an attempt to build our understanding of the role of demographic forces, Samuels' contribution to this volume explains how urbanization altered municipal leaders' political incentives under the military regime (they continued to be directly elected despite military rule) and encouraged an unprecedented process of municipalitization as democratization proceeded.

On the other hand, sociostructural factors also help us understand the *limits* to decentralization. Economic development has proceeded only so far. Urban governments—in both the developed and less-developed world—cannot provide all public services, so the effect of urbanization can also go only so far. Moreover, extreme regional inequalities persist within most Latin American nations. Decentralizing revenue-raising authority obviously cannot help poorer regions if there is little revenue to be raised. In countries with dramatic regional disparities, decentralization might actually exacerbate regional inequalities. Thus, national as well as subnational leaders may face contradictory incentives: subnational leaders might desire the autonomy that decentralization promises, but they dare not bite the hand that feeds them by limiting the central government's capacity to address pressing public needs. Or, national politicians from different regions (even those within the same party) may face opposing pressures to decentralize or not.

In summary, we believe that the recent salience of decentralization in the region should not blind scholars to the potentially critical importance of underlying structural factors that have path-dependent consequences. As several of the chapters in this volume reveal, political, social, and economic legacies, sometimes going back to the late nineteenth and early twentieth centuries, have shaped the politics of centralization and decentralization in more recent years.

Political-Institutional or "Electoralist" Approaches

We believe that to understand decentralization, one must understand the incentives of politicians at all levels of government and the resulting political relationships between national and subnational politicians. These incentives arise from electoral institutions, the internal structure of political parties, and most importantly, politicians' strategic competition, which aims at "political survival" (Ames, 1987). Because decentralization involves shifting power and resources vertically between branches of government, institutional and electoral explanations of decentralization should focus on the way in which subnational politicians are linked to or claim leverage over national politicians and parties. More specifically, such approaches suppose that politicians' incentives to decentralize will be a function of the competitiveness of electoral contests, the relative importance politicians ascribe to subnational (state and/or municipal) versus national elections, politicians' relative dependence on national versus subnational government resources for career advancement or party growth, and the relative importance of national versus subnational "power brokers" within political parties. These approaches assume both that existing political hierarchies exert a path-dependent effect on politicians' choices *and* that politicians are strategic and forward-looking and may attempt to redesign existing institutions to serve an expected future political goal (compare Eaton, Beer, Samuels, Penfold-Becerra, and O'Neill in this volume).

Such approaches take several specific forms in the literature. One variant is exemplified by Willis, Garman, and Haggard (1999), Haggard and Webb (this volume), and Eaton (this volume). These authors start from a "comparative statics" analysis and argue that decentralization varies in degree and form as a function of the interests and location of the party brokers—the political leaders who exert the most influence over political careers. For example, these authors suggest that the relative degree to which subnational political elites (such as governors) influence candidate selection for elections to the *national* legislature helps explain the differences between the more decentralized cases (Argentina and Brazil) and the less decentralized cases (Chile, Mexico, Venezuela and Uruguay). Two contrasting hypotheses emerge from these studies: (1) *where party brokers are national, subnational elites have incentives to satisfy national interests. Thus decentralization will occur if it serves the interests of national party elites;* and (2) *where party elites are subnational, national elites have incentives to satisfy subnational interests by decentralizing resources and authority, if decentralization serves the interests of those subnational party elites.*[12]

Although arguments that highlight the importance of electoral institutions and party system structures have inspired our contributors, we believe that this framework cannot offer a complete explanation for decentralization. For example, O'Neill finds in her study of Bolivia that the presence of closed-list proportional representation (PR), an electoral configuration that Willis, Garman, and Haggard (1999) might have predicted would favor national party control over subnational actors, did not prevent significant decentralization. Other factors proved more important. Elsewhere, Montero (2001) compared a "strong" versus a "weak" national party system (Spain versus Brazil, respectively) and found that—contrary to what one might predict—subnational governments succeeded in decentralizing in the former and central elites (the presidency in particular) were able to recentralize in the latter over the course of the 1990s. This points to the need to explain a greater range of variation in decentralization, particularly over time.

A variation on this political-institutional theme emphasizes the *dynamically changing* expectations of national or subnational party elites.

For example, O'Neill argues in this volume that where national party elites believe their copartisans have good chances to win power at the subnational level, they will preemptively (re)distribute authority and resources to those arenas. In contrast, under more uncertain electoral circumstances, national party elites will discount the expected "political efficiency" gains of decentralization and opt not to devolve scarce resources. The Bolivian case fits this hypothesis well: the national party in power (*Movimiento Nacional Revolucionario,* or MNR) opted to decentralize when its electoral support at the national level was weakening while at the same time its subnational (i.e., regional) support was increasing. O'Neill's argument also explains the form decentralization took in Bolivia. While there was substantial discussion of decentralization to regional governments, which are based in the departmental capitals, the MNR gained more votes from municipalities outside the departmental capitals. Therefore, the MNR shaped decentralization as municipalization rather than departmentalization.

Beer's treatment of Mexico uses a similar "dynamic expectations" approach, but she focuses on the incentives facing *subnational* elites to mobilize for additional fiscal transfers from the center. Her argument is that distinct levels of political competition across the Mexican states produced a diverse national pattern of fiscal decentralization. Like O'Neill, Beer's work explains the form decentralization took in an otherwise fiscally centralized Mexico by highlighting its heterogeneity. In the process, she also provides a more nuanced hypothesis concerning the link between democratization and decentralization by demonstrating that uneven patterns of democratization across the Mexican states produced a more patchwork pattern of fiscal decentralization.[13]

Still other approaches in this volume mix a "party brokers" and a "dynamic expectations" approach. For example, Samuels (this volume) argues that both the location of party brokers as well as the change in political career patterns in Brazil help explain the particular form that decentralization took in the 1980s (see also Penfold-Becerra, this volume). Regardless of the specific form electoralist arguments take, they offer a common insight into the political logic of decentralization: the linkages between national and subnational politicians affect the relative leverage of both, and this balance of power subsequently affects the scope and form decentralization takes. Thus, subnational politicians cannot influence national elites if there is a relatively large degree of political separation between national and subnational politicians, even those of the same party. Penfold-Becerra's examination of the Venezuelan case in this volume illustrates this point. Although the decomposition of the Venezuelan party system and the erosion of central authority created opportunities for subnational political elites to escape the confining spaces of the old party system in the late 1980s and 1990s, they were unable to expand *fiscal* decentralization in a manner proportional to the degree of *political* freedom they attained. Thus, the weakness of linkages across levels in the Venezuelan party system short-circuited the mechanisms of leverage that might otherwise have predicted more substantial decentralization. Similarly, in the Uruguayan case that Eaton analyzes, the two-party system remained highly organized as democratization advanced, but subnational interests (i.e., departmental governments) never emerged as important influences within either the Colorado or Blanco parties. This kept the country fiscally centralized, a condition that only reinforced the weakness of departmental government interests within the parties.

How can scholars identify these linkages across levels within political parties? One of our most important findings is that political career patterns are excellent tools for understanding patterns of intergovernmental leverage. Political career paths—whether careers are made within national party organizations, within the national legislature, or in subnational offices—point to where the peaks of the pyramids of power lie in a given country, and thus reveal whether national or subnational politicians have relatively more or less leverage. For example, the two most decentralized cases in Latin America—Argentina and Brazil—have also tended to have the most powerful subnational elites in the region, despite episodes of recentralization and authoritarian rule. The historic power of state and provincial party bosses to influence the political careers of national legislators in these two countries sets them apart from more recent cases of decentralization, such as Venezuela and Chile (see Samuels, 2003, on Brazil; Jones et al., 2001, on Argentina). They also stand in sharp contrast to one of the most centralized systems in the region, Mexico, where careers have long been made within the national parties (see, e.g., Smith, 1979; Langston, 1995). As Beer's chapter illustrates, Mexican governors and mayors have only recently asserted their *political* autonomy as the regime has changed with the weakening of the PRI's monopoly. Subnational politicians' historical dependency on national political leaders helps to explain why Mexico has been relatively slow to decentralize (Ward and Rodríguez, 1999).

The electoralist framework has emerged as the most powerful in the literature, and the chapters in this volume provide encouraging confirmation of its utility in explaining decentralization. Yet even when it is supplemented by an understanding of distal and macro factors, an electoralist approach is often not entirely successful in explaining all aspects of decentralization. Various contextual factors, or events that are exogenous to "political society," such as economic crises, corruption scandals, and popular protests, have also encouraged decentralization at times and in places where electoral incentives did not. For example, Eaton (this volume) finds that disinterest toward decentralization cannot explain why local officials under Chile's Parliamentary Republic failed to use their expanded taxation authority. In fact, these politicians may have had a strong incentive to employ expanded tax authority, but another factor overwhelmed this interest and offers a more likely explanation: windfall revenues from nitrate extraction, which produced resistance to collecting local taxes. Local politicians thus had no need to risk the prospect that increasing local tax collection would alienate their supporters, because they were awash with funds from other sources. In the Venezuelan case, Penfold-Becerra (this volume) also refers to extra-electoral factors to explain why the dominant parties in Venezuela enacted direct elections for governor in 1989. The timing of the decision to decentralize, a move calculated to buy popular support, was clearly affected by the disruptive events of the *Caracazo* that year.

Economic and other kinds of governability crises may also trump electoral factors. Bahl and Linn (1992) hypothesize that a "crisis effect" will weaken incentives for national governments to decentralize and instead strengthen their interests in recentralizing. Yet the role of crisis effects may well depend on the *types* of crises. Penfold-Becerra's findings contradict Bahl and Linn and suggest that governability crises can create incentives for central government elites to decentralize, not centralize,[14] but the opposite may be true of macroeconomic crises. For example, in recent cases of recentralization, economic crises in Argentina and Brazil have shifted leverage back to presidents who have been able to implement neoliberal stabilization policies, including fiscal restraints on subnational governments (Burki, Perry, and Dillinger, 2000: 41–44). Profound crises of the political party system may also present causes for recentralization. Such dilemmas, coupled with significant economic turmoil, prompted recentralization under President Hugo Chávez in Venezuela.

In summary, we believe that arguments that focus on political institutions and electoral-partisan dynamics offer the best avenue for progress in cross-national research on decentralization. Indeed, we argue that political-institutional dynamics are necessary elements of *any* explanation of decentralization. This does not mean that scholars should ignore nonpolitical factors. However, we suggest that scholars should focus on how contextual (both distal and proximate) factors filter through electoral and party institutions to shape politicians' micro decisions, and how these dynamics help to explain change over time.

THE CONSEQUENCES OF DECENTRALIZATION IN LATIN AMERICA

While this volume is primarily concerned with the political *determinants* of decentralization in Latin America, our observations have implications for what we view as the next phase of the research program: an evaluation of the policy *effects* of decentralization. In thinking about the consequences of decentralization, we realize that other scholars have already ventured into this area.

The most obvious assumption that much of the policy literature brings to the table is that subnational (and particularly local) governments are more accountable to citizens and their demands. Proximity begets efficacy in this framework, and decentralization is therefore normatively a good thing. This conclusion is difficult to deny in the face of numerous studies of innovative policy making at the subnational level in Latin America (e.g. Tendler, 1997; Evans, 1997; Abers, 2000; Montero, 2002). However, ascertaining *why* these success stories emerge in some parts of the region and not in others (or why in some parts of some countries and not in others) must be part of the next phase of the research program. A careful examination of the relationship between the political determinants of decentralization and subnational governments' subsequent policy performance ought to provide substantial insights into this question. For example, the finding that democratization, decentralization, and effective economic management may be linked under certain circumstances may help explain when and where "good subnational government" emerges. The attention of both Wibbels and of Haggard and Webb (this volume) to hardening soft budget constraints is instructive in this regard. More generally, the motives of politicians in national government who seek to decentralize will continue to affect the performance of subnational governments. For example, where such decentralizers are willing to devolve policy responsibilities but not the necessary financing to cover these obligations, decentralization will be less likely to promote effective policy making.

Decentralization also holds great promise for reducing regional inequalities and consolidating equity-enhancing reforms. Katzenstein (1985) and other scholars of the "democratic corporatist" and "consociational" countries of Western Europe have demonstrated the impact that central-government policies can have along these lines. In Latin America, however, decentralization has not shown the same potential to reduce regional inequalities. The transfer of policy authority without adequate financial support has been more common than adequately financed programs of decentralization (Bahl and Linn, 1994; Wibbels, this volume; Haggard and Webb, this volume). In countries such as Brazil with long histories of uneven regional development, fiscal decentralization has actually empowered already industrialized states with large tax bases, further widening the gap between these regions and the poorer ones (Montero, 2000). Beer (this volume) finds a similar pattern in Mexico, which is much more fiscally centralized than Brazil. In these cases poorer regions tend to rely more on transfers, which are an inefficient means to correct regional imbalances (Rezk, 1998). The fault for continuing regional disparities lies not with subnational governments but with their national counterparts, because subnational governments by themselves cannot resolve nagging regional imbalances without the credible commitments of national government (Prud'homme, 1995: 202–3). Yet national authorities are often unwilling or incapable of correcting regional inequalities even though they are best placed to redistribute resources across subnational boundaries. Ultimately, this problem returns to the issue of linkage between national and subnational officials. Subnational politicians may have entrenched interests in supporting the institutional status quo, which may perversely prolong regional inequalities, because their political survival depends on these existing arrangements and because they perceive that the costs of transforming the bases of their political support networks are too high.

Moreover, national leaders' commitments to reducing regional inequalities in Latin America are likely to be muted to the degree that executive-branch economic policy-makers remain focused on macro-economic stability and "signaling" foreign investors. These goals often contradict the goal of making decentralization a tool of good government, because keeping prices stable has meant cutting transfers and spending while raising taxes, all the while undercutting the ability of state and municipal governments to respond to local demands for better housing, education, health care, and infrastructure. Brazil's Fiscal Responsibility Law may be a good example of this unfortunate contradiction. It is doubtful that voters understand the conflicted logic that demands both inflation control at the national level and budgetary streamlining at the subnational level. Under these conditions, continued vertical imbalances between expenditures and revenue assignments undermine the attempt to redress the horizontal imbalances of cross-regional disparities. It may seem obvious to say so, but if subnational governments cannot individually address local constituents' demands (and we can expect historically poorer regions to be particularly vulnerable in this regard), then it is unlikely that decentralization will be able to correct regional inequalities.

Greater decentralization of policy authority and fiscal resources may also ameliorate some problems while creating others. Since tax revenue is finite, any decentralization of revenue reduces the importance of the national budget in correcting interregional inequities. Interjurisdictional competition for investments and the significant coordination problems involved in keeping such competition from spiraling into a "race to the bottom" also tend to aggravate extant inequalities. National government may effectively regulate this competition and thereby even out the equity effects of decentralization (Breton, 1996), but Latin American states apparently lack the political will or policy-making structure to produce the "good" fiscal-federal results seen in Europe (see Haggard and Webb, this volume).

Even if decentralization fails to improve the effectiveness and efficiency of public policy, it might favor democratization. Bland makes the strongest claim in this regard by highlighting the way that decentralization in Chile removed authoritarian enclaves (unelected subnational leaders) during the transition to democracy. Yet it bears considering whether decentralization in a broader sense, not just during transitions to democracy, is itself democratizing. Decentralization empowers non-governmental interests by creating multiple points of access to policy making. This is a major reason why the theme of decentralization has become popular among nongovernmental organizations in Latin America and why the social movement literature has associated decentralization with "deepening" democratization (e.g., Yashar, 1999: 86). Another factor that suggests that decentralization contributes to the "deepening of democracy" is the association between country size and survivability of democracy. Diamond (1999: 117) notes that 75 percent of states with populations smaller than one million were democratic in 1998 as compared with 60 percent of larger states. Since country size and scale of government are closely related (Dahl and Tufte, 1973), it may well be that decentralization, by reducing the scale of government to citizens, produces greater accountability and responsiveness.

These are *demos*-enabling qualities that decentralization *may* provide to local governments, but whether decentralization actually results in across-the-board "good" local government is an open empirical question. Indeed, such generally optimistic assumptions about decentralization may be unfounded. Numerous recent studies have demonstrated that decentralization can empower "bad" local governments as much as "good" local governments, leaving the overall balance open to multiple interpretations (J. Fox, 1994). For example, subnational populists and patrimonial political machines can utilize the proceeds from decentralization to reinforce their privileged economic and political positions (Prud'homme, 1995; Diamond, 1999: 133–34; Stepan, 2000). Snyder (1999, 2001a) has demonstrated that neo-liberal decentralization in Mexico effectively allowed traditional clientelistic elites to extend and consolidate their oligarchical grip on policy-making in some states. Under these conditions, decentralization can actually undercut the likelihood of greater accountability at the local level.

Another important qualifier to the democratizing consequences of decentralization is provided by Wibbels (this volume). Even if decentralization accompanies a transition to democracy, as it did in Argentina, subsequent tensions between decentralization and market-oriented reforms may lead to a rolling back of the *demos*-enhancing qualities of decentralization through recentralization. In short, the greater accountability of elites that some associate with decentralization may not be sustainable in the long term, particularly in the face of significant socioeconomic crises.

The impact of decentralization on local and national democratization and on economic growth, equity, or efficiency are all areas for future research. Theorists of democracy such as John Stuart Mill, Robert Dahl, and Robert Putnam have described the "empathic understanding" that fosters collective bonds of community and "civic virtue" in local polities.[15] Whether these qualities are primordial and antecedent to political institutions or whether they must be "scaled up" by political statecraft[16] is a subject for a volume dedicated to the decentralization-democratization link. However, the historic role played by government institutions and political leaders in organizing civil society in Latin America (Collier and Collier, 1991) suggests that the focus should remain on the impact of government policy itself in this regard—whether at the local, state, or national level. That is, "social capital" may be a consequence of good government and not its cause (Tendler, 1997; Montero, 2002). In short, the political consequences of decentralization depend on the political origins of decentralization.

CONCLUSION

Developing a single approach to the study of decentralization has been difficult, and we believe it will be so for some time. Different approaches may better explain some aspects of decentralization over others. However, some generalizations are possible based on our initial assessment. The essays in this volume find substantial common ground across regime types, historical periods, and countries. First, historical-institutional and socioeconomic legacies matter. For example, the emergence of municipalization in Brazil in contrast to the weakness of municipal demands for decentralization in Chile are different responses to these kinds of legacies. Future research should abandon the tendency toward a presentist bias and explore these patterns in broader longitudinal as well as cross-sectional perspective.

Second, democratization and neoliberal reform are neither necessary nor sufficient to explain decentralization. Moreover, the literature that associates democratization or neoliberal reforms with decentralization tends to be apolitical, and thus has not made clear how, why, or to what extent these factors can truly be considered *causes* of decentralization. This is an important corrective to many of the initial assumptions of the policy literature.

Finally, we believe that institutional and electoralist approaches, supplemented with analysis of macro and distal factors, offer the most promising avenue for research. That is, scholars who avoid *either* the macro *or* the micro level are selling their research short. The research frontier for the study of decentralization should move toward a cross-national integrative approach, one that incorporates long-term factors, a micro logic, and events particular to each country's context. This analytical apparatus must also avoid the tendency to be static. It must be consistently useful for understanding *change* in the distribution of inter-governmental policy authorities and resources, particularly in the cases that lack significant changes in demographic patterns or electoral and party systems. This suggests that other proximate causes, perhaps some exogenous to political society such as the advent of macroeconomic and governability crises, shape decentralization.

In terms of the consequences of decentralization, the chapters in this volume confirm the view of the policy literature that decentralization is not a panacea (e.g., Rondinelli, 1989; Prud'homme, 1995), but they emphasize that *political* factors help explain why decentralization is not always a good thing. We agree that the policy outcomes of decentralization depend upon the institutional design of policy. Yet policy design is not where analysis should begin; political choices and institutions shape design options and policy implementation, and antecedent, distal, and macro factors shape both the range of political choices as well as these institutional constraints. The purpose of this introduction as well as this volume as a whole is to call attention to the *politics* of decentralization. By focusing on the political determinants of decentralization, scholars will be better able to assess the causes of policy success as well as policy failure in cross-subnational and cross-national perspective.

NOTES

1. Our primary influence is the work of Willis, Garman, and Haggard (1999).

2. In this volume, the contributors refer to the first tier of subnational government with the names specific to their cases: states, provinces, departments, regional governments, and so on. The local tier is typically municipal government.

3. See Karl (1986) for the argument.

4. Willis et al. (1999: 8) conflate this dimension of decentralization with subnational policy autonomy into one rubric: "functional" decentralization. We prefer to divide resources from authority to illustrate cases in which asymmetries between the two dimensions affect policy making.

5. For example, see Rondinelli (1981, 1989). Bland (this volume) employs the term "deconcentration," but in a very specific (and useful) fashion: to describe the transfer of functions to subnational offices of the central administration during the Augusto Pinochet regime. Another conceivable example of this is Mexico's National Solidarity Program (PRONASOL), which was mostly administered through federal offices at the local level. Our cases do not include many instances of deconcentration, but we believe that this is a very different process from the one we call "decentralization." Deconcentration is most often associated with changing patterns of service-provision within the bureaucracy of the central government, while all forms of decentralization involve a transfer of resources and/or authorities to subnational governments and agencies that are autonomous from the central government.

6. Despite this conclusion, we believe that future research might still ask the question whether one approach is superior. Penfold-Becerra's treatment in this volume of the Venezuelan case is the most thought-provoking in this regard. During the period that the traditional parties controlled the national government, decentralization did not occur. National leaders implemented political decentralization only when they faced a severe governability crisis during the late 1980s and early 1990s. Bottom-up pressures did not emerge significantly until *after* national leaders opted to decentralize, and these pressures were not enough to deepen decentralization when the crisis of the center led to the collapse of the traditional party system. Therefore, we ask two related research questions: (1) Is bottom-up decentralization possible when the center is strong? (2) Can bottom-up decentralization proceed once the center weakens? Can it proceed if the center becomes more coherent?

7. This tendency mirrors that found in democratization studies between sociohistorical analyses and the "transitologists" who focus on the strategies and institutions governing regime change. See Montero (1998).

8. To be sure, as Beer (this volume) argues, macro factors do not provide sufficient explanations for decentralization, but their consideration is indispensable for understanding the more proximate factors that analyses such as hers favor.

9. The "competitive federalist" logic is most often associated with Charles Tiebout (1956).

10. For an examination of the Brazilian case, see Cavalcanti and Prado (1998).

11. Perhaps the first comprehensive study of decentralization in Latin America by a major IFI was that by IDB (1994).

12. Note that this argument does not lead to simplistic hypotheses such as "federal systems will tend to be more decentralized." As the cases of Mexico and Venezuela versus Argentina and Brazil demonstrate, a de jure federal constitution is much less important than the de facto location of the "party brokers" in these four countries.

13. This conclusion for all of Mexico is strongly supported by Snyder's (1999, 2001a) analysis of re-regulation in the coffee sector.

14. Another Latin American case of governability crises leading to decentralization that is not covered in this volume is Colombia. Guerrilla and paramilitary violence, drug trafficking, and the erosion of the judiciary in this case contributed strongly to decentralization through the 1991 Constitutional Reform, new revenue sharing laws during the early 1990s, and the transfer of territory ("de-militarized areas") to the largest guerrilla organization, the FARC. We thank Kent Eaton for this point.

15. See Mill (1958), Dahl (1992), and Putnam (1993).

16. For a response to the "primordial social capital" argument in Latin America, see J. Fox (1996).

PART 11

The Political Origins of Decentralization

CHAPTER 2

Decentralization in Bolivia

Electoral Incentives and Outcomes

KATHLEEN M. O'NEILL

While decentralization in its many forms has swept through most of Latin America, Bolivia stands out as one of the most surprising decentralizers in the region. With its small population (at approximately eight million, Bolivia's population roughly equals that of the capital city of neighboring Colombia), one of the lowest levels of economic development in the region, and a long history of extremely centralized rule, Bolivia hardly seems an obvious candidate for radical decentralizing reform. Yet Bolivia not only decentralized power, it did so earlier than many of its neighbors and to a much larger extent.[1]

In this chapter I explore the puzzling development of decentralization in Bolivia. While one might expect that decentralization in Bolivia represented a capitulation to either insistent domestic or international pressures or a response to one of that country's many fiscal crises, I find an alternative explanation more compelling. My analytical approach fits firmly within what Montero and Samuels label "political-institutional and electoralist approaches" in their introductory chapter. I argue specifically that Bolivia's decentralization experience has been shaped by parties seeking to distribute power to the arenas in which they are likely to gain access to it. Parties with electoral strength at the national level face incentives to centralize power, while those with reliable support at subnational levels and waning support at the national level may find the devolution of power to be in their best interest in the long term. I argue that electoral considerations played a critical role not only in the central government's decision to decentralize, but also in determining the contours of Bolivia's decentralizing reforms and the evolution of those reforms over time.

Unlike Brazil, Argentina, Venezuela, or Mexico, Bolivia has a long history of unitary government. Even Colombia, a unitary state for most of its history, had experienced a period of strong federalism during the nineteenth century. For Bolivia, the decentralizing reforms of 1994 represented the first time in its history that the central government did not control the public policies of its component territories. Bolivia is comprised of 9 departmental jurisdictions, 112 provinces, and—at the time of decentralization—301 provincial sections. Beyond these territorial divisions there are 1,408 cantons (Nickson, 1995: 107). Bolivians have exercised the vote in the national elections that have intermittently decided its presidents and congressional members throughout its history (and continuously since 1982); however, only a small percentage of the population enjoyed electoral power at the subnational level prior to 1995. Before then, municipal elections occurred only in the country's most urban areas in 1963 and 1968; they were held continuously beginning in 1985. Elected municipal officials served two-year terms and controlled precious few resources:

> In these [124] "cities" [which accounted for 58 percent of the population] there were municipal elections, they had representatives and mayors, but only 24 administered sufficient resources. There were 100 decorative cities that were on the map and that existed as geographic spaces, but that did not have resources with which to resolve their problems. (Molina Saucedo, 1997: 34)

The 1994 Popular Participation Law (*Ley de Participación Popular,* or LPP) dramatically altered this structure.

Bolivia's 1994 LPP and the constitutional reforms that embedded decentralization in the country's charter drastically reconfigured Bolivia's political power structure. Prior to decentralization, which placed development policy squarely in the hands of locally elected officials and territorially based grassroots organizations, the national government had overseen development through nine development corporations (one for each department). These development corporations were centrally directed, located, and funded; positions within these corporations were parceled out by each new administration, providing an attractive source of pork. In addition, regional civic committees—made up of representatives of each regional capital's top business interests—were also granted formal representation within them. Positions within these corporations, which were invested with 10 percent of the national budget, were attractive. From a development perspective, however, these corporations promoted little improvement in the poorest areas of the country. Despite their purported development focus, they spent 90 percent of their funds in the three most developed departments (La Paz, Cochabamba, and Santa Cruz), and 92 percent of spending occurred in departmental capital cities (Barbery Anaya, 1997: 46). Only 8 percent was spent in the countryside, despite the fact that 42 percent of the population were classified as rural in the 1992 census (Molina Saucedo, 1997: 42).

The LPP scrapped the centralist blueprint and devolved power to municipalities.[2] Municipal elections had been going on in the country's largest cities, but there was no municipal identity in the rest of the country. The LPP literally reconfigured the map of the country, creating 308 municipalities out of 301 provincial sections—a designation that had previously denoted a mere administrative unit.

In addition to changing the physical jurisdictions of the country, the LPP granted real powers to municipalities, allowing the public election of municipal officials—a municipal council and mayor—and granting substantial transfers of central-government funds to the new governments. According to the LPP, 20 percent of the central budget was to be divided among the municipalities based purely on each municipality's share of the population. The law also enumerated several tax categories available to municipalities for raising their own revenue apart from the central government's transfers. The LPP not only created a legitimate voice at the local level to call for changes in public policies, it also gave local governments their own resources for local development. Decentralization through the LPP thus fits the criteria for political, fiscal, and administrative decentralization laid out by Montero and Samuels in their introductory chapter.

One of the LPP's most innovative features was the complex system it created to encourage community involvement in local government. Community involvement was supposed to go well beyond the ballot box, extending to frequent interaction with the elected government on major decisions. The text of the LPP begins by granting formal recognition to territorial grassroots organizations (*organizaciones territoriales de base*) such as indigenous communities, neighborhood associations, and peasant associations. The law encourages these entities to form a municipal oversight committee, selected through the customs and practices of the community. This oversight committee is charged with monitoring the elected local government. Oversight committees can petition the central government to suspend a municipality's fiscal transfers in the case of bad management, giving this vigilance bite.

Envisioned as an important curb on the tyranny of an elected mayor, the law includes a censure provision. Municipal councils can vote to remove the mayor after one year of tenure, replacing him or her with another member of the council. This can occur once a year throughout the term of the local government (which the law expanded from two to three years). In fact, this provision has attracted a great deal of criticism as mayors have changed frequently in municipalities across the country. Municipal governments are often highly unstable, and many policies are designed merely to respond to the government's extremely short-term incentives.

Through these measures, the LPP dramatically reshaped power relations between national and local levels of government. Bolivia's power was once firmly concentrated in the national government, and the presidency, in particular; today it is shared with over three hundred elected mayors and their municipal councils. What could lead to such an extreme shift in power? Given that decentralization had been debated for over a decade—in fact, twenty-two legal projects for decentralization were debated over thirteen years (Molina Saucedo, 1997: 35)—why did it occur when it did? How has it evolved over time, following the initial reform? These questions dominate the remainder of this chapter. I begin by articulating several alternative theories for the adoption of decentralizing reform and discuss why each one does or does not appear to fit the Bolivian case. I marshal evidence to support a theory that decentralization in Bolivia coincided with the electoral incentives of the party in power when the reform was adopted. Next, I develop a secondary implication of this theory, namely, that the shape of the reform itself best advanced the electoral prospects of the governing party. Finally, I look at how decentralization has evolved over time. If parties in power use decentralization when it suits their support structure, parties that subsequently reach power might change the level of decentralization to fit their own desires. I look at how decentralization has changed under the presidency of Hugo Banzer Suárez and discuss which aspects of decentralization appear most resistant to change and which are most likely to change over time. In my conclusion I discuss the relevance of this theory to other decentralization experiences in the region and also some of its limitations.

THEORIES OF DECENTRALIZATION

With control of state resources such a large and rewarding prize, why would the central government allow its powers to be devolved to municipal governments? Why would the president allow the election of potential rivals, particularly in large regional[3] capitals? Several theories have sought to explain the adoption of decentralization by strong centralized governments. Montero and Samuels, in their introduction to this volume, have succinctly catalogued the major approaches for explaining decentralization. I will briefly discuss such approaches here, focusing on the question of how well they explain Bolivia's experience. The failure of several of them to fit the Bolivian case should not be perceived to invalidate their usefulness in explaining other cases; not all countries decentralize for the same reasons. However, I agree with Montero and Samuels that electoralist and institutionalist approaches offer the most generalizable and powerful explanatory frameworks. In this section I evaluate five classes of theories that view decentralization as a response to fiscal crisis, pressures from the international financial community, pressures from below, sociostructural causes, or pressures from within the party and electoral incentives. Revealing my hand ahead of time, I will argue that the electoral incentives theory best fits the evidence for the Bolivian case and, further, that it explains not only the adoption of decentralization in Bolivia in 1994, but also why it was not adopted earlier, why decentralization took the form it did, and how it has changed under a successive administration.

Fiscal Crisis

Given the onset of this latest round of decentralizing reforms in Bolivia in the mid-to-late 1980s and throughout the 1990s, it is tempting to consider it a part of the larger move toward neoliberal reform that occurred during this period. Montero and Samuels, by taking a longer historical perspective, find little support for a theory linking decentralization to any particular economic model. A related theory suggests that decentralization may be a response to fiscal crises that also began to occur throughout the region at approximately the same time. This approach begins from the premise that decentralization may be a cheap way to shirk responsibility for providing local public goods. When the national budget sinks into deficit, devolving responsibilites for local spending to subnational governments should free up funds at the national level to balance the budget. In this scenario, shortfalls in local goods become the responsibility of local officials, taking the political and economic pressure off the center. While this theory may explain some instances of decentralization in the region, it does not explain the decentralization of fiscal resources to new municipalities in Bolivia, nor does it explain why decentralization occurred at a time when the budget was relatively balanced. Although Bolivia experienced colossal deficits between 1982 and 1985 (up to 40 percent of GDP), subsequent years saw budget deficits well under 5 percent of GDP. As I will describe later, a subsequent regime has used an incipient fiscal crisis as a justification to recentralize power by cutting fiscal transfers. Indeed, other authors in this volume note that decentralization appears to occur during fiscal good times, and recentralization appears to follow fiscal hardship (see especially the chapter by Eaton). Perhaps decentralization can only be "afforded" by the central government in times of budget balance. Fiscal balance may be a necessary, but not a sufficient, condition for decentralization.

International Pressure

A second set of arguments finds the impetus for decentralization in the international economic arena. Specifically, international pressure may tip the balance toward decentralization by raising the costs of not decentralizing. This pressure may come from international public opinion or from international lenders, who press the point by tying funds to policies. While I would not claim that international support for decentralization played no part in Bolivia's reform, I believe that international pressures played, at best, a supporting role in explaining the LPP's introduction. International opinion on decentralization did not suddenly congeal in 1994. Why did the Sánchez de Lozada administration cave in to this pressure while previous regimes did not? One explanation may lie in the country's vulnerability to international lender pressure. Yet Bolivia was not particularly vulnerable in 1993 or 1994. It had been much more susceptible to international pressure in the mid-1980s, when it experienced one of its worst financial crises. That Bolivia did not decentralize during this period does not accord with a theory that international pressures cause decentralization. Of course, the idea of decentralization's desirability had not reached its peak in the mid-1980s. I would argue that the international consensus on decentralization's desirability has its greatest impact on actual policy making when it coincides with other political incentives that make decentralization attractive.

Pressure from Below

A third class of theories links decentralization not to domestic or international economic trends, but to the general movement toward democracy that occurred shortly before it. While Bolivia's LPP occurred more than a decade after its democracy was reestablished, a more sophisticated model links decentralization to democracy through the space that democratic regimes offer for making demands from below. Popular movements demanding greater local autonomy or a deepening of democratization could so destabilize a government that the cost of giving up some of its centralized power over local politics could be outweighed by the benefit of keeping the peace. In general, central governments lose popularity when they stand against organized civic movements seeking greater democracy. Decentralization may occur as a capitulation to active or incipient social pressures from the grass roots.

Bolivia's 1994 LPP was not preceded by massive demonstrations for increased democratization or local rule. Municipal governments were not clamoring for more autonomy—in most of the country they did not exist as such. To the extent that there was a call for greater subnational autonomy, that call arose from civic committees (somewhat like chambers of commerce) in the regional capitals. These were groups of elite businessmen (overwhelmingly male) who were seeking greater autonomy for regional governments. In Bolivia, the president appoints regional prefects (they are still appointed today). Civic committees pressed for their election, perhaps believing that elected executives might bend more readily to their influence. In the end, decentralization skipped the regional level, devolving power to municipalities and giving the civic committees little of what they wanted. In fact, civic committee members participated in the development corporations that controlled 10 percent of the national budget. The LPP rerouted this 10 percent of the budget, doubled it to 20 percent, and transferred it to municipalities, leaving civic committees in a much worse position.

As the Latin American country with the largest indigenous population, one may wonder whether Bolivia's organized indigenous groups pressured for greater decentralization. In fact, they were originally opposed to the new decentralization law. While several indigenous leaders and intellectuals were involved in the small committee that crafted the LPP, pressure from this constituency did not occasion the law: "there was no coherent political movement for the radical transformation of state-society relations from below, apart from the weak indigenous organizations and the writings of politically impotent intellectuals" (Van Cott, 2000: 150). Finally, the closed nature of the committee meetings that crafted the LPP also signals that the law was not a capitulation by the central government to popular demands; in fact, it was essentially a top-down process. Drafting a reform through the meetings of a small group of advisers would have been nearly impossible under intense popular pressures for change.

Sociostructural Causes

A fourth category of theories, labeled "sociostructural" causes in the introductory chapter, links decentralization to changing demographic and sociological conditions. Inspired by modernization theory, these explanations stress factors such as increased economic development and urbanization as triggers for decentralizing reforms. Comparing Bolivia to its neighbors, these theories provide little explanatory purchase by themselves: while economic development and urbanization in Bolivia have increased since democratization, they remain well below the levels of neighbors who have decentralized far less. In fact, Bolivia is one of the least economically developed and least urbanized countries in the region.

Political-Institutional and Electoralist Theories

These theories refer to more explicitly political incentives to decentralize. One finds the impetus for decentralization within individual party structures, while the other looks to the electoral incentives of political parties competing against one another for access to political and fiscal resources.

Party Pressures

One reason a party might decentralize is if it faces strong pressures from within its organization for increased access to power through subnational elections. Parties in which regional elites or power brokers exert strong indirect pressures on national politics may make support for a candidate conditional on greater direct access to political and fiscal power at subnational levels. For example, Willis, Garman, and Haggard (1999) make a strong case for this type of motivation in the Brazilian case.

In the Bolivian case, this theory holds little explanatory promise. National elections throughout the period have been organized on a closed-list, proportional representation (PR) system. National leaders have strong control over the selection and placement of candidates on these lists.[4] Parties have been extremely centralized, with very little reach into regional and local areas (Zegada, 1998). In general, parties have been tightly controlled by the personalities at their centers, as the following brief histories demonstrate. The MNR (*Movimiento Nacional Revolucionario,* or National Revolutionary Movement) began as the project of three personalities: Victor Paz Estenssoro, Juan Lechín, and Hernando Siles Zuazo. As the three began to disagree on policies, the party split, with the traditional wing of the MNR following Paz and the more left wing following Siles and Lechín. This latter group formed the UDP (*Unidad Democrática y Popular,* or Popular Democratic Unity) and won the 1980 election, the results of which were instated in 1982. After a disastrous presidency from 1982 to 1985, this wing of the party dispersed, and the MNR came more firmly under the control of Paz and a new generation led by Gonzalo Sánchez de Lozada. The ADN (*Acción Democrática Nacionalista,* or Nationalist Democratic Action) was formed as the legitimate democratic vehicle for former dictator (1971–79) Hugo Banzer Suárez. Not surprisingly, he has retained tight control over its direction. When he temporarily retired from politics in 1993, the party fell into bitter factions; unity only returned with Banzer's political reemergence in 1995. It is significant to note that Banzer has been the ADN's presidential candidate in every election since 1978; Jaime Paz Zamora has been the MIR's (*Movimiento de Izquierda Revolucionario*, or Movement of the Revolutionary Left) presidential candidate since 1985; Victor Paz Estenssoro served as the MNR's presidential candidate until he passed the mantle to Sánchez de Lozada, and he continues to exert a firm grasp on the party leadership today. Finally, strong leaders have indelibly marked Bolivia's smaller parties. These include CONDEPA's (*Conciencia de la Patria,* or Conscience of the Fatherland) Carlos Palenque, and the UCS's (*Unión Cívica Solidaridad,* or Civic Solidarity Union) Max Fernández (and in the wake of his death, the emergence of his son, Johnny Fernández).

A further strike against this theory in the Bolivian case is the fact that the results of decentralizing legislation failed to benefit local and regional power brokers in a significant way. In the decentralized system, central party structures continue to draw up and approve the lists of candidates at the local level. Local and regional power brokers continue to exist at the margins of power. Candidates for office at the local level cannot bypass these party structures and run as independents; only candidates from recognized parties may appear on local ballots.

Finally, the one group that might have played a strong role in securing national votes—the highly organized civic committees in the regions— generally opposed municipalization, preferring a decentralized system that would empower departmental governments. Not only did they lose the battle over the level of subnational elections, but the decentralization of funds took the 10 percent of the federal budget of the development corporations (on which civic committees enjoyed representation) and folded it into the 20 percent of the federal budget that bypasses the regional level on its way to municipalities.

Electoral Incentives
This theory links decentralization to electoral competition. In this formulation, decentralization becomes attractive to those holding central power when they believe they can gain strong support in the new elective positions and when they believe their control over the central government may be in jeopardy. A party that believes it can continue to control the center faces few incentives to give power away to subnational levels, where competing parties may gain significant footholds of power. A party that imagines it may lose control of the center, however, has

strong incentives to decentralize if it believes it can gain those footholds of power for itself. This is particularly true if the party believes it may be entirely shut out of national politics in the future. Oporto Castro (1996) eloquently describes this trajectory: a party "may find in decentralization the opportunity to relaunch itself, making itself strong first in local and regional elections, so that from there it can advance to the heart of power in a dynamic sequence from below upward, from the periphery to the center, from local power to the state" (54).[5] As this quote demonstrates, such an electoral strategy promises long-term rewards.

Decentralization imposes up-front costs in the form of lost power at the center during the present administration, with the benefits accruing in the future. For this reason, parties that enjoy reliable bases of support are most likely to undertake such long-term electoral strategies. Parties whose future support at either the national or subnational level remains highly uncertain may heavily discount future time periods where the pay-off to decentralizing would be realized. There is no reason to think that political parties are averse to risk; in the absence of clear evidence that they would do better by decentralizing, parties may prefer the risky strategy of competing for a single, powerful prize. If parties were risk averse, decentralization would have been enacted much earlier in Bolivia and would have swept through the region much more quickly.

Given the logic above, it follows that parties are most likely to decentralize when their electoral support at the national level is weak, their subnational support is strong, and the reliability of their electoral base at all levels is substantial. The Bolivian government in 1994 fits this profile exactly.

This theory has much in common with the literature on political survival in Latin America. In the seminal work on political survival, Barry Ames (1987) makes a strong case that executives seek to ensure their political survival by using public expenditures to build coalitions that can sustain them in office. An electoral theory of decentralization suggests that, when executives realize they cannot sustain themselves or their party in central power, they may seek to distribute authority over public expenditures to levels of government where they or their political allies can exploit them to rebuild party popularity. This theory does not in any way suggest that once a party no longer controls the presidency, it cares only about subnational elections; decentralization might be viewed as a way to rebuild a party's popularity at the subnational level in order to launch a new campaign for central dominance.

There is also a clear affinity between the electoral theory and the literature on bureaucratic structures in American politics. In that literature, which focuses on principal-agent relations, politicians are assumed to use bureaucratic rules and procedures strategically to protect their interests from future opponents who may gain office and seek to roll back their policies. Each administration seeks to insulate the bureaucracies that will carry out its programs from future administrations who may prefer different programs (McCubbins, Noll, and Weingast, 1987, 1989; Horn and Shepsle, 1989; Moe, 1990). In the decentralization scenario, politicians seek to protect their party's access to power in subsequent administrations by creating elected bodies with guaranteed resources—usually meted out through a thoroughly specified formulaic schedule to prevent future tampering—who will find it in their interest to resist recentralization under future regimes.

In the following sections I argue that a theory of electoral incentives explains not only why the MNR decentralized in 1994, but also why previous democratic governments did not decentralize, why the MNR chose municipal rather than regional decentralization, and how decentralization policy has evolved over time as new parties win the presidency and face the same electoral logic. I explain each of these three facets of Bolivia's decentralization using the electoral theory sketched above as a guide.

THE ROAD TO DECENTRALIZATION IN BOLIVIA

Bolivia rejoined the family of democracies in 1982, after years of instability under alternating civilian and military governments. Since then, democracy has endured through five elections and presidents from four different parties. Electoral results for contests during the 1980s and 1990s are summarized in Table 2.1.

In the 1980 elections, three parties won the vast majority of the vote; these were the left-wing UDP (favoring Siles), the centrist MNR (led by Paz Estenssoro), and the more conservative ADN (led by former dictator Hugo Banzer). The UDP administration, led by Siles Zuazo, proved inept at managing the country's major financial crisis and quickly alienated its coalition partners. The most important of these defections was the UDP's major coalition partner, the MIR. By 1985 Siles agreed to end his term, a full two years early. With this action, the UDP disbanded and the MIR replaced it as the strongest party of the left in the 1985 election.

Table 2.1.   National Election Results in Bolivia, 1980–97

Party	*Percent of the Vote Won by Each Party*				
	1980	*1985*	*1989*	*1993*	*1997*[a]
MNR	20.2	30.4	25.8	35.6	18.2
ADN	16.8	32.8	25.4	21.1	22.3
MIR		10.2	22.0		16.8
UDP	38.7				
UCS				13.8	16.1
CONDEPA			12.3	14.3	17.2
PS1	8.7				
MNRI		5.5			
IU			8.1		
MBL				5.4	

Source: Bolivia's National Electoral Court.
Note: Only those parties receiving more than 5 percent of the vote are shown here.
[a] The 1997 results reflect the multimember district vote. The single-member district vote totals are similar to the results tabulated here: MNR, 17.9 percent, ADN, 22.2 percent, MIR, 17.3 percent, UCS, 14.1 percent, CONDEPA, 14 percent, and MBL, 6.3 percent, breaking the 5 percent barrier.

In 1985 the MIR won slightly more than 10 percent of the vote, while the MNR and ADN won just over 30 percent each. Although the ADN won the plurality of the vote, Bolivian law requires the legislature to choose the president from the top three candidates if no party wins an outright majority of the vote.[6] In this case, the MNR constructed a majority ruling coalition and Victor Paz Estenssoro acceded to his fourth presidency.

Bolivia's economic crisis entered its worst phase in 1985, when the country experienced severe hyperinflation in the first six months of that year. The Paz administration imposed orthodox austerity measures, guided by the minister of finance, Gonzalo Sánchez de Lozada. While these measures cured the problem of inflation, they led to a predictable recession, hurting the MNR's popularity in the midterm municipal elections of 1987.

By the national elections of 1989, the MNR had recovered from the nadir of its popularity, winning a bare plurality above the ADN and the strong, third-place showing of the MIR. Despite its plurality, the MNR was denied the presidency through the unusual coalition of left- (MIR) and right- (ADN) wing parties, which instituted a MIR presidency under Paz Zamora.

In 1993 the MNR won a plurality with almost a 15 percentage-point lead over the runner-up, ADN. By this time two new parties had reached the ten percentage-point threshold: the UCS and CONDEPA. In 1997 fortunes changed again. Under a new electoral system that required roughly half the lower chamber of the legislature to be selected through proportional representation at the national level and the other half to be chosen through sixty-eight single-member districts, the ADN won a plurality of the votes, and the MNR placed second in both single-member and multi-member legislative districts. In the former, the MIR placed third, with the UCS and CONDEPA nearly tied at fourth and fifth, respectively. In the latter, CONDEPA managed to surpass the MIR (which came in fourth) and the UCS. This race witnessed a tightening of the field: not more than one percentage point separated the second-place MNR from the third-place party in either type of district.

THE TIMING AND LEVEL OF DECENTRALIZATION

Each party that won the presidency had an opportunity to decentralize power, although it was not until 1994 that the government, controlled by the MNR, devolved power to municipalities. Decentralization was not newly discovered in 1994, however: it had been a national issue since the return to democracy in 1982.

> From 1983 to the present [1996], 18 legal projects [to advance decentralization] have been presented to the National Congress. . . . Nevertheless, there has been no real advance since then in the legislative treatment of this law. At this point, there is no doubt that, despite its historical importance and even taking into consideration the complexity of the issue, the most important factor is the lack of political will of the major parties to allow the passage of the law. (Oporto Castro, 1996: 48)

Using the electoral theory sketched above as a guide, I will examine why there was little political support for decentralization from 1982 to 1994 and why the MNR finally chose to decentralize. I describe the national and subnational support of each administration over time, illustrating that the MNR regime from 1993 to 1997 was the only administration with strong electoral incentives to empower local governments.

Electoral incentives to decentralize failed to spur decentralization by any administration prior to the 1993 MNR presidency. Siles and his UDP lost too much support, at too rapid a pace, to make them strong contenders for future positions at any level of government. The MNR administration of Paz Estenssoro was distracted by financial crisis in the first half of its tenure and thereafter faced a steep dive in its subnational support based on the consequences of its fiscal austerity plan. The MIR-ADN government made a lukewarm attempt to decentralize power to regional governments, but the different subnational strengths of its component parties attenuated its enthusiasm for a strong decentralization reform. Finally, the MNR realized the benefits of decentralizing in 1993. Decentralization played to the strength of the MNR, given its strong support in rural portions of the country and the difficulty of retaining national power in a multiparty system where the left and right had proven a willingness to conspire against the center party.

The first democratic regime, the UDP administration of Siles, began to lose support almost immediately. With loss of support at all levels, decentralization made little sense: while the UDP could not expect to be returned to the presidency, it also could expect little real support in subnational contests. With low subnational prospects and such high uncertainty over its future electoral viability in general, the UDP did not decentralize. In fact, the party disbanded when Siles stepped down from the presidency.

The MNR won the presidency in 1985 without winning a plurality of the national vote. It also faced the same and worsening financial crisis that had led to Siles's early departure from the presidency. Under these circumstances, the party could not take its continuance in national power for granted. At the same time, the MNR did well in the local elections that took place in the same year. Given the MNR's relative weakness at the national level and its strong showing in local elections, one might expect steps toward decentralization during this administration. This is particularly true since the MNR had the longest history of support of any party in the country and thus the greatest expectation of continued support in future elections. In fact, the Paz Estenssoro presidency engendered no decentralization.

Bolivia's severe financial crisis may account for the administration's lack of action on this front. The MNR spent the early years of its administration combating the country's worst inflationary period in its history, with annual inflation rates of over 8000 percent. Though the orthodox "shock" program worked, the MNR paid a high cost in support as unemployment and poverty skyrocketed. Once the stabilization program produced positive results on the inflationary front, the government refocused on ameliorating the effects of this austerity plan on Bolivia's poorest citizens. Progress was slow, however, and by the midterm municipal elections in 1987, the MNR had lost substantial support. Its national percentage of the municipal votes fell from just over 30 percent in 1985 to a mere 12.8 percent in 1987, less than half the percentage won by either the ADN or the MIR. The MNR's future electoral support at the local level appeared uncertain, at best. Given this turn of events, the long-term benefits of decentralization in the form of "safe" subnational electoral districts evaporated.

The MIR's Paz Zamora ruled as the junior partner in a coalition government with the ADN. Although this administration also did not decentralize between 1989 and 1993, decentralization emerged as an important issue of public policy. Most notably, regional conferences sponsored by civic committees discussed and promoted decentralization in 1991 and 1992, and a decentralization proposal was adopted in the Senate but defeated in the Chamber of Deputies in 1993.

The MIR came to office with a third-place finish in national elections, demonstrating a fairly weak national base of electoral support. Notwithstanding this third-place showing, support for the MIR had increased since 1985, almost doubling by 1993. Its local support in 1989 is difficult to gauge because the MIR and ADN ran coalition candidates in that year's municipal elections, winning a plurality of the national votes. The MNR placed a distant second, despite its efforts to reestablish its local support. The MIR's future seemed bright but uncertain.

Given the strong influence exerted by the ADN in the coalition government, it is also important to look at its electoral record at various levels of government. Like the MNR, the ADN enjoyed fairly stable vote shares over time and stable, but not overwhelming, support in national contests. While it had always done respectably in local contests, the ADN appeared to do better in regional capitals than in the smaller cities and, therefore, may have expected to fare poorly in the countryside.

Again, its local fortunes in 1989 are difficult to disaggregate from the votes received by the coalition candidates put forward that year by the ADN and MIR.

In the 1991 municipal elections, the MIR-ADN alliance won a majority of the votes on a nationwide level, but the MNR had significantly rebuilt its strength. Most importantly, the alliance failed to win a majority in five regions, including the key departments of La Paz, Oruro, and Santa Cruz.

The MNR's comeback was complete in 1993, when the party won a plurality of the vote nearly fifteen percentage points above its nearest contender, the ADN. Joined by the growing UCS, which received nearly 14 percent of the vote, and the MBL (*Movimiento Bolivia Libre*), which won approximately 5 percent, the MNR once again acceded to the presidency, with Gonzalo Sánchez de Lozada as president. In addition to strong national support, the MNR had done well across regions and in local races. Given its strong national support, it may seem surprising that this government passed a sweeping decentralization law in 1994. Looking more closely, however, the benefits of decentralization become clear.

Despite winning a plurality in 1989, Sánchez de Lozada had been denied the presidency. This outcome may have seemed particularly unusual; the MNR was edged out by a coalition of left and right against the centrist MNR. Without assurances that national support would continue or be great enough to secure future presidential bids by the party, and with Sánchez de Lozada ineligible for a second consecutive term, the adoption of decentralization by this relatively stable party with strong support throughout the country makes sense. In fact, the MNR underwent a massive reorganization in 1990, becoming the first Bolivian party to develop a territorial structure with a presence throughout the countryside (Zegada, 1998). At the time, this reorganization was an attempt to rebuild its strength after the turbulent elections in 1987 and 1989; international development consultants suggested the specific approach of creating a territorial structure. This presence throughout the country and the MNR's strong association with the popular agrarian reforms of the 1952 Bolivian Revolution (Molina and Arias, 1996) made the MNR the most likely party to benefit from a broad, territorial decentralization in 1993. Also, the MNR had regained its historically dominant position in subnational contests. In cantonal elections for *corregidores* in 1993, the MNR won a plurality of the vote in just over 71 percent of the contests.

While success was uncertain at the time of the reform, the MNR's decentralization strategy paid off in future electoral contests. In 1995 the party won a plurality of the votes in more municipalities than any other party.[7] It is also important to note that the Popular Participation Law became the administration's most popular reform—and the Sánchez de Lozada administration enacted several major reforms, including privatizing pensions, a major educational reform, and several significant privatizations. Despite this popularity, the MNR lost the 1997 presidential elections to the ADN. The MNR reverted to its role as the political opposition at the national level, but won a good deal of the mayoral positions in municipal elections. While I do not have systematic data that cover the entire country, Zegada (1998) notes that the MNR won the greatest number of mayoral positions in the key departments of La Paz and Cochabamba in 1997. It also won a plurality in the greatest number of municipal contests in elections held in December of 2000.

Municipal versus Regional Autonomy

If political actors look to their electoral support in determining whether or not to decentralize, it seems logical that the shape of their electoral support should also determine the level to which they decentralize power and how they distribute resources to decentralized units. When the MNR devolved power in 1994, it chose municipalization over the much more openly discussed plan of regionalization. In fact, the LPP was drafted in an atmosphere of secrecy largely because the administration feared opposition from regionalists. In this section I argue that decentralization occurred along municipal lines because the MNR stood to benefit most from this type of reform. In order to discuss these issues fully, it is important to begin with a summary of Bolivia's decentralization debate, beginning in 1982.

Bolivia has always operated with a rather centralized administration. Steps toward decentralization have been debated occasionally throughout the country's existence, but no real progress occurred until 1993. In Bolivia's 1839 constitution, municipal councils were to be popularly elected; however, this provision languished until a referendum in 1931 showed strong support for administrative decentralization to departments. A new constitution, promulgated in 1938, called for a more decentralized state structure; again, this provision was ignored in practice. Once again, the 1967 constitution made decentralization to regions official policy, but successive military and civilian regimes thereafter failed to translate this provision into practice.

The earliest years of democratic rule, from 1982 to 1987, were devoted to Bolivia's overwhelming financial crisis. Spawned by the profligate spending of the numerous governments that alternated in power between 1979 and 1982, this crisis was compounded by the social spending of the 1982–1985 Siles Zuazo government. Once financial stability reemerged, issues of deepening democracy and expanding electoral participation resurfaced with renewed vigor.

The most strident calls for decentralization can be traced to the civic committees of the regional capitals, particularly the strong civic committee of Santa Cruz. Bolivia's civic committees have never been internally democratic. Still, these committees, acting as the "National Civic Movement," rallied popular support behind their proposal for greater departmental autonomy. In particular, they sought the direct election of departmental governments (legislatures and a governor) to replace the regional prefects appointed by the central government. They specifically argued that these departmental elections should not be concurrent with national elections, in order to keep the national elections from overshadowing regional contests. It is likely that the civic committees believed they could more easily influence a popularly elected government than an appointed prefect, particularly given their strong organization and proven ability to mobilize the public. This proposal resonated with regular citizens who clamored for a greater voice in making local policy. Molina Monasterios (1997) describes this process: "The rebirth of decentralization [as an issue] was a real impulse, begun by the regional elites (for motives that mixed idealism with an interest in increasing their power), but it was seconded by the community. For this reason, few parties and individuals with political aspirations could afford the luxury of clearly saying what they thought about it" (116).

In response to the growing support for decentralization, the MIR presented a legal project to the legislature in 1990 that would provide the outline for decentralization. Paz Zamora's measure, which viewed decentralization as a process that needed to develop gradually, seemed more symbolic than real. The law did not even mention the possibility of electing prefects; it promised no financial resources to subnational governments; and while it promised elected regional legislatures, it assumed that the number of legislative members, their duties, and the manner of their election would be decided in future laws. In effect, this law merely postponed further debate on decentralization, echoing rather than improving upon the decentralizing language in the 1967 constitution.

Debate could not be postponed for long. Civic committees were restless for more concrete measures and found allies in both nongovernmental organizations and in the legislature. A "grand national commission of coordination" was organized to further study and debate decentralizing reforms. The impulse behind this commission came from the president of the Senate's commission for regional development, José Luis Carvajal. Meetings were held throughout the country in 1991 and 1992, the most important occurring in Cochabamba in 1992. This meeting was attended not only by representatives of the civic committees, but also by members of all the major political parties and by a few national deputies, senators, and government ministers. The executive played no role in organizing this meeting; in fact, the administration sent only second- and third-tier officials as its representatives. Sensing that the government would not make forward strides on the issue, several of the national deputies who attended bought return tickets for the next day, even though the meeting was expected to last three days. All of them stayed for the duration of the meeting (Molina Monasterios, 1997: 135).

In January of 1993, a legal project that was heavily influenced by the 1992 meeting gained acceptance in the Senate. The lower chamber debated this law, changing several of its provisions regarding the composition of departmental assemblies and the distribution of resources between the departments. These issues pit region against region as those who benefited from the status quo (the three most powerful departments—La Paz, Cochabamba, and Santa Cruz—received the overwhelming majority of the central government's financial transfers) resisted efforts to create a more progressive distribution of income. The law became mired in these debates and was not ultimately approved.

While plans to decentralize power to the regional level were the most highly developed in the public sphere, the idea of municipalization had been firmly established through several popular texts of the time. These included Luis Ramírez's *Municipio y Territorio* (Municipality and Territory), Rubén Ardaya's *Ensayo Sobre Municipalidad y Municipios* (Essay Regarding Municipalization and Municipalities), Ivan Finot's *Demo-*

cratización del Estado y Descentralización (Democratization of the State and Decentralization), and Carlos Hugo Molina's *La Descentralización Imposible y la Alternativa Municipal* (Impossible Decentralization and the Municipal Alternative). Still, the discussions of decentralization that occurred between 1990 and 1993 included almost no reference to municipalities. Neither did municipal authorities play a significant part in the debates and meetings held in 1991 and 1992 where the possibility of decentralization was discussed. Empowering regional governments was the primary goal of the plans worked out by the civic committees and their allies. A few of these plans mentioned the possibility of decentralizing power to municipalities or provinces, but the timeline and specific provisions of such a decentralization remained vague.

When Sánchez de Lozada began to craft a decentralization reform, he faced at least two options: regionalization and municipalization. Although decentralization had been a much-publicized plank of his campaign platform, the idea had not been developed before he won office. Policy-makers who were brought together to elaborate the idea upon the MNR's electoral victory were shocked by the lack of a clear policy plan (Molina Monasterios, 1997: 198). The new president quickly assembled a skillful team of experts to craft a decentralization reform. Two characteristics of this team foreshadow its drift from the regional decentralization plan already developed by the previous government: the closed nature of its meetings and the strong position within the team of Carlos Hugo Molina, perhaps the nation's strongest proponent of municipalization.

Despite decentralization's popularity, this policy team met behind closed doors—not in a public forum—to create the Law of Popular Participation (LPP). The value of this secrecy was proven in the breach: when working documents from the policy team were obtained by the Santa Cruz Civic Committee, their response was so bellicose that the policy team spent considerable resources and time distancing themselves from the early draft. In addition, further drafts were treated with the utmost security, with no written material allowed to enter or leave the policy meetings.[8]

While not attending every meeting of the team, Sánchez de Lozada played a crucial role in the process. He met frequently with the team, read each revision of the reform, and shaped future meetings of the team with his clear direction. The policy team that drafted the LPP might be misperceived as a group of technocrats operating within a political vacuum; though its meetings were closed and the personnel were highly trained professionals taken largely from outside the political elite, the nature of this committee was patently political. Meetings were closed not to ensure the purity of the resulting law, but to keep political opponents from changing the president's very political agenda. President Sánchez de Lozada did not choose his team and then close the door on them; he visited them almost daily, taking a very keen interest in the group's debates and adjudicating between different versions of the policies proposed. When asked how municipalization was chosen, Luís Lema, a member of the policy-making team, replied: "In the talks that were held, throughout the entire period, with the leader of our party, Gonzalo Sánchez de Lozada" (Archondo, 1997: 150).

When the policy team completed its plan, the government launched a major campaign to educate the public about its new legal proposal. In meetings held throughout the country, citizens began to learn what "popular participation" would mean in practice. Perhaps due to this widespread publicity, the law was passed unanimously within the legislature when it was formally introduced.

In order to assess how Bolivia's parties would have benefited from different configurations of decentralizing reform over time, it is necessary to look at the voting record at the local and regional levels in much greater detail than they are treated in Table 2.2.

Table 2.2.   Local Voting Results in Bolivia, 1985–93

	Percentage of the Vote[a]				
Party	1985	1987	1989	1991	1993
MNR	31.4	12.8	19.3	24.8	34.9
ADN	25.1	28.6	33.6[b]	28.5[b]	7.8
MIR	10.1	26.1			9.4
CONDEPA			18.8	12.6	19.6
UCS			16.5	22.9	8.4

Source: Bolivia's National Electoral Court.
[a] These figures represent the percentage of the municipal vote in the 1985–91 elections and the percentage of the cantonal vote in 1993.
[b] In 1989 and 1991 the ADN and MIR ran joint candidates in municipal elections.

Table 2.3 documents the varying strength of parties in regional capitals versus more rural areas within each of Bolivia's nine departments. The voting results come from municipal elections that, before 1995, were held only in the most urban areas of the country. The results for 1993 reflect votes at the cantonal level, aggregated up to the municipal level. A quick study of the tabular results reveals three noteworthy trends. First, new parties emerge over time, demonstrating an ability to win a significant proportion of the vote. Second, the ADN always does at least as well—and sometimes quite a bit better—in capitals as it does in noncapitals. Third and finally, the MNR consistently performs better in rural contests than in the regional capital cities. The strength of the MNR in rural areas is most striking in the 1985 election, where the ADN won a plurality of the vote in all but one regional capital, while the MNR won a plurality of the noncapital vote in every department for which disaggregated data are available.

Table 2.3.   Urban and Rural Voting Patterns in Local Elections in Bolivia, 1985–95

	Number of capitals (urban) and noncapitals (rural) in which each party wins a plurality of the vote[a]									
	1985		*1987*		*1989*		*1993*		*1995*	
Party	*urban*	*rural*	*urban*	*rural*	*urban*	*rural*	*urban*	*rural*	*urban*	*rural*
MNR	1	7[b]		2		1	6	8	1	4
ADN	8		4	3	6[c]	6[c]			1	1
MIR			3	4			1		1	
MBL			1				1		2	1
FRI			1				1		1	
UCS					1	1			2	1
CONDEPA					1	1	1		1	1
IU			1							1

Source: Bolivia's National Electoral Court.

[a] Numbers are based on restricted municipal contests before 1993, cantonal voting results in 1993, and real municipal returns in 1995.

[b] Two municipalities did not present disaggregated results in 1985, but the MNR won a plurality in the remaining 7.

[c] In 1989, the MIR and ADN ran joint candidates in municipal races.

With the MNR's economic plan still in force, support for the MNR waned in the 1987 midterm elections. Still, the MNR captured a plurality of the noncapital vote in three departments, while failing to capture a plurality in any departmental capital. While the overall vote for the MNR was down, it was still stronger in rural areas than in the big cities. This is recreated in the 1989 contest, when it won no capitals but received a plurality of noncapital votes in one department.

Unfortunately, disaggregated results of the 1991 municipal elections are not available. On an aggregate basis (see Table 2.2), the MNR's support had begun to rise once again. That rise was cemented in the MNR's overwhelming victory in the 1993 elections. In this contest, the MNR won a plurality of noncapital votes in every department except La Paz, where CONDEPA was dominant. In addition, the MNR won a plurality of the votes in six of Bolivia's nine department capitals.

Bolivia's first free election of financially empowered municipal governments demonstrated a wealth of new political strength in the departmental capitals in 1995. Seven different parties won pluralities in Bolivia's nine departmental capitals: the ADN, CONDEPA, FRI (*Frente Revolucionario de Izquierda*), MBL, MIR, MNR, and UCS. Despite losing ground in departmental capitals, the MNR won a plurality of noncapital votes in nearly half the departments and the greatest number of mayors of any party in the system. In all, the MNR won a plurality in 120 municipalities (38.5 percent) and placed 121 mayors (Zegada, 1998: 93).

While precise data are not available to generate tabular representations of either the 1997 or 2000 municipal elections, the MNR's continued electoral strength shaped both of these contests. The MNR won the greatest percentage of municipal votes in the 2000 elections, with 19.7 percent of the total.

If we look at the political landscape of 1993 with a view to the parties' historical patterns of electoral support, it is clear that municipalization promised greater electoral benefits to the MNR than a decentralization plan based on strengthening departmental governments. Given the preponderance of departmental capitals in departmental vote totals and the inability of MNR candidates to reliably win these capitals in municipal votes, the MNR rightly decentralized power to hundreds of rural municipalities (in addition to urban municipalities) in an effort to empower its supporters. Since the reform, this strategy has borne the

expected results: the MNR has lost numerous municipal races in departmental capitals, but has claimed a high percentage of the rural municipal councilors and mayors. In fact, in each of the three municipal elections since 1993, the MNR has won the greatest number of mayoral
posts and municipal council positions of any party in the system. It has
won few of the mayoral positions in the departmental capitals, however.

In addition to shaping the location of power under decentralization,
electoral concerns are also likely to influence the mechanisms chosen for
delivering resources to municipalities. If the MNR is electorally strongest
in rural municipalities, then why does the LPP mandate the distribution
of fiscal resources by population rather than using some formula that
would more clearly benefit its rural strongholds? Many countries in the
region, including Colombia and Mexico, include progressive measures
in the formula for distributing resources, thus favoring poor and largely
rural municipalities; presumably a savvy MNR might have done the
same. In seeking to understand how population came to be the sole cri-
terion for financial transfers, several factors must be considered. According to one author,

> The president chose to distribute resources according to population
> for two reasons. First, there was no consensus on the exact formula
> for calculating inequality or deprivation, a formula that could be jig-
> gled to advantage particular municipalities or departments. Second,
> the creation of this mechanism would require at least several months
> of work to gather the necessary data, choose from a range of mea-
> sures, and calculate the appropriate amount of resources to be dis-
> tributed. In order to avoid such a delay, and the possible political
> manipulation of the distribution mechanism, the team chose the
> path of least resistance—distribution according to population. (Van
> Cott, 2000: 156–57)

THE EVOLUTION OF DECENTRALIZATION UNDER SUCCESSIVE ADMINISTRATIONS

If parties with weak national support, strong regional or local support,
and reliable electorates should decentralize power, will subsequent regimes
with strong national power, weak subnational support, and short-time

horizons recentralize power in the presidency? I maintain that decentralization, particularly its political component, is difficult to reverse.

Before looking into the details of the Bolivian case, it is worthwhile to discuss recentralization at the theoretical level. There are many reasons to think that recentralizing power may be difficult once power has been devolved. Most importantly, voters who have become accustomed to selecting their representatives through an electoral process are unlikely to allow the central government to revert to appointing subnational executives without protest. Likewise, elected officials with popular backing are unlikely to remain quiet while the national government takes away legislated fiscal transfers and taxation powers; once subnational units have gained political legitimacy through elections, they become political counterweights to recentralization efforts in their own right. Recentralization of power may be difficult on a procedural level because laws are hard to change in a popularly elected legislature or, if decentralization has been enshrined in the constitution, because changes to the constitution require supermajorities. Whether for procedural or for popular reasons, decentralization is difficult to reverse.

A full reversal of decentralization may be nearly impossible, but subtle changes in decentralization can be achieved. Decentralization is a multifaceted reform. Some aspects of it may be difficult to roll back, while others may be more permeable to revision. In particular, while the election of local officials may be difficult to reverse, changing electoral laws for municipal contests (so that they benefit the reformer's party) may be possible. In fact, Alberto Fujimori did just that in Peru when he reinstated local elections after a brief pause in 1993. Another arena in which decentralization is vulnerable to change is along its fiscal dimension. Changing highly technical aspects of the fiscal transfer process may significantly affect the reform's beneficiaries without leading to major protest from voters. Finally, symbolic changes in the discourse about decentralization's desirability or in the importance accorded to decentralization may signal change in an administration's stance toward decentralization.

The Bolivian case invites research into the evolution of reform under successive administrations. Hugo Banzer Suárez, the head of the ADN, took control of the presidency in 1997, although he was compelled to step down in 2001, due to poor health, before the completion of his term. I present here a preliminary assessment of his administration's policies toward Popular Participation. I have shown that support for Banzer and his ADN party appears stronger in urban than in rural areas, in contrast to the MNR. Decentralization to departments might have been more in the interest of the ADN than the broad municipal decentralization enacted by the MNR. Given that Banzer inherited this popular municipal decentralization plan, theory predicts that he may try to amend the reform in subtle ways to take power away from his political rivals and redirect it toward his political allies.

Decentralization became embedded in the constitution in 1994, erecting the barrier of constitutional reform against subsequent governments who might want to recentralize power. In addition, decentralization remains the most popular reform of the Sánchez de Lozada administration. These factors make recentralization quite difficult in Bolivia.

A subtle, but significant way in which the LPP has been downgraded by the Banzer government has been in the administrative structure of its program. While Sánchez de Lozada created a Secretariat of Popular Participation, Banzer has reorganized the state apparatus, placing the responsibility for this program in the Vice Ministry of Strategic Planning and Popular Participation, within the Ministry of Sustainable Development and Planning.

More importantly, while the 2000 municipal elections were held on schedule and without any restrictions imposed by the central government, it parceled out campaign funds in a series of payments. The government claimed that fiscal problems necessitated this change in previous practice. This change caused a large public debate in which the National Electoral Court demanded that at least half of the money be transferred to the parties at once. As reported at the time, "Authorities of the National Electoral Court and party leaders believed that the situation reflected the [fiscal] crisis and a lack of liquidity in the national treasury, but were not in agreement that the first installment should be made in pieces" (*La Razón*, September 23, 1999).

In addition to the controversy surrounding campaign funds, municipal governments have also criticized the government for failing to even out the payment of fiscal transfers promised by the LPP. This, among other demands by the Bolivian Association of Municipal Governments, led to a twenty-four-hour strike in mid-August of 1999 that paralyzed the country (*Los Tiempos*, August 18, 1999). Again, the government explained its restriction with reference to fiscal difficulties of the central government. It remains unclear to what extent monies are being retained in the center due to fiscal crisis and to what extent this is a strategic maneuver to keep financial resources in the central government's hands.

The consensus on the Banzer administration's treatment of the popular participation program seems to be that, while he has not rolled it back, he has not furthered it. During his tenure, the program's emphasis has shifted away from the local level and toward the departmental governments.

> The motivation for this is obvious: ADN militants hold all nine departmental prefectures, but the party is weak at the municipal level. Greater resources and responsibilities have been shifted to this level of government to enhance the ADN's future electoral chances and to facilitate the proportional distribution of patronage jobs among coalition partners. It also indicates a response to pressure from the Civic Committees, which are closer to the ADN than to the MNR. (Van Cott, 2000: 211)

An early act of Banzer's government (undertaken within the first month of his presidency) liberated departmental prefects—all ADN partisans—from having to present written quarterly reports to the departmental assembly and also from the necessity of attaining the general director of the department's signature on administrative resolutions of the prefecture. This measure, enacted in Supreme Decree 24833, also enhanced the prefect's power relative to provincial subprefects in the provinces and *corregidores* in the cantons (Urenda Díaz, 1998: 83–85). While none of these changes has greatly damaged the impact of the LPP on devolving power to municipal governments, each represents a subtle, but meaningful step toward reining in the process of devolution.

CONCLUSION

Since 1982, Bolivia has enjoyed its longest uninterrupted era of democratic elections. Democratic competition has weathered the country's worst economic crisis; it has witnessed the alternation in power of four different parties and even more numerous coalitions; and it has created the impetus for deepening democracy through decentralization. Com-

petition in national elections is tight, and no party has yet won a majority of the vote, which would allow it to bypass the coalition-building
process in the legislature and claim the presidency outright. History has
tempered any party's assumption of natural coalition parties—most notably when the rightist ADN and the leftist MIR teamed up to exclude
the centrist MNR from gaining the presidency in 1989. In short, no party
can take its ability to control national power for granted. With power
concentrated in the presidency, a loss at the national level before decentralization meant at least four years of exclusion from national power.
This context created the incentives for a party with strong support at the
subnational level throughout much of the nation's territory to decentralize power and therefore retain access to decentralized positions, even
when national power was out of its reach. Decentralization allowed the
parties to exchange high-risk competition over one largely indivisible
prize for a set of competitions for hundreds of smaller prizes, where virtually every party would have a chance to prove its ability to govern on
a small scale.

While this chapter has been devoted to the Bolivian case, the theory
developed here may be useful in understanding decentralizing experiences outside Bolivia's borders. At the same time, it should not be interpreted as a universal theory of decentralization; as other authors, including several in this volume, point out, decentralization has occurred under
widely varying conditions and for many different reasons. Looking across
Latin America, however, an electoral theory seems to hold out the most
promise in explaining cases of decentralization where both political and
fiscal resources were simultaneously decentralized under democratic auspices. Initial phases of decentralization in Chile, Argentina, and Brazil
appear to be conversions back to the decentralized state structure that
preceded authoritarian rule; further fiscal decentralization may be a capitulation to pressures from popularly elected mayors or governors, or
it may reflect a budget-rationalizing strategy at the national level. The
advent of meaningful decentralization in Mexico may represent a concession to growing opposition parties who could cite constitutional language allowing subnational political contests before the ruling PRI (*Partido Revolucionario Institucional*, or Institutionalized Revolutionary
Party) recognized opposition victories. Alternatively, its coincidence with
growing PRI insecurity in the central government could signal an electoral motive for decentralization (see Beer, this volume).

The electoral basis for decentralization appears to fit the Colombian and Peruvian cases best. In Colombia, municipal elections were legislated (1986) under a Conservative president elected in 1982 due to a split in the nearly hegemonic Liberal Party. Based on national legislative voting results from 1982, the percentage of the vote won by the Liberal Party differed by less than a percentage point from its 1978 tally, and it had a considerable margin over the Conservatives in that body. Under these conditions, Conservatives could be expected to have little hope of continuing to hold the presidency if the Liberals coalesced behind a single candidate in the future (which they did). In Peru, decentralization began through a constitutional assembly in which the American Popular Revolutionary Alliance (APRA) predominated—a party with widespread and stable support throughout the country, but one that proved unable to attain the presidency. The election of governors was also legislated during an APRA presidency; as the 1990 election approached, the APRA saw its chances of regaining the executive evaporate. Although the APRA lost the national contest to Alberto Fujimori, the party picked up the vast majority of gubernatorial posts. After his sweeping national victory, Fujimori—a president who created and discarded party machinery with every new election—erased the election of regional governors, ridding himself of opposition leadership in Peru's departments. He also reshaped the political and economic rules governing local mayors and councils, stacking the electoral rules against the remnants of Peru's traditional parties, and making financial resources almost entirely subject to his own discretion. Given Fujimori's national popularity and his party's inability to place its candidates in lower offices (Cambio 90 candidates won less than 5 percent of the mayoral positions in 1993, the first local elections of Fujimori's tenure), this recentralization of power follows from the electoral theory.

I have argued here that both the impetus for Bolivia's decentralizing reform and the shape that the reform took were critically influenced by the electoral considerations of those parties in a position to affect power relations between levels of government. The MNR—a party with strong and relatively stable support throughout the countryside—decentralized power. It devolved national power to the municipal level, playing to its electoral strength in rural areas of the country. In doing so, it bypassed a much debated and fairly well-developed plan to devolve power to departments. In this alternative plan, urban votes would have swamped rural votes, granting power to the MNR's greatest political rivals. Electoral considerations shaped not just the timing but also the very form of decentralization in Bolivia.

Major decentralization reforms signal the beginning of a process that inevitably changes over time. Bolivia is no exception to this rule. Just as electoral considerations have helped to shape the devolution process up to this point, we should expect them to continue to do so. We should look to electoral incentives when predicting shifts in decentralization over time. The final section of this chapter has discussed how, despite many legal and popular obstacles to reversing decentralization, successor administrations with different electoral incentives may attempt to recentralize power. In Bolivia, the ADN's Hugo Banzer has attempted to rein in some of the decentralizing effects of the Popular Participation Law he inherited from his predecessor. As new governments rise to take his place, I am certain that these same forces will result in an ebb and flow of power from central to local government and back. Once decentralization has been put into place, however, the shifts over time should be fairly minor.

Notes

1. Bolivia's decentralizing reforms compare favorably with those of Venezuela, Peru, Chile, and Ecuador—all countries with larger populations and more advanced economic development.

2. The government did not devolve increased powers to the regional level, making this a case of one-tier decentralization in the framework of Montero and Samuels.

3. Throughout this chapter I use the terms "region" and "department" interchangeably.

4. In the 1997 reform this formula was changed somewhat so that half of the Chamber of Deputies is now elected in single-member districts.

5. All quotes presented in this paper are my translations from Spanish.

6. A 1994 constitutional change now limits the legislature's choice to the top two candidates in the national election.

7. Selecting mayors resembles the presidential selection process. If no party wins a majority of the votes, the municipal council determines the mayor from

among the municipal council members. The fact that the MNR won a plurality in more municipalities than any other party does not, therefore, mean that the MNR placed more mayors than any other party.

8. Author interview with Federico Martínez, a member of the policy team under Sánchez de Lozada that designed the LPP, La Paz, January 1997.

CHAPTER 3

The Political Logic of
Decentralization in Brazil

David J. Samuels

Even before the wave of decentralization hit Latin America
in the 1980s, Brazil was the most highly decentralized country in
the region. Historically, federalism has contributed to this comparatively decentralized system, whether the political regime
was democratic or authoritarian. Being relatively decentralized,
however, does not explain swings toward or away from centralization over time, and we must therefore ask, Does the process of democratization Brazil began in the 1980s explain the
swing toward decentralization to states and municipalities begun
around the same time? Some have argued or at least implied that
the answer to this question is yes (e.g., Nohlen, 1991; Nickson,
1995; Souza, 1997; IDB, 1997; Bird and Vaillancourt, 1998).

In this chapter I argue that the "democratization leads to
decentralization" argument is inadequate. At the most basic
level, correlation is not causation: democratization is too general a concept to explain the extent and form of decentralization. We must explore the particulars of every country's transition to understand why politicians decentralized extensively in
some countries and not in others, even as all moved toward democracy. More specifically, democratization cannot sufficiently

explain decentralization in Brazil because decentralization in the current democratic period differs significantly from the decentralization that took place during Brazil's first experience with democracy between 1945 and 1964. In particular, in contrast to previous eras, the contemporary period has witnessed decentralization of significant power and resources to Brazil's states *and* its municipalities, the country's lowest level of government. This is a particularly noteworthy development: for the first time in Brazil's history, local governments have significant fiscal and political autonomy. Indeed, the degree of municipal autonomy in Brazil now exceeds that in any other Latin American country (Nickson, 1995). Decentralization to municipalities complicates the pendular swings of centralization to the national government and decentralization to state governments (and back again) that have characterized Brazilian history since 1889, when a centralized hereditary monarchy was overthrown. Because the two democratic experiences with decentralization differ, the end of a dictatorship and the start of free and fair elections is insufficient to explain the particulars of the decentralization process. In this chapter I explain why, in contrast to previous eras, decentralization in Brazil has included both states and municipalities.

What explains decentralization in Brazil, if not democratization? First, one cannot explain decentralization under democracy without reference to whatever centralization occurred under dictatorship. Moreover, democratization cannot explain decentralization in Brazil because decentralization to states and municipalities actually began prior to the restoration of democracy. Some policies that could be candidates for decentralization were decentralized before the 1988 constitution, while others remain in the hands of the central government to this day. This points to the importance of understanding the particular political logic of decentralization, for decentralization has not been immediate or wholesale following redemocratization. An explicitly political logic that involves federal, state, and local executive-branch leaders has determined which policies are decentralized, to what extent, and how rapidly.

This chapter attempts to paint a picture of the general trend to decentralize power and resources away from the central government since the 1980s.[1] In terms of decentralization to Brazil's states, I argue that it resulted from the inability of the military regime to transform the Brazilian political elite's preexisting organizational structure, which was and continues to be based on state-based networks as opposed to strong, centralized national party organizations (Hagopian, 1996). Given the continuity of its organizational structure, when the regime began the transition process Brazil's political elite retained strong incentives to mobilize to amplify state governments' resources and powers at the expense of the central government. In addition, the electoral calendar during the first decade of the transition intensified these state-based political incentives, because the schedule of elections forced politicians to organize around state-based political interests and networks.

The story for municipal governments is somewhat more complex. Decentralization to municipalities initially and somewhat ironically resulted from the unintended consequences of two policies the military adopted to *limit* municipal autonomy. First, while the military ended presidential and gubernatorial elections, gutted Congress's powers, and deliberately destroyed the pre-1964 party system following its coup, it maintained the schedule of municipal elections. Thus, aspiring politicians found that they could play an important role at the municipal level during the military regime, as opposed to the state or national level. Second, shifting away from long-established practice, the military regime deliberately attempted to sidestep state governments' role as intermediaries between national and local governments, and instead dealt directly with municipalities, in a less politicized and more bureaucratized fashion. This freed municipalities from state-government tutelage and, in combination with Congress's and the states' military-imposed debility, left municipal mayors as the only politicians able to claim credit for implementation of government programs or projects at the local level.

These two policies would only become significant later on, since the process of urbanization also set the stage for municipal decentralization. As in other countries, urbanization shifted the mass of Brazil's electorate from the countryside to the cities during the 1960s and 1970s. This transformation has had far-ranging political consequences: although municipal interests were largely rural interests up through the 1964 coup, by the 1980s urbanization forced the vast majority of Brazilian politicians to focus on providing government services to urban voters. Thus, as free elections returned in the 1980s, politicians increasingly realized that their own careers depended on bolstering ties with municipal government officials. In fact, by the 1980s a surprising number of Brazilian politicians sought to make their political careers at the municipal level; urbanization and the military's policies had made the position of municipal mayor a significantly more attractive political position. Given these factors, upon redemocratization politicians had far fewer incentives to return to the pre-1964 situation, where state and national governments dominated municipalities. Instead, because municipalities had become a relatively more important part of every Brazilian politician's career, politicians in the 1980s sought to cement municipal political autonomy.

In summary, the consequences of military rule and urbanization help us understand how a political-electoral logic drove decentralization to both states and municipalities during the democratic transition.[2] That is, democratization and electoral considerations are necessary ingredients to an explanation of decentralization, but they are not sufficient. In this chapter I first briefly explore the historical swings between centralization and decentralization in Brazil from 1889 to 1964. I then explore in greater detail the ways in which the 1964–85 military regime attempted to centralize power, and explain why these policies had limited success. Together with an exploration of the political consequences of urbanization, I then explain how the military's policies helped create the conditions for decentralization. Subsequently, I explore the specific choices that Brazilian politicians made during the 1980s to decentralize resources and power. The final section offers some conjectures about the future of Brazilian federalism.

Federalism under the "Old Republic," 1889–1930

Brazil's hereditary monarchy was overthrown in 1889 and replaced with a republican form of government in 1891. This period, which lasted until 1930, has been characterized as the "Politics of the Governors" because a dramatically decentralized federal system emerged in which governors of the most powerful states dominated the country's politics. The federal constitution at the time granted extensive powers to states, such as the ability to impose export and import taxes on interstate trade within the country. Brazilian states could recruit troops, and many formed what were essentially independent armies. They could write their own civil, commercial, and penal codes (unlike Mexico and Argentina, two other federal systems) and had exclusive control over subsoil mineral rights. They could also negotiate international loans without central-government authority (Love, 1993: 186–87). State governors dominated politics within their states, playing municipal bosses off each other (Castro, 1987; Brasileiro, 1973). In stark contrast to the other emergent de jure federalisms in Latin America at the time, Brazilian federalism granted extensive de facto power to states during this period.

FEDERALISM AND DICTATORSHIP, 1930–45

Getúlio Vargas, a former governor of the state of Rio Grande do Sul, led the overthrow of the Old Republic in 1930.[3] In 1937 Vargas engineered a coup d'etat and declared himself dictator, beginning a short but important period (until 1945) known as the New State (*Estado Novo*). He proclaimed the literal end of Brazilian federalism; Brazil became a unitary state officially, with the states now called "administrative units." Vargas abolished all state parties and directly nominated state "interventors," who replaced the elected state governors. In a famous demonstration of his intention to destroy federalism, Vargas publicly burned each state's flag. However, this centralizing project hid important continuities. The "ex-states" continued to administer much of the government apparatus: state tax receipts from 1938 to 1945 were 56 percent of national tax receipts, while in Mexico at the same time (a de jure federal state), state tax receipts accounted for only 17 percent of national tax receipts (Love, 1993: 218). Although both the centralizing goals of those who led the *Estado Novo* as well as Vargas's personal impact on Brazilian politics from 1930 to his death in 1954 have received substantial attention,[4] more recent historiography has ascertained that a high degree of continuity with the 1889–1930 republic characterizes the 1930–45 period, in that the basis of elite political competition, coordination, and organization never shifted away from the states (e.g., Camargo, 1993, 1999). Unlike Juan Perón in Argentina, for example, Vargas was unable to create a national movement or party that could compete for control of the nation. The *Estado Novo* did move Brazil in a centralizing direction, but the options open to Vargas were circumscribed by the historical "stickiness" of Brazilian federalism. The same logic holds for the other eras I discuss, in particular the contemporary phase of decentralization, which was conditioned by the actions of the previous military regime.

FEDERALISM, DEMOCRACY, AND DECENTRALIZATION, 1945–64

Following the ouster of Vargas in 1945, Brazil began its first experience with mass democracy. This is a crucial period to examine along with the post-1985 period, because in both periods direct election of mayors and governors was allowed. If one supposes that decentralization follows democratization, we might expect that decentralization to both states and municipalities would follow dictatorship in both 1945 and 1985.

Indeed, as in the 1980s, pressure for decentralization immediately following Vargas's ouster was intense, and a general "electoralist" logic
of decentralization appears to hold for the 1945–64 period. Recently
elected politicians wanted to decentralize power and resources to both
states and municipalities, because they wanted to remove control over
policy, resource distribution, and patronage from the hands of central-
government bureaucrats and Vargas appointees who had dominated during the previous period. However, an examination of this period shows
that decentralization mainly benefited states, not municipalities.

After 1945, states and state governors regained powers lost under
Vargas. Most importantly, direct elections for governor returned, giving governors independent control over substantial pools of revenue and
patronage. In turn, this provided governors with substantial influence
over the careers of *national* legislators from their state, because legislators need these state-level resources to advance their own careers (Abrucio, 1998). Thus, when free elections began in 1946, governors regained
their position as key players in national executive-legislative relations. In
short, despite Vargas's efforts from 1930 to 1945 to centralize and promote a nationalization of politics, and his creation of ostensibly national
parties in 1945, political elites retained their state-based political allegiances throughout his reign and into Brazil's first democratic period
(Camargo, 1993, 1999). Moreover, state governments benefited considerably from fiscal decentralization after 1945. The onset of democracy re-
invigorated states' and state actors' influence in Brazilian national politics.

In contrast, municipalities did not experience similar political gains,
despite a strong pro-municipal lobby, which gained momentum following
the demise of the *Estado Novo* (Mello, 1965). This lobby even managed
to obtain increased municipal autonomy in Brazil's new constitution; for
the first time in Brazilian history, the constitution mandated that all municipal officials would be elected.[5] Municipalities also gained the freedom to organize services according to local needs and, most importantly,
gained increased revenue transfers from the state and federal governments. Since nearly all municipalities at the time lacked their own revenue sources, the new fiscal transfers promised "a large windfall" (Mahar,
1971: 71), and municipal leaders believed that increased political autonomy would follow from the intended funding increases. Scholars therefore concluded that Brazil's 1946 constitution boded extremely well for
municipalities (Mello, 1955: 29; Sherwood, 1967: 38).

Unfortunately, as has been common in Brazilian history, politicians did not comply with the written rules. Nearly all municipalities remained penurious and politically dependent, because both the state and federal governments ignored the constitution's revenue-transfer rules. In many years the federal government delivered its payments late, in other years it disbursed only partial payments, and in some years it disbursed nothing at all (Sherwood, 1967: 124; Mahar, 1971: 73). In addition, except for three relatively wealthy states, state governments during the entire 1945–64 period never disbursed what they ought to have transferred to municipalities, and the three remaining states only did so sporadically and according to political criteria that reduced municipal political autonomy (Mello, 1965: 23; Ferreira, 1965: 423). Thus, although it appeared that municipalities would gain along with states in terms of decentralization, the formal rule changes were ignored. Municipalities remained politically subordinate to federal and, in particular, state-government whims. Brazilian scholars observed this fact soon after Congress had promulgated the new constitution; one analyst wrote that state governments *could* neutralize the pro-municipal constitutional rules (Xavier, 1950: 222), and others noted that political connections, not formal rules, actually *did* determine whether a municipality would receive the funds it was due (Mello, 1955: 42–43; Sherwood, 1967: 38–39; Brasileiro, 1973: 105).

In summary, despite a vocal *municipalista* lobby and pro-municipal rules, the 1946 constitution did not decentralize resources and autonomy to Brazil's municipalities. Instead, state governments regained powers lost under Vargas, and the federal government continued its expansion. Municipalities remained locked in their traditional role as passive recipients of government services—if their leaders had the right political connections. In 1946 *municipalismo* did not resound with a broad enough audience for its ideas to be put into practice. This would occur only later, in the 1980s. I now turn to the question of *why* this later decentralization occurred, beginning with the policies of the 1964–85 military regime.

MILITARY RULE: STATE AND MUNICIPAL CIRCUMSCRIPTION

The generals who ended Brazil's democracy in 1964 initially had no clear plan to modify intergovernmental relations. However, the military soon perceived the need to increase their control over subnational authorities when several of its favored candidates lost in important state gubernatorial elections held in October 1965 (Abrucio, 1998: 10–12). The military quickly understood that subnational political autonomy, particularly at the state level, and the concomitant independence of political elites from national-government control could threaten its rule. Thus, soon after this stinging defeat, the military extinguished all existing political parties and decreed that all subsequent presidential and gubernatorial elections would be indirect (state assemblies would elect governors, after the military had approved their nomination). The regime then established a "government" party (ARENA, or National Renewal Alliance) and an "opposition" party (MDB, or Brazilian Democratic Movement).

Importantly, the regime did not eliminate all direct elections: citizens continued to vote for mayor and city council members (in almost all municipalities) and for state and federal legislators, despite frequent changes in electoral laws and limits on competition. The continuation of local-level elections turned out to be a crucial element in explaining decentralization to municipalities, as I will discuss below. The military believed that such limited political competition would not impede its plans to centralize control over both municipal and state governments. In a 1967 fiscal reform, the military government created two "Participation Funds," one for states (*Fundo de Participação dos Estados*, FPE) and one for municipalities (*Fundo de Participação dos Municípios*, FPM). Ten percent of the national-level income and excise taxes were to be pooled and then divided equally between the two funds for distribution. These transfers (as well as state-to-municipal transfers) were made automatic, and ought to have increased municipal revenue, especially given their pre-1964 situation. However, just a year after the funds' implementation, the military halved the share of the taxes designated to the FPE and FPM and placed restrictions on how state and municipal governments could spend funds they received or raised (Oliveira, 1995: 22). This tied subnational policy increasingly to central-government directives, and the reductions in revenue also tended to limit subnational political autonomy. Table 3.1 shows the effect of the 1967 reforms on state and municipal finances through 1980.

The federal government gained 17 percent in terms of final expenditures as a proportion of the total, while states lost 34 percent and mu-

Table 3.1.   Division of the Fiscal Pie in Brazil, 1960–80

	Share of Total Revenue (%)			Share of Final Expenditures (%)		
Year	Central	State	Municipal	Central	State	Municipal
1965	63.8	30.9	5.9	54.8	35.1	10.1
1970	66.7	30.6	2.7	60.8	29.2	10.0
1975	73.7	23.5	2.8	68.0	23.3	8.7
1980	74.7	21.7	3.7	68.2	23.3	8.6

Source: Rezende (1995); Varsano (1997), Tables 5 and 6.

nicipalities lost 15 percent. Subnational governments (states especially) would lose on other fronts as well, as the national government increased its administrative and legal powers with the promulgation of a series of decrees that imposed national administrative guidelines (Abrucio, 1998: 64–82). In short, in the early years of its rule, the military regime implemented a number of policies specifically designed to reduce state and municipal government autonomy.

THE MILITARY'S FAILURE TO ELIMINATE DECENTRALIZING FORCES AT THE STATE LEVEL

To understand how states regained power and resources during Brazil's recent democratic transition, we must understand why politicians continued to act on behalf of state interests once the military regime ended. In brief, decentralization during the democratic transition resulted from the military regime's inability to transform the Brazilian political elite's organizational structure. Since at least the period of the "Politics of the Governors," Brazil's dominant political elites have derived their power from state-based support networks. Although the military strove to alter this form of political organization and reduce the influence of federalism in Brazilian politics, they ultimately failed. Consequently, once the military made it clear that they would relinquish power, politicians once again reasserted their state-based allegiances and interests.

The maintenance of semicompetitive elections at various levels during the dictatorship, even given the reductions in state-government political, financial, and administrative autonomy, meant that governors remained important political players. This was due to the logic of patronage politics in Brazil; historically, politicians at all levels have depended on *state* government machines for access to politically valuable goods. The military recognized that governors were the key to this system, and that in order to maintain the support of Brazil's traditional political elite, they would have to control who became governor. Thus, the military nominated "technical" governors—men with nonpolitical backgrounds, fewer links to traditional state politicians, and tighter links to the central government (Nunes, 1996: 90–91; W. Santos, 1971: 123–28). This tactic, the generals reasoned, would allow the government to construct a new political elite, one decidedly different from the "traditional" politicians who reigned prior to the 1964 coup.

However, this strategy failed to eliminate state political elites' autonomy and destroy their state-based organizational structure in the long term, for two reasons. First, the regime did not change how politicians accessed the system. Although the military could have decreed that central party organizations in ARENA and the MDB would control nominations for federal deputy and senator, it instead permitted state political machines to maintain nomination control, as they had prior to 1964. Thus, politicians maintained their state-based ties, and despite the façade of national bipartisan politics, both ARENA and the MDB continued to be federations—"islands" of largely independent political elites, mostly rooted in pre-1964 arrangements. Second, and more importantly, although the regime continued to rely on conservative political elites, and these politicians continued to rely upon traditional forms of clientelism (Sarles, 1982; Cammack, 1982; Hagopian, 1996), these same elite politicians resented and resisted the imposition of *técnico* governors, who tended to ignore their demands for clientelistic goods. The *técnicos'* different governing style—and the fact that many of them attempted to construct their own political bases independently of existing networks—estranged governors from many of the regime's own ARENA supporters. Consequently, the *técnico* governors ended up politically isolated and had great difficulty controlling state ARENA machines (Sarles, 1982: 49).

The military suffered an embarrassing electoral defeat in 1974, despite having carefully selected the gubernatorial candidates and manipulating electoral laws to favor ARENA. The military high command concluded that opposition victories at the state level would mean the loss of important niches of power and potential loss of control over the transition. Likewise, ARENA governors perceived that their power grew after the 1974 election, because the military increasingly needed them to help generate ARENA majorities and weaken the MDB opposition. The regime, finally perceiving that *técnicos* reaped few votes, and desperate to strengthen its allies, began to cede power to state governments through traditional (non-*técnico*) ARENA elites in the mid- to late 1970s. In 1978 the military nominated more *políticos* for governor (Nunes, 1996: 90–91), loosened control over ARENA machines, and allowed traditional politicians to reestablish links with organs of the state executives (Hagopian, 1996: chap. 7).

In addition, the military attempted to strengthen elites in less-developed states and to weaken the richer states, where the opposition was stronger. To this end they adopted a six-point plan: (1) greater government investment in less-developed states through the Second National Development Plan, which aimed to strengthen government allies in those states and to reduce the weight of the state of São Paulo within the Brazilian federation (Ames, 1987; Silva and Aguirre, 1992); (2) electoral reform through the so-called April Package in 1977 that increased congressional representation of poorer, conservative states; (3) creation of "bionic" senators, one-third of the total, to be chosen indirectly (as were governors) by state assemblies (all except one of which ARENA controlled); (4) creation of an additional poor and conservative state (Mato Grosso do Sul), which increased the representation of regime allies in Congress; (5) an increase in politically negotiated transfer payments to state governments, especially to the less-developed states. Such transfers rose 208 percent between 1976 and 1982 (Afonso, 1995a: 22); and (6) a gradual increase in automatic transfer payments to states (and municipalities), which amounted to the beginning of the process of fiscal decentralization that culminated with the 1988 constitutional convention (see below). This plan guaranteed a regime victory in all state governments except one in 1978, yet the MDB posted additional electoral gains that year. In 1982, ARENA's successor party (the PDS, or Social Democratic Party) would only win direct democratic elections for governor in states where it had reestablished close ties between the state executive and the traditional state political elites.

In summary, in terms of intergovernmental relations, following the coup the military high command realized that gubernatorial strength and traditional politicians' state-based allegiances might undermine its centralizing plans. Thus, the military attempted to reduce governors' power and cut state political elites off at the knees. However, this policy backfired. Traditional elites resisted military meddling in their affairs, and *técnico* governors failed to unite state elites behind the regime's project. This weakened the regime's base of support. In 1974, because of this weakness and because of overblown economic expectations, electoral disaster resulted. Subsequently, the military faction favoring *abertura* and a gradual transfer of power to the regime's civilian allies won the upper hand, and the military began to return power to state governors and reintegrate state-based elites, who remained formally allied to the regime and who of course did not want to lose power to the MDB. The regime's relative losses in the 1974 and 1978 elections had already begun to alter the federal balance of power in favor of the states—without the opposition actually winning more than one of the elections—because the bargaining power of traditional political elites increased as the military's own position became more precarious. In Brazil, decentralization began *under* military rule, not *after* it.

The military failed to dramatically alter the state-based organizational structure of Brazil's dominant conservative political elite during its rule. Political elites in all states successfully survived central-government imposition of state executives and preserved their traditional organizational structure, based on state politics (not surprisingly, this held as well for the emerging MDB opposition elites). Contrary to their early centralizing plans, by decentralizing power and resources to states during the *abertura,* the military increased the political importance of state governors and turned the conservative political elites against the central government—and in favor of additional decentralization—as the transition advanced.

STATE-BASED POLITICAL INTERESTS AND THE TRANSITIONAL ELECTION CALENDAR

The incentives for Brazilian politicians not only to defend a state's interests but to augment state power intensified as the transition wore on. A turning point came in 1982, when the military moved from liberalization to democratization of the process and held (mostly) free and fair elections for all offices except president. Brazil's "transitional" electoral calendar—the sequence of elections for president, governors, Congress, and so forth—helps us get a handle on the particular electoralist logic behind the demand for decentralization to states during the democratic transition, because the gubernatorial races instantly became the focus of electoral competition around the country.

Brazil held two democratic elections for governor, senators, and state and federal deputies in 1982 and 1986, before conducting its first national (presidential) election in 1989 (another nonconcurrent election for governors and Congress was held in 1990). After 1982, while the military retained control over the presidency and the central government bureaucracy, democratically elected governors grew increasingly independent of the central government and controlled state-government bureaucracies. Because subnational elections were held first (unlike in other democratizing Southern Cone countries), the political elite's electoral energies focused on state politics and conquest of state offices, to the detriment of national parties. Thus the rise of gubernatorial influence at the state level combined with continued military control of the presidency during this time increased the importance of subnational actors and interests in national politics, to the detriment of national parties and national issues.

Nonconcurrent gubernatorial elections accentuated the importance of state politics because candidates for federal deputy must, despite the individualistic nature of the electoral system, ally with a political "boss" who is a candidate for state-wide office. These state leaders form groups that provide the resources and connections necessary for a successful congressional campaign. In exchange, candidates for deputy promise to support the governor once he wins office (Abrucio, 1998: chaps. 4–5). Historically in Brazil, the governor's race, and not the presidential race, has determined electoral coalitions for legislative elections within each state. Gubernatorial candidates provide a focal point for all campaigns, pulling in votes and sweeping candidates into office on their coattails (Samuels, 2000a; 2000b).

Gubernatorial elections served as an electoral focal point even before 1982. In 1979, when the regime indicated that the 1982 gubernatorial elections would be direct, politicians immediately began to scramble for position at the state level, literally downplaying national partisan attachments (see, e.g., *Veja,* September 5, 1979: 28–29). By allowing the direct election of governors, the regime admitted that any and all governors, and not just opposition governors, would be free from central government tutelage. Given the control governors can exert over federal deputies in their states, gubernatorial independence echoed within the halls of Congress, transforming executive-legislative relations years before the last general left the presidential palace. In short, once the announcement was made that the 1982 elections would be free, the façade that the (P)MDB and ARENA/PDS were national parties dropped away, and politicians in both parties fought for space where it first opened up: at the state level.

Brazilian politicians organized themselves for subnational democratic elections for ten years before a direct election decided a national political contest. As a result, throughout the 1980s and even into the 1990s, the political fates of all deputies, senators, and governors have been tied to state-level disputes and de-linked from national electoral-political disputes. The divorce between subnational and national political contests during Brazil's transition accentuated the power of state governors, increased federal deputies' state-based orientation, and contributed to the comparatively low degree of electoral nationalization of most of Brazil's parties. Together with the military regime's unsuccessful efforts to undermine the state-based nature of elite political organization in Brazil, the electoral calendar accentuated the incentives Brazilian politicians had to decentralize power and resources to states during the transition to democracy.

Urbanization and Military Rule: Shaping the Context for Decentralization to Municipalities

When the transition to democracy began in the late 1970s and early 1980s, a strong state-based dynamic was already reemerging in Brazilian politics. However, decentralization in Brazil has been significantly greater to the municipal level in the 1980s and 1990s than to the state level, and in this section I explain the factors that encouraged this transformation.

Prior to the 1988 constitutional convention, politicians held numerous "pro-municipalist" meetings that attracted a good deal of media attention. The *municipalista* lobby appeared prominently in the debates prior to the 1988 constitutional convention, as it had during the 1946 constitutional convention. It is useful to recall that municipalities achieved significant "paper gains" in 1946, but only because this reminds us that strong pro-municipal sentiment is an insufficient explanation for decentralization. Increased municipal autonomy and power do *not* necessarily follow from democratization, and did not in 1946. Why did the 1988 changes go much further on paper and—more importantly, in contrast to the aftermath of the 1946 convention—why have they stuck? Here I focus on two sets of forces that helped set the historical stage for 1988: the political consequences of military rule, and the political consequences of urbanization. Both factors affected individual members' of Congress electoral and career interests, which is the key to understanding the actual decision to decentralize.

THE POLITICAL CONSEQUENCES OF MILITARY RULE

I suggested above that the military's own policies ultimately set the stage for demands for decentralization to Brazil's states. Similarly, two policies the military government adopted resulted in greater incentives for politicians to decentralize power and resources to municipalities. First, the political attractiveness of municipalities increased as an unintended consequence of the military's initial policy of *restricting* municipal (and state) autonomy. Under military rule, federal-government bureaucrats gained a freer hand to exclude subnational authorities from policy making and execution. As a result, during the dictatorship municipal participation in planning and execution of government programs was minimal, and municipal authorities were rarely consulted prior to a program's implementation. Resource allocation also reflected the central government's priorities and not—even in highly populous municipalities—local-level needs or desires (Instituto Brasileiro de Administração Municipal, 1976: 37–38). As part of this process of centralization, the military deliberately curtailed state governments' historic role as intermediary between federal and local governments (Schmitter, 1973: 220; Cammack, 1982: 67; Medeiros, 1986). Through 1964, state-level politicians had often diverted federal resources that were destined to municipalities, but by 1976 the central government had blocked state-government officials from interfering with federal-municipal contacts (Instituto Brasileiro de Administração Municipal, 1976: 18). The military also reduced the capacity of states to politicize municipal-level resource distribution by making fiscal transfers to municipalities automatic, in contrast to the highly politicized pre-1964 system. Although the military did reduce the amounts transferred following the 1967 fiscal reforms, automatic transfers assured municipal-level politicians that they would receive *all* funds they were allotted, without political interference. One Brazilian scholar concluded that "Municipal governments' greatest conquest in the 1967 fiscal reform was not in the volume of funds, but in the certainty of receiving the federal quotas" (Mello, 1971: 56). This "bureaucratic rationalization" of disbursements to municipalities would have a positive impact in the long run.

Second, given the circumscription of state-level political involvement in municipal affairs, we must consider the impact of the military's decision to continue to hold direct mayoral elections in all municipalities except state capitals[6] throughout its rule. Given continued elections, and despite municipalities' reduced fiscal resources, mayors continued to appeal to and depend on popular approval and were closest to citizens' day-to-day problems. In contrast, throughout the military period congressional deputies had no access to the budgetary pork barrel and little influence over national policy, and state-oriented politicians faced relatively greater difficulty in obtaining and distributing patronage. Thus, during the military regime winning election at the municipal level became relatively more politically profitable than it had been under the previous democratic regime (see Samuels, 2003: chaps. 3–4). The relative attractiveness of municipal positions increased particularly after 1974, when the military lost ground to the opposition MDB party and subsequently increased the distribution of patronage to its ARENA allies at the municipal level (Medeiros, 1986; Ames, 1987).

The Political Consequences of Urbanization

The military's policies would not have affected Brazilian politicians' decision to decentralize if not for two dramatic demographic transformations that characterize post-1945 Brazil: population growth and urbanization (M. Santos, 1994; Power and Roberts, 2000). Urban population growth increased most rapidly during the dictatorship, growing faster in the 1970s than overall population growth. And unlike other Latin American countries, which have one or at most a few large urban centers, Brazil in 2000 had twelve cities with a population of over one million and 203 cities with a population between 100,000 and one million (TSE, 2000).

Members of Congress have strong incentives to lend a close ear to municipal-level demands, because they depend on connections with municipal government leaders and with local-level popular groups to advance their political careers (Mainwaring, 1999; Ames, 2001). This tendency is exacerbated by Brazil's electoral system, in which federal legislators are elected in at-large electoral districts that conform to state boundaries, and in which citizens can choose a candidate's name instead of a party label when they vote. Given the statewide electoral district, candidates must campaign in urban areas, where they benefit relatively more from media exposure and economies of scale in campaign advertising. Thus even candidates with rural bases also campaign in urban areas.

It is true that politicians during the 1945–64 period also depended heavily on municipal bases of support (Ames, 1987), but far fewer municipalities were urban during that period. The system that Nunes Leal (1977) characterized as *coronelismo* operated in mostly rural municipalities. The key point is not simply that there are more voters now and that more of them now live in urban areas, but that residents of urban municipalities have different needs and present different demands than do residents of rural municipalities. For example, housing and transportation are generally more expensive, and crime more rampant, in urban areas. As the democratic transition progressed, such demands rang increasingly loudly (J. Costa, 1996: 115).

In addition, while many urban politicians continue to this day to seek votes by providing particularistic goods, urban voters are typically less integrated into clientelistic machines than are rural voters. For example, given the success of parties such as the PT (Workers' Party) in larger cities (Nylen, 2000), urban residents are more likely to vote on policy issues than on whether they received particularistic goods such as jobs or money. For politicians interested in building their reputation on responding to broad popular pressures, holding municipal office provides such an opportunity. Even for those politicians still primarily interested in distributing particularistic goods, the municipal government apparatus provides a structure for exploitation. In short, as voters poured into urban areas during the military period, and with these voters presenting different demands than rural voters, politicians increasingly have had to pay close attention to urban popular pressures.

Urbanization, the continuation of a degree of real political competition at the municipal level, and the circumscription of state governments' political powers made municipalities a better prize—and a more
profitable political investment—for an ambitious Brazilian politician during the dictatorship. Even though less money was coming into each municipality's coffers, at least during the dictatorship it came in automatically. And even if they were largely dependent on government transfers,
municipal mayors still made the final call on hiring and firing, and gained
recognition for implementing public-works projects within the municipality. Thus, given that during the dictatorship federal-government bureaucracy became more "technically" oriented, that the federal government limited the ability of states to interfere in municipal politics, and
that federal deputies had lost influence over distribution of pork-barrel
funds, municipal mayors were the *only* ones who could claim political
credit for "getting the job done" in a municipality. This transformation
has had important consequences for democratic representation in Brazil,
for it altered mayors' historic role from that of passive recipient of state-
and federal-government largesse to one where active, creative problem
solvers could have a great impact. Likewise, at the national level it also
implied a change in the role of federal deputies. By the 1980s, at least in
the medium-to-large cities, mayors had far more political weight than
federal deputies; deputies acted as intermediaries on behalf of mayors by
attempting to pry resources from federal and state governments.

PINPOINTING THE POLITICAL CAUSES OF INCREASED MUNICIPAL AUTONOMY

Urbanization and the ironic consequences of military rule increased the
importance of the municipality within Brazilian federalism. These factors set the historical stage for decentralization to municipalities in the
1980s, but they are insufficient to explain why politicians voted to codify
municipal autonomy in the 1988 constitution. Upon the renewal of democratic elections, politicians could have chosen to revert to the pre-1964
situation, where state governments would regain their relative dominance over municipalities. Given the state-based nature of political campaigns in the early 1980s, this outcome might not have been surprising.
However, upon redemocratization, politicians instead decided to *augment* municipalities' power relative to the other two levels of govern-

ment. To understand why they did so, we need to explore in greater detail how the "macro" factors described above encouraged politicians to see the local level not only as a place to reinforce their support bases, but also as a place to actually develop their political careers. Given this motive, during the transition politicians strove to increase the payoff to holding office at the municipal level (particularly as mayor) by decentralizing to that level.

Ambition theory suggests that "a politician's behavior is a response to his (or her) office goals" (Schlesinger, 1966: 9–10). Because most federal deputies serve only one or two terms in Brasília but then continue their political careers outside the legislature, understanding the nature of political careers in Brazil can help us understand policy decisions taken while politicians are serving in the Chamber of Deputies. Prior to 1964, Brazilian politicians generally sought to build a long-term political career in executive-branch positions in state and/or national government. (Long-term legislative careers—as in the U.S. House of Representatives, for example—have never been common in Brazil.) In particular, deputies' connections to state governments help explain the continuing importance of state-based federalism during the 1945–64 period (Samuels, 2003). Aspiring politicians in earlier eras might have held municipal office prior to holding office at the state or federal level, but more recently politicians have come to regard holding municipal-level office as a career goal in and of itself. This fact helps us understand the more recent trend to decentralize to the municipal level.

We can observe the increasing importance of municipal-level positions in Brazilian politicians' careers beginning in the late 1960s and early 1970s, when the municipal-level executive branch began to accrue significantly more power both in absolute and in relative terms, as described above. This holds particularly in larger cities, where the mayor has a large budget and a large bureaucracy to control. Municipal legislatures are very weak, but the mayor controls hiring and firing, implementation of public-works projects, and execution of various public policies. On the other hand, federal deputies typically find that they play only a minor role in the national legislative process, and, compared to the power of a mayor, that they have little access to politically useful government-provided goods.

Data on political career paths indicate the way in which municipal mayor has risen in the hierarchy of political offices in Brazil. For example, since 1945 many sitting congressional deputies have abandoned their seats soon after winning election, *during* a legislature, in order to take a political position outside Congress. Table 3.2 provides the percentages of sitting deputies who took a position outside of Congress during the legislature from 1945 to 1998.

The percentage of deputies going to national-level positions was relatively higher in the 1945–64 period than it is today, while the percentage of deputies going to state-level positions is slightly higher in the current democratic period than it was during the earlier democratic period. The most dramatic change is the percentage of deputies leaving for municipal positions, which begins its increase in the late 1960s and proceeds throughout the military period and into the current democratic period.[7] This indicates that politicians began to see municipal-level positions as more attractive long before the transition to democracy began (Samuels, 2003: chap. 3). It should be noted that the number of deputies who *run* for mayor is typically between three and four times greater

Table 3.2.   Percentages of Deputies Going to Municipal, State, or National Positions in Brazil, 1945–94

Legislature	% Municipal	% State	% National
1945	0.0	11.2	4.3
1950	0.3	5.3	3.0
1954	0.9	7.1	2.8
1958	0.0	7.7	7.1
1962	0.2	5.4	3.9
1966	*0.5*	*5.4*	*2.2*
1970	*1.3*	*1.6*	*0.0*
1974	*3.0*	*5.2*	*0.6*
1978	*0.7*	*8.8*	*0.7*
1982	*3.6*	*9.0*	*1.9*
1986	4.7	8.8	2.5
1990	6.8	11.1	3.0
1994	7.8	8.6	1.4

Source: Samuels (2003: chap. 3).
Note: Italics indicate years of military rule.

than the number who actually win and thus leave the Chamber. Unfortunately, detailed information on the number of deputies who ran for mayor prior to 1988 is incomplete, but about 20 percent of all sitting deputies have run for mayor in each legislature since then (and, of course, some untold higher number may have considered running) (ibid.).

Many deputies not only run for mayor during their term, but also continue their careers at the municipal level following a brief stint in the Chamber. Again, by the 1963–66 legislature, career patterns had begun to change. Only 5 percent of deputies elected from 1945 to 1958 pursued a municipal-level career following service in the Chamber. In contrast, 21 percent of deputies elected between 1962 and 1978 pursued a post-Chamber municipal career, and this number rose to nearly 25 percent of those elected from 1982 to 1994 (Samuels, 2003: chap. 4).

Clearly, Brazilian politicians' career ambitions have shifted over the last fifty years. In the past, relatively more politicians sought a long-term career in state government or in the national bureaucracy. Currently, many more politicians seek power at the municipal level. This signifies a dramatic transformation in the place of municipal government within the hierarchy of government institutions in contemporary Brazilian politics. When few prominent politicians seek to enter municipal politics, we can be relatively confident that municipal politics is a place for novices, and that holding office at the municipal level may serve as a stepping-stone to higher office.

Today, the situation is different: municipal politics is now a place for seasoned politicians, and serving in state politics or in the national legislature may serve as a stepping stone to holding office as mayor. In short, the most important change in the structure of political careers in Brazil following redemocratization was not a revitalization of national political parties, but rather a revitalization of offices at the municipal level. Given urbanization and the unintended consequences of military rule, this desire helps explain Brazilian politicians' actions to decentralize. Following the logic of ambition theory, incumbent deputies who seek office at the municipal level are likely to act to increase the attractiveness of municipal-level office, much in the same way that members of the U.S. House have acted to increase the advantages of incumbency because they prefer to win continued reelection (Samuels, 2003). Thus, by the early 1980s the career interests of incumbent Brazilian deputies favored states *and* municipalities. Upon redemocratization, instead of returning to the pre-1964 balance of intergovernmental relations, members of Congress acted to institutionalize increased municipal resources and autonomy. In the next section I describe some of these changes, focusing on fiscal decentralization.

DE JURE AND DE FACTO DECENTRALIZATION TO STATES AND MUNICIPALITIES IN THE 1980S

As I have noted, the process of decentralization in Brazil actually began prior to the resumption of democratic procedures. In 1967 the military dramatically centralized fiscal resources, and both states and municipalities suffered revenue reductions as well as limitations in how they could spend the revenue they raised or received via transfer. Rapid economic growth from 1967 to 1974 muted criticism of fiscal centralization, but when the economy took a downturn in 1974, state- and municipal-based politicians (ostensibly allied with the government) began to lobby for more resources (Afonso, 1995b: 354). Beginning in 1975 the military leadership responded, attempting to fortify its allies by decentralizing resources to subnational governments. Changes in the FPE and FPM followed: a series of increases after 1975 more than doubled the amounts transferred via those two funds by 1982. In addition, in 1979 the regime eliminated the centralizing administrative requirements that states spend only in certain areas, providing mayors and governors with additional political autonomy (Oliveira, Fabrício, 1995: 62).

The 1982 elections returned political autonomy to Brazil's states, as governors were once again elected directly. Municipal elections were also held that year, except in state capitals, which would not elect their own mayors until 1985. The pace of decentralization increased following these elections, and an electoralist logic drove newly elected governors and mayors to pressure the military president and Congress for additional decentralization. Congress, populated by deputies who knew that the era of military centralization was coming to a quick end and who possessed state- and municipal-directed political connections and careerist ambitions, responded positively by passing the Passos Porto Amendment in December 1983, which decentralized additional resources to states and municipalities. Thus, decentralization was one of Congress's first steps toward reestablishing its political autonomy and authority during the transition to democracy. After the Passos Porto Amendment, governors and mayors continued to press for more resources. Congress responded, passing the Airton Sandoval Amendment in 1985, decentralizing revenue to states and municipalities even further.

The Constitutional Congress in 1987–88 capped the fiscal decentralization process. Once again responding to gubernatorial and mayoral pressure, career-minded legislators increased the revenue distributed to states and municipalities to the point where today, the rate of FPE and FPM disbursements is nearly four times the rate during the high point of the military regime. Table 3.3 shows the shifts from 1980 to 1995 in the relative balance of Brazilian fiscal federalism. The central government's share of total expenditures began to decline in the 1980s. Starting in 1980 state governments gained, but municipal governments gained much more—nearly a 100 percent increase in their share of final expenditures. Municipalities currently receive relatively much more than they did during the 1945–64 period.[8]

Fiscal decentralization has provided municipalities with an unprecedented degree of political autonomy, because the lion's share of fiscal transfers are now made automatically. Automatic fiscal transfers, as a percentage of the central government's budget, increased by 200 percent between 1978 and 1994, while "politicized" transfers were cut in half during the same period (Nogueira, 1995: 28). Politicians chose to increase automatic as opposed to discretionary transfers, a conscious choice to reinforce state and municipal autonomy and avoid a return to the

Table 3.3.   Division of the Fiscal Pie in Brazil, 1980–95

	Share of Total Revenue (%)			*Share of Total Expenditures (%)*		
Year	Central	State	Municipal	Central	State	Municipal
1980	74.7	21.7	3.7	68.2	23.3	8.6
1985	72.8	24.9	2.4	62.7	26.2	11.1
1990	67.0	29.6	3.4	58.9	27.6	13.5
1995	66.0	28.6	5.4	56.2	27.2	16.6

Source: Rezende (1995); Varsano (1997), Tables 5 and 6.

pre-1964 situation. These changes had important political ramifications; increased automatic transfers (and decreased discretionary transfers) reduced the ability of the central government to meddle in state and municipal affairs, but also reduced the capacity of state governments (to a lesser degree) to meddle in municipal affairs, and gave municipal leaders greater leeway to make policy choices.

The gains of municipalities go beyond fiscal decentralization. Under the 1988 constitution, for the first time in Brazilian history, municipalities gained legal status as federal entities. This eliminates the ability of the state and federal governments to interfere with municipal organic laws. Municipalities also gained exclusive authority to organize and provide public services of local interest (largely defined as public transportation), to organize municipal zoning laws, and to legislate and develop urban development plans. In other cases, such as preschool and primary education, social welfare, and health care, the constitution describes the municipality as the policy "executor," with technical and financial assistance provided by state and/or the federal governments.

These changes provide Brazil's municipalities greater relative autonomy compared to municipalities in other Latin American countries. For example, in Argentina the provinces retain the power to organize municipalities, and of seven other major Latin American countries, only Brazilian municipalities currently have the power to pass legislation on their own. In the other six countries, municipalities may be delegated powers, but this decision always emanates from another level of government. This provides Brazilian municipalities with a degree of formal autonomy unheard of across the continent (Nunes, 1995: 196; see also Nickson, 1995).

Municipalities have also gained a new role as policy provider in many areas (Almeida, 1994; V. Costa, 1998), although the extent of decentralization to local government is limited by the existing structure of policy-delivery instruments, economies of scale, the penury of most Brazilian municipalities, and of course, political considerations (which may also vary from state to state or even municipality to municipality). Regardless, Afonso and Serra (1994: 21) argue that "as never before, municipalities have become extremely important in Brazil's public sector. . . . municipalities have rapidly increased their expenditures and their basic governmental services such as education, health and sanitation, urbanism, and even public safety." This has allowed substantial opportunities for local-level innovation (Figueiredo and Lamounier, 1996; Larangeira,

1996; Silva, 1996). The political logic of decentralization across different policy areas to municipalities, and especially whether decentralization and/or policy innovation pays off politically at the state and/or municipal level, merits further investigation.

CONCLUSION

What lessons can we learn from the Brazilian experience with decentralization? First, I have argued that the "democratization leads to decentralization" hypothesis is inadequate, because the process of decentralization began prior to democratization in Brazil. Moreover, the *form* that decentralization took cannot be explained simply by some general "logic of democracy." Rather, demographic change during the dictatorship and policies that the military regime had enacted to enhance its interests generated the incentives for politicians to choose to decentralize in particular ways when democracy did return. To understand decentralization in Brazil, these distal factors must be coupled with any proximal causes.

Second, I have suggested that we must couple both the macro and micro dynamics for understanding the political logic of decentralization in Brazil. Understanding the background dynamics that set the stage for decentralization under democracy are as important as exploring the electoralist logic of those choices themselves. This connects the macro to the micro factors—the strategies of those who made the actual decisions to decentralize, that is, the elected politicians. When democracy returned, state governors and municipal mayors pressured their representatives in the national government to continue to decentralize, especially fiscal resources. Deputies and senators respond to this kind of pressure because their careers depend on fortifying their state- and municipal-level support networks, and because they also typically continue their postcongressional careers at the subnational level. At a micro level, these politicians therefore had tremendous incentives to continue the process of decentralization, especially in ways that would benefit their own careers. This is why fiscal decentralization was resolved long before more complicated issues such as decentralization of social policy were addressed.

Third, the details from the Brazilian case demonstrate that, given the general importance of subnational politics for politicians' career advancement, pressures for decentralization in the 1980s and 1990s in Brazil did not divide along partisan lines. The form or degree of decentralization advocated by politicians from different parties varied, but the general pressure for decentralization was consensual. No "Federalist versus Anti-federalist" division emerged among elected politicians; no party picked up the banner of "saving" the federal government from being parceled out to the state and municipalities; the few who actively opposed decentralization included members of the national executive-branch bureaucracy (see Samuels, 2003, chap. 8). However, these bureaucrats were unable to create counterincentives for the state- and municipal-oriented elected politicians, and of course following democratization these bureaucrats lost political influence.

Brazil may be the most decentralized country in Latin America, but the form that decentralization took was not simply a return to the country's "natural" state following a period of authoritarianism. Decentralization followed a particular path because of the way that particular social and political developments affected politicians' strategic calculations. The Brazilian case aptly illustrates Montero and Samuels' arguments that historical-institutional and socioeconomic legacies matter, that democratization is neither necessary nor sufficient to explain decentralization, and that one must supplement an institutional or electoralist approach to explaining decentralization with analysis of macro and distal factors.[9]

Notes

This chapter is partly based on my "Reinventing Local Government? The Evolution of Brazil's Municipalities," in *Democratic Brazil,* ed. Peter Kingstone and Timothy Power (Pittsburgh: University of Pittsburgh Press, 2000), and on an article written with Fernando Abrucio, "The 'New' Politics of the Governors: Federalism and the Brazilian Transition to Democracy," *Publius: The Journal of Federalism* 30, no. 2 (Spring 2001): 43–61. I thank Al Montero and the reviewers for comments.

1. In focusing on fiscal decentralization and attempting to provide a general explanation for a broad and multifaceted process, I necessarily ignore variation across policy areas as well as across space within specific policy areas. However, this does not mean that the explanation for decentralization in other policy areas will be "less political." Indeed, my argument parallels more detailed research (see, e.g., Montero, 2002). For example, as Arretche (2000) has recently argued, although differences across policies and across regions may be partly a

function of path-dependent institutional attributes, fiscal capacity, and other "structural" attributes, these can never provide fully sufficient explanations. Like the argument in this volume, Arretche's explanation for social policy decentralization is also explicitly political: decentralization is a function of the deliberate political calculations of executive-branch office-holders at the national, state, and local levels. See also Arretche and Rodrígues (1998) for a cross-policy study within one state (São Paulo) that comes to similar conclusions about the importance of political-electoral considerations.

2. This argument implies that although an electoral dynamic was important, one cannot map national party preferences onto the process of decentralization in Brazil. All political parties advocated decentralization, especially of fiscal resources. Of course, this therefore tells us almost nothing about why decentralization took the form and extent that it did in Brazil.

3. For a very brief introduction to the forces behind the 1930 revolution, see Skidmore (1967: 3–12). A more extensive treatment is Fausto (1987).

4. See, e.g., Skidmore (1967), Wirth (1970), Sola (1987).

5. Except mayors of capital cities in some states, whom the governor continued to appoint for several years.

6. State governors appointed the mayors of state capitals. Elections were also not held in about 180 municipalities designated as important to national security, which included municipalities with a large military presence, some border municipalities, municipalities with hydroelectric installations, etc.

7. I explain the 1978 decline as well as provide a more detailed explanation of the trends, in Samuels (2003: chap. 3).

8. In the late 1990s, the federal government's *relative* share of total revenue and expenditures began to increase, giving the impression of a fiscal recentralization. However, this resulted from the effects of increased federal-government efforts to collect taxes it did not have to share with states and municipalities, and not from a deliberate policy of recentralization. In fact, in *absolute* terms, state and municipal revenue also increased, just not as fast as the central government's. See Samuels (2003: chap. 9).

9. For a discussion of the evolution of intergovernmental relations under President Cardoso, especially the issue of the extent of recentralization, see Samuels (2003), Montero (2002), and Abrucio and Samuels (n.d.).

CHAPTER 4

Enclaves and Elections

The Decision to Decentralize in Chile

GARY BLAND

One of the difficulties of examining decentralization in any country is determining where to begin. It is possible to look at decentralization either as a point on a continuum—the state of an intergovernmental political system—or as the continuum itself—the process of decentralization. On the one hand, when viewing decentralization as a process—as the transfer of power from the central government to popularly elected subnational governments[1]—one needs to consider the length of time during which decentralization has taken place. The relevant period may encompass a few years; since institutional developments usually reflect a long course of political change, that period is more likely to encompass decades. On the other hand, if decentralization is considered a state of operation, one has to examine the level of autonomy granted to the subnational system. The case of Chile in particular demonstrates the critical importance of distinguishing between the process and the state of decentralization when attempting to define its effects.

Contemporary *political* decentralization in Chile can be traced to a specific point: the June 1992 local elections.[2] The 1992 elections provided the missing ingredient for the establishment of basic local autonomy, namely popularly legitimized political authority. Decentralization was a direct result of the process of a negotiated democratic consolidation that began after General Pinochet left the presidency in 1990. So, perhaps not surprisingly, the democratic consolidation process significantly influenced the nature and extent of the decentralization reforms. And, of course, decentralization was equally integral to democratic consolidation. One of the first of the antidemocratic enclaves left by the Pinochet regime to be dismantled was the appointed mayoralty, which was abolished by the decentralizing 1992 elections.

In addition, Chile demonstrates how hard bargaining over elections and electoral issues—because the negotiators knew well how elections and the rules that translate votes into seats would strongly shape their relative political strength—can be a constant issue in the debate over decentralization. If election laws are under consideration as part of larger decentralization reform, they are likely to take center stage. Indeed, the subnational reform effort nearly collapsed as Chile's political elites quarreled over the details and ramifications of electing or appointing municipal and regional officials. Therefore, this chapter follows the conclusions of many of the other chapters in this volume in claiming that electoral incentives shaped and, in turn, were shaped by the process of decentralization.

THE CENTRALISM OF TWO PRECEDING REGIMES

The Pre-Coup Period

Since the 1930s, Chile has been ruled by three distinct regimes: the pre-1973, centralized democracy; the Pinochet dictatorship from 1973 to 1989; and the current period of democratic consolidation. From 1935 to 1971, acting under the 1925 constitution, Chile convened municipal (also known in Chile as "commune" or "communal") elections every four years without interruption. Elections proved to be highly competitive; the typical municipality was highly politicized. Councilors tended to be political party representatives operating within a system of strong national parties and often looking to advance their political careers. They generally did not view the municipal government as a vehicle for advancing community welfare. By the 1960s, the mayor, who was chosen by the elected councilors from among their group, presided over council meetings, executed council decisions, directed municipal administration, and served as community spokesperson.

Few would question that Chilean municipalities prior to the 1973 coup had few actual functions, however. For decades in Chile, as in the rest of Latin America, the belief in state-led development dominated politics. The national government gradually nationalized many functions that once belonged to municipal governments or took responsibility for any new ones that emerged (Gil, 1966: 132; Cleaves, 1969: 11, 29–30; Pascal, 1968: 40–41; A. Valenzuela, 1977: 28–32, 42–44). Although provinces existed as politico-administrative units, there was no other subnational level of government. On paper, local officials were responsible for a wide range of development-related and other activities. In practice, however, by the early 1970s they had been relegated primarily to licensing vehicles, disposing of garbage, and keeping the community clean and pretty (Cleaves, 1969: 33; A. Valenzuela, 1977: 43–44; Raczynski and Serrano, 1987: 129). As one observer wrote at the time,

> Legislation and political practice have more and more been buttressing the powers of the officials of the central government and restricting the activities and jurisdiction of municipalities to administrative matters of relatively minor importance. Centralization today has advanced to the point that self-government in municipalities has little or no reality. (Gil, 1966: 132)

If Chilean municipalities had few functions during this period, their financial situation was not any better. Since the national government collected municipal taxes first and then distributed them to the municipalities, it was Santiago that exercised ultimate control over these finances. In particular, the central government regularly failed to return substantial amounts of income tax funds that under the law belonged to local governments. In fact, the Ministry of Finance owed local governments substantial sums of money (Cleaves, 1969: 24–30; A. Valenzuela, 1977: 44–46). Adding to these problems, two-thirds of local residents did not pay license fees, a major source of funds. Elected officials refused to take the unpopular step of raising tax rates, and the national tax collection agency was years behind in updating local property values, thus depriving municipalities of additional tax income (A. Valenzuela, 1977: 44–46).

Finally, if the central government had not put the final nail in the coffin of municipal autonomy, local governments themselves surely undermined their case for greater self-government. Municipal officials devoted the large majority of the scarce resources they did receive to operating costs (wages and benefits), and the amount dedicated to development projects was small and declining. The rampant patronage engaged in by mayors and councilors further drained local budgets (A. Valenzuela, 1977: 47–50; Campbell, 1990: 6).

Municipal officials did work hard to address local problems and serve their clients, for their political careers depended on it. One of the most significant and enduring features of the municipal system prior to the 1973 coup was the linkage between the center and locality. Local leaders, usually the mayor, secured projects they could never have financed alone through the use of party ties and other contacts in Santiago. In this regard, political brokers—senators and deputies who would in most instances allocate funds in the national budget for projects in their districts—served as the main intermediary or facilitator. The national Congress, often acting in response to municipal interests, was the focus of considerable give-and-take, the home of classic pork-barrel and log-rolling politics (A. Valenzuela, 1977: 89–97, 137–47).[3]

Municipal dependence on brokers was one of the clearest demonstrations that party-dominated centralization was the order of the day. If local elected officials held a fair degree of political autonomy, their administrative and financial authority was weak and in continual decline. Local self-government remained an ideal.

The Pinochet Regime

The military dictatorship dismantled this system within eight days of the 1973 coup and then quickly created a corporatist hierarchy of subnational administration controlled from the center. This meant the establishment of thirteen new regions, which were subdivided into fifty-one new provinces. The provinces were subdivided into ultimately 335 municipalities.

The national bureaucracy was "deconcentrated"[4] to the regions with the idea that Santiago was not to engage in any activity that could be performed more efficiently at the regional and local levels (Canessa, 1979: 17–18; Castro and Méndez, 1992: 57–72). The military regime wanted to replace the antiquated existing system with a politico-territorial division that would break up the concentration of economic and political power in Santiago, particularly the traditional influence of organized labor, and reverse migration to the cities. The deconcentration of the bureacracy was a central facet of the regime's bold strategy of economic liberalization, with its emphasis on opening the Chilean economy to international competition, efficient use of resources, investment planning, and modernization of the public sector. The rationale for this new subnational structure also included a geopolitical component. The military was deeply concerned with national integration both internally, to control any dissent, and externally, given the unusual territorial extent of the country and perennial border conflicts with neighbors. Regionalization, it was hoped, would promote balanced development, strengthen the national presence in underpopulated areas, and protect against subversion (Cumplido, 1983: 6–13; author interview,[5] October 16, 1995).

The deconcentration of bureaucratic authority was accompanied by the severe repression of political activity, particularly party politics, at all levels. Civil liberties were extinguished; political autonomy evaporated. Pinochet established a rigid, vertical politico-administrative structure, appointing high military commanders as regional *intendentes* and provincial governors (who were subordinate to the *intendente*) and appointing primarily civilians as local mayors. This allowed the regime to penetrate deeply into the localities and exert tight control over the subnational bureaucracy. Often not a resident of the municipality, the mayor was imposed on the community, occasionally in the face of local opposition (Rehren, 1986: 62, 96–97).

Regionalization, coupled with the elimination of political party activity, "not only changed the nature of [political] brokerage, [but also] reduced the scope of the brokerage role of councilors and mayors to the regional bureaucratic setting" (Rehren, 1986: 160). As tight control was imposed by provincial and regional officials, a new "regional centralism" emerged (Rehren, 1986: 162–65; Rosenfeld, Rodríguez, and Espinoza, 1989: 204–5).

Yet the dictatorship's transformation of the subnational system did lay the administrative groundwork for the municipality's emergence as an "agent of development."[6] Continuing with its grand design for economic modernization and elimination of the politics of the past, the Pinochet regime transferred an extraordinary array of new functions to the municipalities. A central objective of a number of decrees, including a 1976 municipal reform law, the 1980 constitution, and the municipal reform law of 1988, was to grant municipalities a lead role in community development. Municipalities were "incorporated into the administrative and financial system of the State, and into the planning, execution, and oversight of communal development by the central government" (Rosenfeld, Rodríguez, and Espinoza, 1989: 195).

Local governments were required to develop an annual budget, zoning ordinance, and municipal development plans. Execution of the development plan required prioritizing community needs, creating local projects to meet those needs, and then working with the local and regional administrations to implement them. Municipalities were thus obligated to establish various departments and hire professional technicians and administrators to head them, most importantly, the communal planning secretary. The Communal Development Council (*Consejo de Desarollo Comunal*, or CODECO) was devised as an advisory body to the mayor, who presided over it, and as the primary participatory channel for community residents. To varying degrees, CODECO members represented neighborhood committees, functional community groups, and representatives of other major community activities. Codified in the 1988 municipal law, they shared a status and value structure similar to the old *regidores*, or town councilors, of the democratic past (Rehren, 1986: 103, 121). CODECOs, however, did not play a significant role because they lacked decision-making power vis-à-vis the mayor, excluded important organizations from participating, and were comprised in large part of members who backed the Pinochet political line (Rosenfeld, Rodríguez, and Espinoza, 1989: 192).

Local employees were ranked according to professional status and were paid better than before, which served to attract young professionals to municipal work, and the number of lower-skilled positions was sharply reduced. Finally, municipalities were given flexibility to contract with the private sector (in fact, they were expected to) for those municipal services that could be best handled by the market (Campbell, 1990: 5). Local government was pushed to operate along the lines of private business (Rosenfeld, Rodríguez, and Espinoza, 1989: 198–202; Raczynski and Serrano, 1987: 129–30).

In another major move, municipalities became public service providers. In the early 1980s, the Pinochet regime began transferring the
administration of primary and secondary education, primary health services, and cemeteries to the municipalities. Under the new system, mu-
nicipalized schools were expected to compete with private schools, the
belief being that such competition would enhance the quality of the educational system. In addition, local governments were charged with ad-
ministering national programs for poverty alleviation, delivery of subsidies
to poor families, and the regularization of squatter settlements (Rosenfeld, Rodríguez, and Espinoza, 1989: 202–3, 218–20; Espinoza and Marcel, 1994: 33–34; Campbell, 1990: 5).

The many new functions taken on by Chilean municipalities would
have proved of little value without the financial resources to back them
up. Municipal revenue improved only slightly during the first years of
the dictatorship, and central government transfers decreased dramatically from 1975 to 1978 (Rehren, 1986: 77–78). In 1979, however, a new
law (the *Ley de Rentas Municipales*) included, among other provisions,
a series of permanent income sources for municipalities. Revenue therefore increased substantially over the next decade—in 1989 it was six times
larger in real terms than in 1974 (Chile, Ministerio del Interior, 1991: 36).
Easily the most important item was the creation of the Municipal Common Fund (*Fondo Común Municipal,* or FCM), to which all municipalities contributed a percentage of the revenue received from three
separate local taxes. The FCM was then used to redistribute resources
from wealthy municipalities in Santiago to the poorest nationwide (Rehren, 1986: 78; Rosenfeld, Rodríguez, and Espinoza, 1989: 210; Espinoza
and Marcel, 1994: 32–33, 38; Campbell, 1990: 13–17). Important municipal income could also be derived from external sources or special project
funds—such as the National Fund for Regional Development (*Fondo
Nacional de Desarollo Regional,* or FNDR) and the Social Fund—
managed at the regional level in conjunction with the national ministries.
Municipalities could obtain these funds by presenting economically
viable projects to compete for available financing.

The national government, however, was transferring income to municipalities to cover the costs of the administration of education, health,
antipoverty, and other programs now administered by local governments.
Often these transfers did not fully cover administrative costs, leaving
local governments, to varying degrees, with growing budget deficits that

they had to cover with their own resources, and thus draining the funds they could otherwise dedicate to investment (Espinoza and Marcel, 1994: 44; Campbell, 1990: 18–19). In addition, tight national and regional controls over the allocation of income to the municipalities, despite the increase in resources, limited financial autonomy. For example, tax rates, personnel ceilings, and salaries were set by national law, and budgets were subject to strict review by regional governments and the Interior Ministry (Campbell, 1990: 7; Rehren, 1986: 84). Municipalities were given broad powers under the law, but they were often subjected to the authority of the regional ministerial heads, and dealing with them was a constant struggle (Rosenfeld, Rodríguez, and Espinoza, 1994: 205).

General Pinochet's creation of regions, the new "territorial base" of the country, was the most dramatic change in the new politico-territorial division. Regionalism generally, it should be noted, has been a part of Chilean history since independence. On several occasions during the post-independence era, regional leaders politically and militarily confronted their counterparts in the national capital. In 1826, Chile actually established a short-lived federal constitution, and on two separate occasions during the 1850s civil conflicts erupted when the province of Concepción and, later, Copiapó revolted against the domination of Santiago. The centralist tradition prevailed, however, and the regions' resentment of strong centralization and of Santiago's authority over them endured. Such feelings—"a dormant force of some significance"—were on the rise again in the 1960s in protest against the neglect of the interior provinces by the capital (Gil, 1966: 132). A degree of regional planning began in the mid-1960s under the Frei government, but in 1974 the military moved well beyond past efforts in creating a deconcentrated administrative structure.

Each of Chile's new regions was headed by an appointed *intendente* and a Regional Development Council (*Consejo Regional de Desarollo*, or COREDE), the regional equivalents of the mayor and CODECO. The *intendente* was the executive and administrative chief, while the COREDE served as the corporatist vehicle for soliciting the participation of regional organizations in development, especially those from the private sector. In practice, the COREDE, like its local counterpart, served an advisory role and lacked any real decision-making power. The intendente did establish a close working relationship with the regional planning secretary, who in turn worked with the new regional offices of the central ministries. Now operating in the regional capitals, offices were charged with formulating budgets, developing programs, providing technical advice for the approval of municipal projects, and coordinating with the national planning ministry (Rosenfeld, Rodríguez, and Espinoza, 1989: 190–92).[7]

Ultimately, then, Pinochet's new subnational system was perhaps more technocratic, more development oriented, and maybe even more market oriented and efficient than the system it replaced. It was not, however, self-governing, most notably at the municipal level, the traditional bastion of Chilean local governance. Local officials now had more administrative and financial strength than in the past, but any semblance of political autonomy had disappeared. For different reasons, then, decentralization was no more a consideration under the dictatorship than it was during the preceding democracy.

Achieving Democracy and Decentralization

The Chilean political landscape remains characterized, as it has been since the democratic transition in 1989, first by the reemergence of a strong multiparty system grouped around two poles: the center-left Concertation (*Concertación*) coalition of parties and a party alliance on the center-right. The center-left is led by the *Partido Demócrata Cristiano* (PDC), the *Partido por la Democracia* (PPD), and the *Partido Socialista* (PS), while the main parties on the right are *Renovación Nacional* (RN) and the *Unión Demócrata Independiente* (UDI). Second, Chile is characterized by centripetal politics, whereby virtually all party leaders emphasize the centrist nature of their policies. In stark contrast to the pre-1973 period, ideological polarization is absent. The electorate itself is considerably more centrist than during the conflictive days of the late 1960s and early 1970s. Thus, since 1990 the Chilean political system has been defined by an ethic described as "moderate pluralism" (Saffirio Suárez, 1995: 30–51; Scully, 1995: 122–37; Scully and Valenzuela, 1993: 6–7).

The principal coalitional pattern of the political system continues to reflect the differences between supporters and opponents of the military regime and its institutional legacy. It is this division—the political reality generated by the movement to defeat Pinochet and the "political learning" that grew out of the transition to democracy—that gave birth to the

[margin annotation: moderate pluralism]

bipolar system. Neither the center-left coalition nor, especially, the center-right alliance is a paradigm of harmonious relations. Until leading political actors find stronger incentives to dissolve or to ally with parties other than those with which they are now grouped, which may occur as the salience of issues involving the legacy of the military regime diminishes, this bipolarity is expected to continue (Scully and Valenzuela, 1993: 7, 24).

Chile was hardly a consolidated democracy, however, when the newly elected president, Patricio Aylwin, assumed office in March 1990. Bastions of institutional authoritarianism—the so-called authoritarian enclaves or "reserved domains" of authority—hampered further democratic progress (Garretón, 1995: 146–58; A. Valenzuela, 1999: 190–247; Rabkin, 1992–93: 119–94; J. Valenzuela, 1992: 64). One of the most obvious was the appointment, required by the 1980 constitution, of nine senators for eight-year terms. By the time Aylwin took power, Pinochet had already installed his loyalists in those nine seats (later reduced to eight), thereby tilting control of the upper house of Congress to the political right. The electoral law promulgated by Pinochet in early 1989 established a binomial system, which induces parties to form broad coalitions and ensures overrepresentation of the second strongest electoral force (i.e., the right) in both chambers of Congress (Saffirio Suárez, 1995: 35–36 n.; Rabkin, 1992–93: 139; Scully, 1995: 125–26). Together, these provisions made the achievement of large majorities to pass laws and reform the constitution a far more difficult process of negotiation with the right, especially since the RN and UDI are certainly not inclined to support changes that erode their own political strength. It was no less significant that Pinochet was to remain, under the constitution, commander of the army until March 1997 and thereafter a senator for life.

Another of the bastions of authoritarianism at the beginning of the 1990s was the continued exercise of power by Pinochet's appointed mayors. The December 1989 national elections did not affect the local and regional systems Pinochet had established. Facing a rather glaring obstacle to the goal of deepening democracy, Aylwin and his Concertation-backed government took up the challenge of reforming the Constitution and relevant municipal law in order to reinstall democratic local government. All parties to this debate understood that the Aylwin administration's plans would be heavily weighted by a single imperative: constitutional reform of any kind would require significant input from the political opposition because the right controlled the deciding votes in Congress.[8] The Chilean constitution cannot be amended without a two-thirds majority vote in both houses of Congress; the revision of "organic" laws requires a four-sevenths majority vote in both houses for passage. As the discussions on local and regional government got underway, and throughout the long and arduous debate, these institutional parameters established the strategic reality that neither the Aylwin government nor the rightist opposition could ignore.

The Push for Reform: The First Year

When President Aylwin submitted his proposal for municipal reform to the Chilean Chamber of Deputies on May 18, 1990, just two months and one week after his assumption of office, the plan was to hold the country's first municipal elections since 1971 the following year. The reestablishment of elected municipal government was a lead item on Aylwin's agenda. As he wrote in his message to the deputies, the proposed reforms "reflect the national feeling directed at the introduction of indispensable changes so as to make the present municipal regime more democratic, decentralized, and participative."[9] According to the interior minister, the municipalities were to become "pluralistic organs" and would "never again become politicized instruments in the service of the central government."[10]

As part of a major restructuring of the municipality, mayors were to be elected directly (but not on a separate ballot) for the first time. Moreover, the municipality was defined not as a subunit of the interior ministry but rather, for the first time in Chilean constitutional history, as a public corporation with appropriate legal rights and administrative autonomy (Chile, Ministerio del Interior, 1992b: 1). Unbeknownst to the president at the time, however, he would have to wait more than two years for the return of local democracy. Despite his plea for action, in January 1991 the Senate refused to consider municipal reform legislation that had earlier passed the Chamber of Deputies (Martner, 1993: 71).[11] The senators on the right would not support the process of state reform as conceived by the government; they wanted something more.

A "long and complex political negotiation with the opposition parties," led by the two largest parties, the PDC and the RN, ensued (Martner, 1993: 71). The result was President Aylwin's presentation in May 1991, almost a year to the day since he announced his first initiative, of

a second constitutional reform proposal including not only the modifications at the municipal level, but also the creation of regional governments—a prospect unprecedented in Chilean history. The new initiative
proposed that the *intendente*, appointed by and responsible to the president, serve as chief executive of the regional government. His cabinet
would be comprised of the regional ministerial secretaries. The regional
government would also include a new entity, the regional council, and
a consultative body, such as a reformed COREDE. In addition, under the
agreement reached with the opposition, the Senate would first consider
constitutional reform and then the revision of the appropriate laws; mean-
while, the Chamber of Deputies would simultaneously address legislation to increase municipal income (Chile, Ministerio Secretaría General
de Gobierno, 1991: 9).

President Aylwin's new proposal directly reflected the political dynamic at work in Chile. The RN and UDI had made a simple, rational
calculation. The right could not expect to win the presidency for years,
and its political power at the municipal level would be greatly reduced
even if it performed better than expected in democratic elections. The
regions, however, promised to generate "new political spaces" through
which "its presence in the state apparatus could be strengthened" (Boisier,
1994: 16). The refusal to address municipal reform without simultaneously considering regional reform generated considerable tension between
the Concertation and the RN-UDI bloc, which was accused of being interested only in delaying the return of local democracy.[12]

Electoral systems, in particular, and subnational government functions and financial resources were to be at the center of these discussions.
By definition, then, the degree to which decentralization would occur
was on the negotiating table as well. Members of the Concertation and
the right suggested the popular election of the regional *intendentes,* a
proposal which, by Chilean standards, would have been a radical departure from tradition, had it been accepted (Fuentealba, 1991a).[13] Yet, the
president did offer another dramatic proposition: the popular election of
the regional councilors, or the creation of so-called regional parliaments
(Fuentealba, 1991a; Chile, Ministerio del Interior, 1992a: 1).[14]

Finally, at the municipal level the electoral system was, according
to the undersecretary for regional government, a "fundamental knot" in
the talks (Fuentealba, 1991b). The president's original plan for electing
the mayor was discarded; others emerged only to be rejected as well. The
Concertation and RN-UDI disputed not only the method but also the

number of municipal councilors to be elected. In short, as the lead actors well understood, the rules under which the game is played significantly determine the outcome. These rules were now in flux, and at times the issues involved cut across coalitional lines to reflect the interests of party size, institutional competition, and historical tradition.

The Push for Reform: The Second Year

The angst generated by the prospects for simultaneous municipal and regional reform were clearly expressed by President Aylwin in his annual address to the nation just four days after his presentation to Congress of the joint municipal-regional initiative. Aylwin explained that support for municipal democratization was "formally expressed" by the "immense majority of Chileans" in the 1990 election, and that there was a "general consensus" on the issue. After noting the objections of the center-right and expressing his support for the joint consideration of municipal and regional reform, he declared:

> The municipality is a traditional institution of our political system, as is also its democratic-representative character. In deliberating on its reform, we rely on a long and rich experience, the product of our own history. On this matter, we are treading on well-known ground. . . . We know well the problems municipal government and management present.

> However, the reform of regional government and administration takes us into *unknown territory*. It means introducing nothing less than a major innovation into our political system. We lack here a history and tradition that allows us direct and sustained experience over time, which is helpful in identifying the problems involved and designing reliable solutions to them. We would be doing poorly simply to copy institutions from other [national] realities . . . . [or] be seduced by principles, which may well be valid in theory, but produce very complex questions in their practical application.

> Understand me well; I am a resolute supporter of a process of regional decentralization, but I think it should be done on a realistic basis and without affecting the unitary character of the Chilean State. (Chile, Ministerio Secretaría General de Gobierno, 1991: 9–10)

Aylwin added that the experience of developed nations demonstrates that regionalization is a gradual process requiring decades to achieve. Avoiding regrettable failures, he concluded, meant that Chile should advance in stages and build on experience.

The commitment to move ahead had been made and a cautious tone set, but the critical details had yet to be resolved. The Aylwin administration, Congress, and the political parties were now faced with the enormous task of negotiating the structure, functions, finances, interrelationships, and electoral systems for two levels of government. Accommodating regionalization within a unitary state, or coping with the strong resistance to any perceived attempt at federalism, was at the heart of the difficulty.

To many Chilean leaders, electing the *intendente*, a figure viewed as the central government's link to the rest of the country, especially in matters of governance and public security, was tantamount to creating a federalist state and risking national fragmentation (author interview, December 23, 1994).[15] How was the attempt to create a regional council, especially a popularly elected one, to be perceived? Would it be the first step toward the election of *intendentes* and federalism? This great bargaining process ultimately also required accommodating the interests of the six or so major parties that comprised the two alliances. Chilean leaders, moreover, could not ignore two additional concerns: macroeconomic balance and the potential for social instability following seventeen years of repressive authoritarianism. No doubt adding to the pressure, municipal democratization had been delayed one year already and the 1993 parliamentary elections were approaching quickly. A Christian Democratic (PDC) leader began threatening that local authorities would again be appointed if agreements were not reached in time.[16]

The focal point of the negotiations that took place from June to August 1991 became the rightist-controlled Senate, particularly the two mixed committees with jurisdiction over the issue. As these joint committee meetings began, members on the political left and the right emphasized that regional reform, although entailing a "profound transformation" of state administration, should be a gradual process of deconcentration that would lead to future decentralization.[17] The sessions made it clear that members of Congress wanted to ensure that regional councilors would not be accorded the political legitimacy to pose a future electoral and broader institutional challenge to them. Most, therefore, opposed the popular election of the councilors. There also seemed to be a consensus among committee members and the executive branch officials who appeared before them that the regional councilors would play a limited governmental role, with their decision-making capacity restricted to questions of regional development. However, these points of general agreement—all three of which were included in the final measure—masked deep discord on many other aspects of subnational reform (Chile, Senado de la República, 1991a).

Because of the significance, complexity, and urgency of the reform process, normal parliamentary procedures were bypassed. Chilean leaders decided to settle these issues as rapidly as possible among a group of some twenty political party chiefs, members of Congress, and executive branch officials—the so-called Negotiating Table. The participants agreed on the principal objective: a single, global accord on all the major issues related to democratizing local government and the deepening of regionalization. But as the negotiators reviewed the eighty-nine provisions under consideration (the first two alone required two and a half hours of discussion), there was some confusion as to the positions of the respective parties, a few provisions proved to be points of severe contention, and deadlines fell by the wayside. Three major issues of disagreement involved the proportion of public investment the regions would handle, the number of municipal councilors and the means by which they would be elected, and the generation and composition of the regional councils. Much of this discussion involved the perceived political advantages and disadvantages associated with the design of various local and regional electoral formulas; no party was about to unilaterally sacrifice their electoral potential.[18] As the talks dragged on, the PS and PPD threatened to leave the table if agreement was not reached as planned by August 20.

That deadline was met. On that day, the negotiators announced that they had reached a "Political Accord on the Reform of Regional and Communal Administration." The protracted negotiations produced a series of political agreements, including the fixing of the date of municipal elections within the first six months of 1992, for subsequent enactment into law. Over the next fifteen months, the provisions of the accord would be pushed through Congress, integrated into the constitution, and developed into the national laws on municipalities and regional government. The process continued to generate intra- and intercoalitional conflict—often centered around, again, who does and does not benefit from proposed electoral designs—and create doubts about each side's com-

mitment to the agreement.[19] But, comparing the present subnational system with the accord's provisions, one can fairly conclude that the essence
of state reform was now simply a matter of time. As in other instances
during the Aylwin government, state reform was "significantly predetermined by extraparliamentary agreements aimed at guaranteeing a
more rapid and effective approval of legislation of great social tran-
scendence" (Varas Alfonso and Mohor Abuauad, 1992: 10). Political
adversaries had come to the negotiating table to reach a compromise,
they succeeded in that objective, and then kept their commitments. The
politics of the center prevailed once again.

As a result, Chile's political elites converted the thirteen regions created by Pinochet into "governments"[20] responsible for regional development. As in the Pinochet years, the executive is the *intendente,* who
is selected by the president. The new regional council, elected by province
by an assembly of municipal councilors from each province, replaced the
COREDE. On the financial side, regional governments would participate
to a greater extent in the nation's public investment, primarily through
the distribution of regional investment projects financed by the FNDR
and the ministries' regional investment programs.

Municipalities were guaranteed legal rights and administrative autonomy under the constitution. Executive authority would lie with the
mayor; the councilors would exercise oversight, budget approval, and
other responsibilities. An even number of municipal councilors would be
elected depending on the size of the municipality. Under the reformed
municipal law, the Communal Economic and Social Council (*Consejo
Económico y Social Comunal,* or CESCO), a consultative body, would
serve as a vehicle for public participation. A separate bill for improving
the municipal financial situation, on the other hand, proved to be less of
a priority. It stalled in Congress and would not be addressed until 1994.
The FCM, the fund used to redistribute municipal income to the poorest localities, would remain the most important source of financing for
the large majority of municipalities.[21]

THE IMPULSE TO DECENTRALIZE

Was the establishment of regional government in Chile and the concomitant debate on decentralization the product of party politics or a

priority that emerged from a society demanding institutional change? One Chilean analyst best expresses the reality of the situation: "I do not deny that today the issues of decentralization and deconcentration are much more relevant than they were two or three decades ago, but neither would I assert that the reform is the result of a regionalist or prodecentralization sentiment that is crystallizing into a new structure of territorial administration" (Abalos, 1994).

The guiding impulse to decentralize was national politics. In terms of subnational reform, the Aylwin government was concerned with democratizing the municipalities and ensuring social peace in support of the new regime during the transition, not regionalization or decentralization per se.[22] As the president stated in his address to the nation, the Chilean people elected him to restore local democracy. The undersecretary for regional development explained that the administration's "first work is to democratize the municipalities" (Martner, 1993: 27). Its ideas for regional reform in June 1990, which had not been formalized, were not as ambitious as they proved to be a year later (Martner, 1993: 27–31).[23] The rightist parties, as a result of their own political calculations and desire to maximize their leverage, clearly pushed the administration in this direction. Yet, at the same time, for all their advocacy of greater regional resources, the center-right also opposed government proposals (such as the direct election of regional councilors) that would have produced greater progress toward decentralization. If one can conclude that the Aylwin government was most interested in stronger municipalities, then one can equally argue that the opposition was primarily concerned with regionalization to improve its political position. The outcome of the negotiations, which was a state decentralized to only the municipal level, was a secondary consequence of each side's promotion of its immediate political objectives.

The lack of a long-term perspective meant the sacrifice of a "logical and rational conformation" to regional government and regional-municipal relations (author interview, December 13, 1994). Leading negotiators lament the "inadequate distribution and equilibrium of functions" among the different levels of government and the "very imperfect" municipal electoral system (now twice reformed) that resulted (author interviews, December 16 and 23, 1994). In some cases, such as requiring an even number of town councilors, which led to serious conflicts because the councilors would often reach a tie in voting for a mayor from among their group, the operation of municipal and regional government was seriously impaired by the deals struck during the negotiations.

As the Aylwin government initiated its plans for the restoration of local democracy in 1990, public support for broader decentralization, regionalization in particular, was diffuse at best. Two sectors that strongly support the transfer of authority outside the national capital adopted the regionalist ideal: modern, dynamic, regional entrepreneurs and emerging regional universities (Boisier and Zurita, 1993: 9; Boisier, 1994: 10–16). Regionalization emerged as an issue during the 1989 national election campaigns, benefiting from the traditional anti-Santiago sentiment. Where advocacy of regionalization was most pronounced, however, it had developed a subtle rightist character. Regional businesses and universities maintained informal ties to the center-right parties (Boisier, 1994: 15). This made regionalism less appealing to Concertation supporters, although segments within the alliance strongly favored it. In addition, during this period other issues of great political consequence, such as human rights accountability and the role of the military in political life, competed for the attention of the Chilean populace and policy-makers. In short, it would be a mistake to characterize the Aylwin government's movement toward regional government as a response to rising public pressure for such a step.

Although forced to address the regional issue sooner than desired, the Aylwin administration (and some politicians on the left and right) did demonstrate support for decentralization on its merits. The president declared to the nation that he supported the process. His government advocated measures, such as the direct election of mayors, more resources for municipalities, and popular election of regional councilors, that would have moved both governmental levels much closer to decentralization. Aylwin's former minister of government later argued that the government's emphasis on municipalization first was "not a matter of lack of confidence in the processes of regionalization, but only a cautious and prudent conduct so as not to force the State to live through two experiments, the municipal and the regional, simultaneously" (Correa R., 1994: 4). The Senate negotiations, however, watered down the bolder ideas from all sides, such that ultimately decentralization occurred on the municipal level, while in the regions there was deconcentration. Regional reform in Chile was a step toward decentralization on the regional level, not its achievement.

The complexity of the negotiations within a political system characterized by two party coalitions is reflected in the debate over the direct election of mayors. Direct election meant that one candidate within a coalition would win at the expense not only of the opposition, but also of the other candidates from allied parties. At least three major proposals were considered, as the problem of meeting the interests of all parties, at times across alliances, proved quite difficult. The smaller parties in both coalitions objected to direct election formulas, which generally favor the formation of two-party systems, because "they feared their positions within their respective coalitions would deteriorate" (Correa R., 1994: 4).[24] This situation produced acceptance of the remaining alternative, the pre-1973 system of indirect election by the councilors from among their group. Even so, to maintain coalition unity, the Concertation selected their council candidates by proportion of each party's past vote and negotiated a national "Protocol" providing the rules on how elected councilors had to vote when it came time to electing mayors (the right apparently failed in a similar effort).[25] Extending coalition unity to the local level, where politics is far more varied, more conflictive, and less controllable, was considerably more difficult than selecting candidates for previous congressional elections. The centripetal tendencies witnessed at the national level lost some of their force in the localities.

The Chilean Congress, for its part, was well aware that decentralization, especially the direct election of regional councilors, posed a threat to its power. When Aylwin government officials presented their plan for the creation of "regional parliaments," Congress balked. Members of Congress, deputies in particular, saw such a step as a significant challenge to their institutional role.[26]

Members of Congress were justified in feeling defensive. The role of the political broker—the nationally elected official using his or her connections and clout to serve the local constituency—is a deeply imbedded tradition in Chile. Chileans expect close ties between their congressional representatives and the public.[27] The 1980 constitution, however, establishes an extremely presidentialist system in which Congress is denied the tools legislators traditionally used to provide pork and develop their clienteles. Rather, the president establishes the legislative agenda and controls the legislative process to an extraordinary degree. Developing particularistic legislation aimed at satisfying the demands of individual constituents or their municipalities is no longer possible.[28] Nor can deputies and senators attach articles to legislation that are not ger-mane to the "central concept" of the measure. Because only the president can propose legislation related to state financing and budget adminis-tration, the president maintains almost complete control over the budget process, which shuts down another traditional avenue for local largesse. Congress can only reduce—not modify or increase—items in the presi-dent's budget proposal. Likewise, the chief executive also retains exclu-sive initiative over legislation related to retirement payments, pensions, and social security norms. Since virtually any major bill either requires some type of spending or involves social and economic concerns on which the president must take the lead, the ability of Congress to propose leg-islation of any significance is quite limited (Siavelis, 1997: 325–30).

Deputies and senators nonetheless do their utmost to serve or be seen by their constituents as brokers to their home communities. Pre-serving their bases of support, they do hundreds of particularistic favors, for example, grease the wheels of the national bureaucracy for mayors, routinely raise constituent concerns on the floor of the chamber, and send thousands of official letters to ministerial authorities requesting infor-mation or action on an issue. Until executive-legislative relations are re-formed and the Chilean public attaches much greater value to the role of national legislators as lawmakers, these activities (which are technically illegal under the constitution) will undoubtedly continue.

Simultaneously, regionalization has moved many of the administra-tive decisions important to local officials to the regional capitals. Hence the regions provided an entry point for building political support, one that would easily be available to a regional legislator or councilor with a specific mandate to promote regional interests and development, espe-cially if that mandate was drawn from victory in a popular election. The idea of creating a regional legislature or council raised the prospect of introducing another level of authority into the political system that could further weaken the relative power of national legislators.

Senators and deputies felt they would face competition for their jobs from ambitious regional councilors and, worse yet, increasing irrele-vancy in the eyes of the public as regional officials began to receive credit for delivering on investment projects or resources. Some claimed that they would be reduced to stronger clientelistic behavior and demagogu-ery if faced with this electoral challenge (Chile, Senado de la República, 1991a). Other objections were raised,[29] but senators and deputies clearly had in mind their own status within the political system, which remains fairly privileged, when they decided to reject the idea. As a former minister and lead negotiator later explained, the Aylwin government believed the direct election of councilors was important:

> But our senators and deputies did not agree, because they felt [the regional councils] were a body that could conspire against their power. A councilor elected in Santiago [would be] elected by the entire metropolitan region. A senator in Santiago [would be] elected by half of the metropolitan region. . . . So they felt there would be a [regional] institution with a lot of administrative capacity—to distribute resources, approve projects—that could constitute a permanent threat to their reelection, to their positions in the Senate or Chamber. We did not address [the regional councilors' possible election in provincial electoral districts]. They did not want anything directly elected. If they were to be elected in each province, the deputies would have considered themselves threatened because many deputies are elected by one or two provinces. And the senators felt they already had enough, having to face councilors elected in the municipalities, elected deputies, and now [potentially] an elected regional council. So again it was, as you can see, a position taken basically according to immediate political interests. (Author interview, December 23, 1994)

When an influential opposition senator was asked if in the future the law would be amended to provide direct election of the councilors, which he opposed, he bluntly responded: "Never. This is not going to be changed" (author interview, December 13, 1994). As an Interior Ministry subsecretary reasoned, the members of Congress "did not share, when the opportunity arrived to generate the basis for decentralization at the regional level, some of the reasoning with which the country has lately become acquainted" (Velasco Baraona, 1994).

Conclusion

In 1992, after at least a century or more, Chile finally transferred enough authority to local governments to allow them to act with a real measure of autonomy. Elections that year provided the critical political legitimacy to a local system that had been administratively and financially transformed during the Pinochet years. Today, Chilean local governments are not only represented by elected officials, they are also responsible for a range of functions and regularly receive or raise sufficient access to financial resources to exercise their primary duties. Whereas regional governments are administrative arms of the central government, they also serve as an important source of project-related resources for the municipalities. It should be emphasized, however, that the Chilean centralist tradition remains among the strongest in Latin America. Although local governments crossed an important threshold in the early 1990s, their level of autonomy vis-à-vis the center and regions continues to be limited by ministerial decision making or interference in purely local concerns and central management of local tax income, among other constraints. Decentralization has advanced significantly since 1992, including municipal fiscal reform and the establishment of additional regional funds for local project finance. Significantly, electoral reform enacted in July 2001 provides for the direct election (on a separate ballot) of mayors beginning in 2004 and allows the presentation of independent candidates.

The Chilean case confirms some of the hypotheses discussed in the first chapter of this volume. First, the process was decidedly "top-down." Chilean national leaders negotiated the municipal and regional systems largely among themselves. This was not an executive proposal to be widely debated, amended, and passed by the national legislature, or a response to popular demand for decentralized government. Second, the nature of democratic transition in Chile affected the impulse to decentralize. Specifically, the interests of democratic elites in removing Pinochet's authoritarian enclaves drove the process. Local government was on the agenda of reform because mayors appointed by the military were unacceptable to most Chileans and the new democratic government and politically untenable for the center-right coalition. Although there has long been a regionalist, anti-Santiago sentiment among the populace and although improved state efficiency and political representation were (and remain) major concerns, Chile's reforms were not a response to heightened public demands for particular characteristics of decentralized government. The progress of decentralization in Chile reflects much more the balance of power and interests among political elites and their political organizations than the impact of decentralization-minded social forces.

Perhaps more than in any other case analyzed in this volume, national political democracy required local democracy in Chile. Decentralization brought about the local democratic transition and, as such, was part of democratization generally. Indeed, the push for renewed democratic institutions almost seeped into the regional system, as the election of *intendentes* and, far more likely, the regional councilors was briefly brought into the debate, despite the strong unitary tradition working against such a move. In the end, in a compromise bow to democratic process, regional councilors with considerable formal responsibilities would be chosen indirectly by the elected town councilors. It bears noting that by 2001, the Lagos administration was seriously considering regional reform to increase regional government functions and even provide for the popular election of regional councilors.

Chile's democratization, not surprisingly, significantly influenced the nature and extent of decentralization. First, democratization set the timing for its emergence. Facing a clear national consensus in favor of democratic government, both the Aylwin government and the opposition were under pressure to remove the appointed mayors. They agreed to a timetable for doing so and forced themselves to meet that goal. Second, the reform agenda as well as specific reforms were framed by what the two sides initially felt they must accomplish to achieve agreement: for Alywin, local democracy that would likely favor his governing coalition; and for the center-right, a subnational system that would maximize their political potential. Hence the agenda included both municipal and regional government. Municipal reform largely revolved around local electoral rules that would be suitable to all parties—fiscal reform was put on hold—and regional reform involved the establishment of appointed and nonpopularly elected regional authorities with a significant role in local development. Third, key decentralization decisions were decided by a small group of elites with minimal public input. The enormous number of details to be addressed, time pressures, and Chile's traditionally oligarchic political culture were important influences here. So was the increasingly routine process of resolving critical governance issues through negotiation between the center-right and center-left blocs, however. In these ways, as discussed in the introductory chapter of this volume, macro-institutional factors set up the micro logic governing the negotiations among elites during the transition to democracy. Finally, the negotiations were not suitable to the development of a rationally designed subnational system. The bargaining required by coalition politics produced electoral rules and other difficulties in intergovernmental institutional relations that negatively affected subnational government performance. Larger political goals easily took precedence over concerns of effective public administration that would likely have arisen under more favorable circumstances. Negotiated democratization's impact on decentralization was not a one-way street. It is fair to argue that the arrival of decentralization—in effect, the emergence of local democracy after nineteen years and the removal of a glaring enclave of authoritarian power—brought Chile a step closer to consolidated democracy. New elections brought the return to local politics of a great many Chileans who had long been excluded, allowed a generation of young, mostly center-left activists to participate in government for the first time, and undoubtedly helped strengthen the legitimacy of the entire political system. A return to military government, even serious consideration of it, would surely be considerably more difficult. In addition, local elections are viewed in Chile as a kind of public opinion poll on the strength of support for each of the political parties and their respective coalitions. As such, local election results will surely influence, favorably or unfavorably for democracy, the policy positions of the two coalitions in future negotiations over the elimination of remaining authoritarian enclaves.

The centrality of electoral issues is reflected throughout the Chilean debates leading to decentralization. Indeed, these issues are shown to be essentially inseparable from the emergence of decentralization. Moreover, immediate political interests—often the perceived electoral implications of one reform versus another—clearly dominated much of the decision making on the part of the negotiators. At the municipal level, majoritarian electoral characteristics (i.e., direct election of mayors) and easier agreement were precluded by the requirement of proportionality imposed by the realities of coalitional politics. At the regional level, the issue of popularly electing *intendentes* and councils highlighted the constraints the existing institutional structure can place on efforts to accord popular legitimacy to governing officials. On the one hand, then, electoral issues came to the fore and were framed by inter- and intracoalitional bargaining. On the other hand, intra-institutional competition and the desire for institutional preservation—in this case, primarily the fears of national legislators—can cut across party and coalitional lines when the vertical redistribution of power is placed on the negotiating table.

The complexity of the situation in Chile can inform further study in Latin America of the links between decentralization and elections, where local electoral rules not only have been central to decentralization programs, but are also subject to constant change and often manipu-lation. In Venezuela, for example, where for more than a decade electoral codes have been modified prior to each election, the 1989 establishment of direct elections for governors and mayors was a major decentraliza-tion reform aimed at improving subnational government responsiveness (see Penfold-Becerra, this volume). As part of their programs, Colombia and Paraguay established elected intermediate levels of government in 1991 and 1993, respectively. Reflecting the institutional change that can emerge through subnational elections, opposition victories in state and local contests gradually weakened the formerly hegemonic Institutional Revolutionary Party (*Partido Revolucionario Institucional,* or PRI) of Mexico (see Beer, this volume). In Honduras, the mere separation of the ballots for local and national elective offices was viewed by the highly centralized parties as a major concession. These and other instances, along with the example of Chile, provide ample indication that there is much to be learned about the impact of strengthening subnational po-litical authority in Latin America.

NOTES

I thank the North-South Center, the Woodrow Wilson International Center for Scholars, IESA in Caracas, and FLACSO-Santiago for their invaluable sup-port in completing the research that led to this chapter. I also appreciate the help-ful comments of the editors of this volume and the anonymous reviewers.

1. The definition for political decentralization used throughout this chap-ter is drawn from the liberal political tradition (see Lipset, 1995: 335). For a dis-cussion of the dimensions of decentralization, see chapter 1 of this volume.

2. A. Valenzuela (1977: 193–210) argues convincingly that Chile experi-enced landmark decentralization to the local level during the Parliamentary Republic (1891–1925).

3. See Eaton (this volume) for a discussion of the causes of low municipal autonomy in the pre-Pinochet era.

4. By "deconcentration" I mean the transfer of functions to subnational offices of the central administration. Subnational officials are appointed and sub-ject to supervision from the center. In Chile this took on a particularly regional form, so I also refer to this process as "regionalization."

5. All interviews cited in this chapter were conducted on an anonymous basis.

6. Many agree that the Pinochet regime, although undeniably antidemo-cratic, did provide municipalities with an important degree of administrative and

developmental potential that could prove valuable in the event of local autonomy under a new democratic system (Raczynski and Serrano, 1987: 129–31; Rosenfeld, Rodríguez, and Espinoza, 1989: 220–33; Rehren, 1986: 76, 84–85; Campbell, 1990; Martelli, n.d.: 21).

7. Governors, who were subordinate to the *intendente*, had little formal power. They could maintain an advisory committee.

8. During the Aylwin government, only three separate constitutional reforms were enacted. They involved granting amnesty powers to the president, reduction of the presidential term from eight to six years, and the municipal and regional reforms discussed here (see Munck, 1994: 16, 31 n.).

9. Message No. 37 of S. E. Patricio Aylwin Azócar, to initiate the constitutional reform related to municipalities, reprinted in *El Mercurio,* "Pidió ejecutivo al Congreso: Modificación constitucional para municipios," May 19, 1990, p. C10.

10. These were the remarks of Minister Enrique Krauss at a news conference on the government's municipal reform proposal. See *El Mercurio,* "Pidió ejecutivo al Congreso," May 19, 1990, p. C10.

11. The government submitted two proposals, a constitutional reform and legislation to reform the municipal organic law, which passed the *Concertación*-controlled Chamber in November 1990.

12. As Gonzalo Martner, Subsecretary of Regional Government, Ministry of Interior, reflected in his remarks, the opposition used the initial absence of a regional initiative by Aylwin as an "excuse to delay" municipal reform. See *La Epoca,* "El Parlamento debe decidir el futuro de la reforma municipal," March 30, 1991.

13. See *La Epoca,* March 31, 1991; and *El Mercurio,* March 17, 1991, p. A12.

14. By the time the president's proposal was formally presented, it stated that the manner of electing the councilors would be determined by law (i.e., in negotiations in Congress).

15. Rarely does a government official discuss regionalization without affirming, as the president's proposal did, that Chile is a unitary state.

16. *El Mercurio,* "Hasta el 9 de agosto: Ampliado plazo para trámite de reformas," June 12, 1991, p. A12.

17. Senator Ricardo Núñez, president of the joint committee and a Socialist, made a point of the lesson he learned from the dramatic experience of Salvador Allende's Popular Unity government (1970–73): Any state transformation that is not "gradual and harmonious" runs the risk of failure (see Chile, Senado de la República, 1991c: 7; 1991b: 18).

18. Regarding the first issue under discussion, the rightist RN-UDI bloc, most interested in strengthening the regions, sought to require that a much larger portion (50 percent) of public investment be handled at that level. The

government, concerned with maintaining control over such politically valuable resources, macroeconomic stability, and the lack of technical capacity in the regions to invest the funds, objected. Second, the Concertation called for an odd number of councilors based on municipality size (i.e., 5, 7, and 9) and for their election on a proportional basis, at which point they would chose the mayor among themselves. As the majority coalition, it would be favored by proportional voting, and an odd number would preclude tie council votes for mayor. The right wanted to fashion a municipal electoral system comparable to the binomial system developed for congressional elections, with an even number of councilors (6) for every municipality, which, they felt at one point, could give them control of 50 percent of the localities with 40 percent of the vote (Fuentealba, 1991b). Third, various proposals were considered regarding the generation and composition of the regional council. The Aylwin government initially advocated the direct election of councilors; important segments of all parties, and members of Congress especially, opposed it. Other key issues included the creation of electoral subpacts (a measure supported by the right) and the vote percentage that would be required for council candidates to be automatically elected mayor.

19. For example, the RN-UDI coalition suffered a vocal public split—the first division between them regarding regional and local reform—over the RN's decision to join the PDC in support of the selection of the councilors by party lists. The right also sought to ensure that independents, with whom they were often allied, were granted the same status under electoral law as a political party.

20. The newly enacted constitutional reforms and laws are paradoxical in the following sense. The municipality basically serves as a local government in practice, but is legally considered an administrative entity ("municipal administration"). At the same time, the "regional government," legally denominated as such, is not actually a government but, rather, the administrator of nationally designated regional investment funds.

21. A fourth level of administration is the province, headed by a governor who serves as an advisor to the *intendente* and can be an influential figure. The Provincial Economic and Social Council (*Consejo Económico y Social Provincial*), an advisory body to the governor, was established to serve as a forum for public participation. The province is, however, of relatively minor governmental importance.

22. These conclusions are supported by interviews conducted by the author with various former ministers, subsecretaries, and advisors to the Aylwin government between September 1994 and February 1995.

23. In this June 1990 speech to a strongly pro-regionalization association, Martner asserted the government's desire to strengthen all levels of government, enact a new law for *intendentes* and provincial governors, and study the "democratization of regional organs of participation" (Martner, 1993: 27).

24. The election of mayors directly and on a ballot separate from the council candidates would have reflected stronger decentralization. A second plan, proposed by President Aylwin, was to elect as mayor the councilor who received the most votes from the party list of council candidates that received the most votes. The final, indirect method for electing mayors included the proviso that councilors who received 35 percent of the vote on the list receiving the most votes would be automatically named mayor.

25. For a discussion of the protocol, see Corporación Tiempo 2000 (1992: 23–30). The protocol "required" councilors (disciplinary action was to be taken against those who ignored the rules), in choosing the mayor, to vote for the councilor who received 22.5 percent or more of the vote. Also, some mayors were predetermined by election formulas and by negotiations after the voting based on each party's performance. The protocol would have worked, it seemed, if its norms had been respected.

26. For the structure, functions, and financing of regional government, see Martelli (1994).

27. A study of Chilean public opinion by *Participa* found that in 1993, confirming earlier polls, 82.5 percent of the respondents either agreed or strongly agreed with the idea that there needs to be greater contact between the people and Congress (Garretón, Lagos, and Méndez, 1994: 63).

28. None of the members of Congress interviewed by this author expressed a desire to return to the old system of clientelistic legislation. According to one congressional leader, this was not even an objective. They did strongly believe, however, that a strengthening of their legislative power was necessary.

29. These included the right's opposition to another forum for the center-left political parties, concern that regional centralism would develop (at the expense of conservative, rural interests) in the regions' capital cities, fears of creeping federalism, and the desire to ensure municipal-regional coordination.

CHAPTER 5

The Link between Political and Fiscal Decentralization in South America

KENT EATON

The recent adoption of decentralizing policies in countries throughout the developing world has focused scholars' attention on the broad, systemic forces behind decentralization. One of the most salient hypotheses about decentralization to emerge in the contemporary period traces the adoption of decentralizing policies to democratization (Bird and Vaillancourt, 1998; IDB, 1997; Nickson, 1995). According to this argument, the historic third wave of democracy that began in the mid-1970s triggered a subsequent and equally profound wave of decentralization in the 1980s and 1990s. As Montero and Samuels argue in their introduction to this volume, scholars have articulated a variety of causal connections through which democratization might lead to decentralization. According to the hypothesis I evaluate in this chapter, it is the democratic election of subnational officials in particular that unleashes powerful and ultimately irresistible pressures from below for greater fiscal decentralization. In this view of decentralization, fiscal authority follows elections.

As a result of political and fiscal decentralization in the last two decades, more mayors and governors are currently elected in Latin America than ever before, and more of these subnational officials now enjoy significant fiscal and economic powers in their own right. Though the substantive importance of these changes is beyond dispute, is it the case that political decentralization has caused fiscal decentralization?

In assessing the causal connection between political and fiscal decentralization, most of the literature has focused on the contemporary period. After all, in much of Latin America the holding of elections for subnational office is unique to the third wave of democracy, making it impossible to explore the impact of earlier experiences with subnational elections on fiscal decentralization (Willis, Garman, and Haggard, 1999: 11; IDB, 1997: 152). For example, none of the following countries had significant experiences with subnational elections before the most recent wave of democracy: Bolivia, Colombia, Ecuador, Panama, Paraguay, Peru, and Venezuela.[1] Instead, the power of national executives to appoint subnational offices in these countries was the norm throughout their histories as independent republics. In these countries, the newness of elections for subnational office is an obvious candidate for explanations of the dramatic upsurge in decentralizing proposals and policies in the last twenty years. According to this view, decentralization failed to occur before for the simple reason that local elections were not regularly held.

Neither political nor fiscal decentralization are entirely new in Latin America, however. This chapter examines four countries that experienced earlier and significant periods of subnational elections in order to determine whether the historical record offers broad support for the argument attributing decentralization to democratization. Argentina, Brazil, Chile, and Uruguay are unique in Latin America for their long histories of elections at the subnational level, predating by decades their most recent transitions to democracy. Did the holding of elections for mayor and governor lead to decentralization in earlier time periods? If so, under what conditions? If not, why does the logic of this hypothesis appear to be limited to the contemporary period? Answers to these questions may allow for a more robust appraisal of democratization as an explanation of decentralization, one that can then be contrasted with other generic explanations including neoliberal reform, international factors, and sociostructural causes.

According to the research presented in this chapter, elections for subnational offices in the twentieth century quite consistently led to fiscal decentralization in Argentina and Brazil, but not in Chile and Uruguay. In using these four cases to deepen our understanding of the relationship between democratization and decentralization, two distinct empirical questions arise. First is the necessity of determining whether subnational officials, subsequent to their election, demanded greater resources and powers from the national level. Second is the question of whether these demands were successful. In the Chilean and Uruguayan cases, where fiscal authority remained centralized despite the holding of subnational elections for decades, we need to determine if subnational officials actually made such demands, and if they did, we need to know the nature of the response to those demands. Evidence of unsuccessful demand making suggests that subnational democratization does generate some pressures for decentralization from below, while evidence of the failure to make demands poses a more direct challenge for the democratization hypothesis. Though analytically distinct, these two questions raise similar methodological problems, given that I am asking them about distant time periods in which key decision makers have long since passed from the scene. Although the quality of the historical record varies across countries and time periods, the historiography is generally richer in its characterization of macro-level variables than in its treatment of the micro-level decisions and demands that are central to this investigation. The case studies that follow reflect this asymmetry.

Despite this methodological challenge, what clearly emerges from the sometimes messy and incomplete historical record is the *absence of significant demand making* by subnational executives in Chile and Uruguay. Why did democratically elected officials push for greater independent fiscal powers from below in some countries but not in others? At first glance, federalism would appear to be part of the answer: Argentina and Brazil are federal in structure while Chile and Uruguay are unitary. Federalism may legitimize and thereby motivate subnational actors to demand the sorts of powers that would enable them to play their constitutionally assigned roles. At the same time, unitary constitutions that deny important roles for subnational officials may inhibit them from making similar demands. Comparative data on subnational spending as a percentage of total spending, however, show that federal systems are sometimes more centralized than unitary systems, and so the question remains as to why subnational officials failed to demand greater fiscal authority in my two unitary cases.

I argue in this chapter that the answer can be found by blending the democratization hypothesis with the institutional factors that Montero and Samuels highlight in the introduction to this volume. Democratization at the subnational level took place in all four cases and brought to office new actors whose fiscal behavior can only be understood in light of the party institutions they inhabited. Different aspects of party systems lend themselves to hypothesizing about decentralization. For example, by raising the number of veto players whose agreement is required for changes in the policy status quo, party system fragmentation may inhibit decentralization.[2] The greater the fragmentation, the greater the number of national party leaders who must be convinced of the merits of shifting power away from the national level. By increasing the ideological distance between parties, polarization of the party system may also pose an obstacle to the adoption of decentralizing policies, though, in practice, decentralization has generated coalitions for and against that seldom respect traditional ideological dimensions.[3]

I also focus on a third aspect of political parties that is especially useful in understanding how subnational officials behave: the degree to which authority is centralized within the party. As Willis, Garman, and Haggard (1999) have argued, Latin American parties vary significantly in the extent to which subnational party officials control the future careers and thus current behavior of policy-makers at the national level. Typically, this control takes the form of participation in candidate selection and appointment for a host of positions to which national legislators aspire. Such control gives subnational actors the ability to leverage future appointments and favors on the passage of decentralization. By contrast, subnational actors who lack this type of control are powerless to secure the requisite decentralizing legislation. Although not all subnational officials are alike in their capacity to secure decentralization, there are theoretically solid reasons to expect that they are alike in their preference for decentralization. Assuming that, like all politicians, subnational officials prefer more power to less, officials who control the careers of national policy-makers should seek independent access to fiscal resources to *supplement* this control. Subnational officials who do not control the careers of national politicians should seek fiscal powers that might *substitute* for the lack of such control. Because it partially refutes the logic of this deductive hypothesis about the fiscal preferences of subnational officials, the Chilean case is particularly important in this analysis.

According to the comparative literature on political parties in Latin America, there is significant variation across my four cases in the degree to which control over access to political careers is centralized. Brazil marks the most decentralized end of the continuum given the salience of governors in the calculations of national policy-makers (Abrucio, 1998; Samuels, 2003). Although greater national party discipline has traditionally weakened federalism in Argentina, the recent literature has emphasized the extent to which national legislators are beholden to governors (Eaton, 2002; Jones, 1997; Tommasi and Spiller, 2000). In contrast, in the current period as in previous periods, Chilean political parties have been among the region's most centralized, with candidate selection for national and local contests alike the purview of national actors (Siavelis, 2000). Similarly, subnational officials in Uruguay are devoid of the power over national decision-makers that their peers enjoy in Brazil and Argentina (Gillespie, 1991; González, 1991).

This chapter proceeds as follows. The next section explores in greater depth the logic of the argument linking subnational elections with fiscal decentralization. The third section discusses the broad patterns that emerge from the historical record with political and fiscal decentralization in Argentina, Brazil, Chile and Uruguay. The fourth section evaluates political and fiscal decentralization and recentralization in each country, highlighting the most important experiences in each case. Rather than describe any one period in great detail, the purpose is to characterize the content of political and fiscal shifts in enough detail to determine whether they support my variant of the democratization hypothesis. While this chapter seeks to capture both the direction and magnitude of the shifts in each period, further research needs to be conducted on the latter question. The final section offers concluding comments.

SUBNATIONAL ELECTIONS AND FISCAL DECENTRALIZATION

Before turning to the historical experience with decentralization in the four case studies, the logic of the democratization hypothesis requires further consideration. Democratization may lead to decentralization through a variety of different causal mechanisms. One important distinction made in the literature contrasts top-down versus bottom-up approaches to decentralization. Does decentralization occur because policy-makers at the center push it "from the top," or because actors at lower levels demand greater control over revenues and expenditures "from the bottom"?

According to top-down arguments, democratically elected national policy-makers may have a variety of reasons to support decentralization. Like chief executives in nondemocratic systems, democratically elected presidents generally stand to lose considerable authority as a result of decentralization. Unlike unelected chief executives, however, presidents may agree to decentralize as a means of bolstering their electoral support among groups who favor decentralization or as a means of incorporating new actors into the political system (Garman, Haggard, and Willis, 1996). Where new democracies are fragile, presidents may favor decentralization as a means of furthering the democratization process itself (Eaton, 2001). Political parties at the center may also support decentralization when they estimate that their electoral strength in the future lies at the subnational level rather than at the national level (see O'Neill, this volume). With respect to national legislators in particular, legislatures may advocate decentralization when they are dominated by opposition parties who seek to decentralize policy-making authority in order to limit the president's power over them (Garman, Haggard, and Willis, 1996).

The bottom-up pressures for decentralization that are unleashed by democracy may also come in many different forms. For example, particularly where the mobilization of civil society played a leading role in the transition to democracy, democratization may open space for demands from below for decentralization. Though civil society actors were often demobilized in the aftermath of the transition to democracy, in many cases they enjoyed significant influence in debates over decentralization. Nongovernmental organizations, citizens' groups and neighborhood associations may support decentralization as a means of shifting authority to government officials over whom it may be easier for them to exercise oversight (Manor, 1995). On the other hand, because of the very persistence of authoritarian enclaves at the local level, progressive actors in civil society may be ambivalent toward decentralization and actually prefer that policy authority continue to be centralized at the national level, where they often have greater influence (Fox, 1994; Schönwälder, 1997). Whatever the attitude of civil society actors toward decentralization, research suggests that grassroots pressure for decentralizing policies has in practice been largely absent from the most significant decentralization episodes in the developing world (Manor, 1999: 43).

According to the literature, democratically elected subnational officials are a much more important source of bottom-up pressure for decentralization than are civil society actors at the local level (Manor, 1999: 31; Souza, 1996b; Samuels, 2003; Penfold-Becerra, this volume). When subnational officials are selected through elections that are free and fair, they have a variety of reasons to prefer the decentralization of revenues and expenditures. Decentralization increases the power of subnational officials relative to the populations they govern and relative to the national policy-makers who effectively concentrated most policy-making authority under previous periods of centralized governance. Dependence on central-government officials for revenue transfers and spending projects may represent a serious constraint on subnational politicians that prevents them from building their own political support coalitions independent of national politicians. The important point is that these pressures for decentralization would have been absent both under the authoritarian governments in Latin America's past, when subnational officials served at the pleasure of de facto authorities at the center, and when democratically elected national presidents had the power to appoint subnational officials.

This argument about decentralizing demands should apply to both the executive and legislative branches of subnational governments. The research presented in this chapter focuses more on the behavior of the chief executives of subnational governments as opposed to subnational legislators, but decentralization should also be important to the latter. Unless subnational legislators are completely denied participation in subnational budgeting and policy making, the devolution of rights and responsibilities to states, provinces, departments, and municipalities should increase the authority and attractiveness of legislative positions at these levels. The argument should also apply to both the revenue and expenditure sides of fiscal policy. By revenue decentralization, I am referring both to reforms that increase the taxing capacity of subnational governments and to reforms that increase their shares of centrally collected and automatically distributed tax revenues. Though the former is a more robust indicator of decentralization than automatic revenue transfers, both can increase the autonomy of subnational actors.[4] By expenditure decentralization, I am referring to changes that devolve responsibility for the provision of services formerly provided by the central government.

HISTORICAL EVIDENCE FROM SOUTH AMERICA

As seen in Table 5.1, the shift toward political decentralization in the form of elections for subnational office is hardly unique to the most recent transitions to democracy in Latin America. Though they did not all achieve the same standards of democratic fairness, all four countries in the southern cone had significant experiences with political decentralization earlier in the twentieth century. In the three-tiered systems of Argentina and Brazil, subnational elections were held for both governor and mayor before the current democratic period. For most of its history, Chile had no intermediate level of government, and first held municipal elections for mayor as a result of the 1891 constitution. In Uruguay, the local and intermediate levels are combined into a single departmental level (sometimes referred to as *municípios*) for which elections were first held as a result of the 1918 constitution. If the democratization hypothesis is not temporally constrained, we should see evidence of fiscal decentralization resulting from these earlier subnational elections.

In addition to earlier periods in which subnational elections were held, each country also had earlier experiences with the reversal of political decentralization in the form of suspensions of local elections. Almost always, the shift toward political recentralization at the local level occurred as part of the breakdown of democracy at the national level (e.g., all Argentine cases, both Chilean cases, Brazil in 1964, and Uruguay in 1934 and 1973), but not in all cases (e.g., Uruguay in 1908). In keeping with the democratization hypothesis, one would expect that the recentralization of political authority after its previous decentralization would lead to the recentralization of fiscal policy authority as well. According to the logic of this argument, central-government officials would take advantage of the absence of democratically elected subnational officials and augment their own power by reclaiming authority over previously devolved revenues and expenditures. Including in the analysis periods that were characterized by both political decentralization and recentralization yields a total of twenty-eight different episodes: eleven in Argentina, seven in Uruguay, and five each in Brazil and Chile (see Table 5.1). Only in Argentina and Brazil were subnational elections followed by significant episodes of fiscal decentralization, and not all of the Argentine episodes support the hypothesis, as explained in the country-specific discussions below.

Table 5.1.   Decentralization and Recentralization Trends in
South America

	Shifts toward Political Decentralization	Shifts toward Political Recentralization
Argentina	*1912–1930*	*1930–1946*
	1946–1955	*1955–1958*
	1958–1962	*1962–1963*
	1963–1966	*1966–1973*
	1973–1976	*1976–1983*
	1983–	
Brazil	*1889–1930*	*1930–1945*
	1945–1964	*1964–1982*
	1982–	
Chile	*1891–1924*	*1924–1935*
	1935–1973	*1973–1990*
	1990–	
Uruguay	*1897–1908*	*1908–1918*
	1918–1934	*1934–1938*
	1938–1973	*1973–1984*
	1984–	

Note: Periods that clearly support the democratization hypothesis are italicized.

In Argentina and Brazil, independently elected governors emerged as powerful advocates for fiscal decentralization in the aftermath of democratization. In Argentina, governors were successful in their demands that the central government increase the provinces' shares of centrally collected tax revenues shortly after the transitions to democracy in 1946, 1959, 1963, and 1983. Furthermore, de facto military governments moved quickly either to freeze or reverse fiscal decentralization when they took power in 1943, 1966, and 1976. In Brazil, the fall of a centralized monarchy in 1889 led to a constitution two years later that expanded the fiscal powers of the states relative to the center. Though elections in this "First Republic" failed to meet the minimum standards of democracy, this period represents one of decentralization relative to the previous monarchy and relative to subsequent efforts by Getúlio Vargas to recentralize power in the *Estado Novo* period (1930–45). Transitions to democracy that placed governors at the center of the political system in 1945 and 1982 resulted in significant fiscal decentralization, in contrast to the centralization of fiscal authority in the intervening period of military government (1964–1982). In both Argentina and Brazil, pressure by subnational actors for decentralization appears to be the paramount factor at play, helping to explain why the two countries are, according to many indicators, Latin America's most decentralized (Dillinger and Webb, 1999; IDB, 1997; Willis, Garman, and Haggard, 1999).

Though Chile and Uruguay both had experiences with political and fiscal decentralization that predate the third wave of democracy, there is little evidence that the former led to the latter. In Chile, victorious forces aligned against the president in the country's 1891 civil war wrote a new constitution that *simultaneously* provided for local elections and increased local taxing capacity. While the constitution endowed municipalities with significant taxing authority, this devolution did not occur in response to pressures from below, and in practice these powers were never used. In Uruguay, political and fiscal decentralization in the country's 1918 constitution was the result of high-level interparty bargaining between the Colorado and Blanco parties rather than pressures from departmental executives for greater power. In both cases, then, political and fiscal decentralization occurred simultaneously as the result of political struggles and bargains at the center; in neither case were fiscal powers devolved in response to demands by independently elected subnational officials. The following section will explore these cases in greater depth.

Four Cases

Argentina

Over the course of the twentieth century, democracy in Argentina proved to be just as volatile at the subnational level as at the national level, on which scholars have focused most of their attention. After the extension of electoral reforms that guaranteed democratic elections in the provinces in 1912, military coups suspended elections in 1930, 1943, 1955, 1962, 1966, and 1976. The Argentine case offers quite strong support for the hypothesis that subnational elections generate pressures for fiscal decentralization. As the following discussion shows, transitions to democracy at the provincial level led to changes in revenue sharing procedures that favored the provinces in 1947, 1959, 1964, and 1988. Most of the military regimes reversed fiscal decentralization, though one military government in the early 1970s was responsible for an important decentralizing reform. It would be hard to understand why fiscal policy in Argentina is as decentralized as it is today without emphasizing the importance of pressure by provincial governors for greater powers.

The first period of relevance to the democratization hypothesis was initiated with the introduction of the Sáenz Peña electoral reform by progressive elements of the governing Conservative Party in 1912, which marks the onset of democracy at the national and provincial levels. In the subsequent eighteen-year period, which ended with Argentina's first breakdown of democracy in 1930, governors had some cause but little capacity to demand greater powers from the federal government. Before the centralization of fiscal policy-making authority in 1934 (see below), fiscal powers were quite decentralized. The country's 1853 constitution had endowed the provinces with important tax powers. According to the constitution, taxes on external trade would be the exclusive preserve of the federal government, while provincial governments had the exclusive right to collect direct taxes. Indirect taxes on domestic tax bases were shared jointly between the federal and provincial governments (Frias, 1980: 13). For much of the nineteenth century, trade taxes mainly financed the federal government, while the provinces depended on domestic indirect taxes (Pírez, 1986). When the financial crisis of 1890 slashed federal government earnings from trade taxes, however, it began to collect domestic indirect taxes as well, leading to a significant degree of overlapping in federal and provincial tax bases (Nuñez Miñana and Porto, 1982). The encroachment of the federal government continued apace throughout the first period of democratic subnational elections.

Although governors in this period were losing fiscal power relative to the center, their ability to protest was limited by the actions of Radical president Hipólito Yrigoyen, first elected in 1916. Once in power, Presi-

dent Yrigoyen behaved in ways that constrained political decentralization. Because governors in Argentina exert much influence over the behavior of national legislators, and because Yrigoyen faced opposition
in Congress to his reform agenda, the president depended increasingly
on federal interventions in the provinces. Designed "to supplant the conservatives and their party machines in the provinces," Yrigoyen decreed
over twenty interventions in his first term (Rock, 1987: 199). These interventions countered the potentially decentralizing effect of the 1912 democratizing reforms.

This first democratic period ended with two political and economic
changes that would have profound consequences for subnational politics and decentralization in Argentina. First, the world economic depression led to a decline in trade receipts that sent the federal executive
branch scrambling for additional tax revenues, further crowding out the
provinces' ability to raise taxes. Second, on the political side, a brief but
important military coup in 1930 brought an end to the previous period
of Radical Party dominance and led to the proscription of the Radical
Party in subsequent elections. Subnational and national elections in this
period were characterized by a great deal of fraud, as reflected in the
"Infamous Decade" label that has been applied to the 1930s. The 1931
elections restored to power groups that had been excluded during the
preceding period of Radical government, including pampas exporting
interests and lesser landowners in the interior provinces. President Agustín Justo's *Concordancia* alliance of conservative and provincial parties
held a majority of seats in the national Congress, thanks almost entirely
to the proscription of the Radical Party (Rock, 1985). Dominated by traditional land-owning elites, these same parties controlled the governorships of most provinces in this period, though their electoral legitimacy
was undermined by widespread electoral fraud and proscriptions.

In this political and economic context, the governing *Concordancia* alliance created a new system of revenue collection and distribution
called *coparticipación* (henceforth, coparticipation). According to this
centralizing measure, the provinces delegated to the national Congress
exclusive rights over certain taxes in exchange for an automatic share in
the revenues collected. This agreement took the form, in late 1934, of a
series of new sales, excise, and income taxes passed by Congress, which
voted to share the proceeds with the provinces on the condition that they
repealed any overlapping provincial taxes.[5] The laws also specified that

how much individual provinces gave up in the way of locally collected tax revenue would be the central factor determining each province's share of the taxes now collected by the federal government (i.e., distribution criteria were initially devolutive) (Nuñez Miñana and Porto, 1983).

With the transition back to democracy in 1946, and with subnational elections that were freer and fairer than those in the preceding decade, pressures emerged from below for fiscal decentralization. In November 1946, just five months after he was elected president, Juan Perón called the first ever conference of provincial finance ministers to discuss coparticipation. These ministers complained about the centralization of tax authority in 1934 by a government that many of them considered to be illegitimate and on terms that many of them considered disadvantageous for the provinces (Pírez, 1986: 25). The Perón administration agreed to raise provincial shares but defended coparticipation as necessary in order for the federal government to carry out the many new tasks associated with state-led industrialization and development (Pírez, 1986: 27). In 1947, Peronist majorities in Congress legislated changes that augmented provincial shares.

When the 1947 coparticipation law expired after the forced exile of Perón in September 1955, the military government that deposed him simply extended the laws for successive one-year periods. Four months after the return to democracy in May 1958 with the inauguration of Arturo Frondizi as president, provincial officials organized a conference in which they demanded that coparticipated revenues be split evenly between the federal and provincial governments (*La Nación*, July 7, 1958). Initially, Frondizi responded that he could not afford to send any more revenues to the provinces and proposed delaying any discussion of the coparticipation system for five years. When the provincial representatives insisted on reform, the president agreed to increase provincial shares from 21 percent to 26 percent. Calling this increase insufficient, subnational politicians responded by successfully lobbying Congress to legislate changes that increased provincial shares to 36 percent by 1963 (Pírez, 1986: 39; *Diario de Sesiones,* December 21, 1958).

After the brief military government of 1962–63, a similar dynamic occurred under the democratic government of Arturo Illía (1963–66). Early in Illía's administration, governors of some of the most important interior provinces, including Catamarca, La Rioja, Salta, and Tucumán, met in Buenos Aires to discuss coparticipation. They reiterated the 1958 demand that the federal government split revenues with them equally by raising the provincial share to 50 percent. Though the president initially refused to raise provincial shares beyond 44 percent, provincial governors successfully pressured legislators in the national congress to increase the share to 46 percent (*Diario de Sesiones,* January 29, 1964).

The steady increases in provincial shares of centrally collected tax revenues that took place over the first thirty years of coparticipation came to an end with the military coup of 1966. Unlike the previous two military coups of 1955 and 1962, the June 1966 coup sought the fundamental transformation of the Argentine economy, polity, and society. By replacing democratically elected governors with military appointees and by dissolving Congress, President Juan Onganía subverted the institutions that formerly mediated provincial and national interests, enabling him to ignore subnational pressures. In March 1967, Onganía's government imposed changes that sharply reduced provincial shares in coparticipation to pre-1959 levels. While the revenue shares of the provinces were reduced 11 percent (from 40 percent to 35.6 percent of total revenues legally subject to coparticipation), the capital city's share alone was reduced 22 percent (from 6 percent to 5.3 percent) in 1967 and an additional 22 percent in 1968 (Nuñez Miñana and Porto, 1982).

The equally ambitious but more brutal military coup that Argentina suffered in March 1976 led to an even more profound reversal of fiscal decentralization. Unlike the earlier Onganía government, what motivated the Jorge Videla government to decrease provincial revenue transfers was not just fiscal stabilization but the attempt to enhance market-driven growth and reduce wage costs by eliminating employer contributions to social security (FIEL, 1993: 146–47). According to the 1980 decree law that abolished social security taxes on employers, the federal government would deduct from the coparticipation pool the funds it needed to finance the national social security system. This "pre-coparticipation" did not alter the provinces' legal shares in the revenue pool, but it effectively reduced transfers by decreasing the size of this pool. As a result of pre-coparticipation, provincial shares were reduced to 29 percent of total revenues legally subject to coparticipation, a 44 percent decrease (FIEL, 1993: 148). In 1981 the military government decreed a law that eliminated entirely the federal capital from the coparticipation law, arguing that the city of Buenos Aires had "sufficient revenues to fulfill its obligations" (Nuñez Miñana and Porto, 1982: 22).

As in 1946, the centralization of revenue under the previous military regime ignited pressures for decentralization after the return to democracy in 1983. Unlike in 1946, however, no single party controlled both the legislative and executive branches, and the Radical and Peronist parties failed to come to agreement about a new revenue-sharing law after the earlier law lapsed in 1984. Between 1984 and 1988, in the absence of a coparticipation law, revenue sharing became the prerogative of the Radical president Raúl Alfonsín. This enabled the president to use revenue transfers to the provinces, the majority of which were governed by Peronists, as a means of getting opposition governors and legislators to support his various policy proposals in Congress (Pírez, 1986). Because this arrangement put Peronist provincial governors at a disadvantage, Peronist governors and legislators quickly engineered the legislation of a new coparticipation law after they won congressional elections in 1987.[6]

Most of the decentralization that has occurred in Argentina over the last sixty years has been the result of pressure exerted by subnational officials, namely, provincial governors. These many different periods offer strong support for the democratization hypothesis. There is, however, one important exception in the 1973 implementation of changes that expanded provincial shares in coparticipated taxes under the outgoing military government of Alejandro Lanusse. This episode is the exception to the rule of military support for recentralization. In response to the Peronist victory in the 1973 presidential elections that the military finally agreed to hold, Lanusse's decision to decrease federal tax shares and increase provincial tax shares can be understood as an attempt to constrain the incoming Peronist government (Saiegh and Tommasi, 1998). Shifting resources to the provinces where conservative politicians would hold greater sway was a means of protecting the military's interests against the types of policies it expected from a third Peronist administration at the federal level.

Brazil

Though Brazil has had fewer than half the transitions that occurred in Argentina between democratic and nondemocratic governance at the subnational level, the country's experience in many respects mirrors the dynamic at play in Argentina. In both countries, the democratic election of subnational officials created pressures for fiscal decentralization, and in both countries, the suspension of elections during periods of de facto government at the center opened up space for fiscal centralization. Unlike the Argentine case, which is notable for the absence of a significant tradition of municipal autonomy (Nickson, 1995), local governments in Brazil emerged as important actors in fiscal decentralization (see Samuels, this volume).

Because national and subnational elections in Brazil's First Republic were restricted to such a limited group of citizens, the 1889–1930 period is not strictly germane to this analysis. Several aspects of this period, however, are important to note. First, the 1891 constitution shifted political and fiscal autonomy to the states and away from the federal level. Under the previous imperial system, Brazil's provinces had no real fiscal power independent of the center (Shoup, 1965: 75–76). In 1892, many taxes formerly collected by the central government passed to the states, and state governors became active in the defense of state interests vis-à-vis the federal government (Abrucio, 1998; Topik, 1987). Between 1907 and 1930, the states' share of total public expenditures increased from 36 percent to 46 percent (Mahar and Dillinger, 1983: 2). Second, municipalities were politically and fiscally weak compared to the state governments (Abrucio, 1998: 38). In twelve of the twenty states, governors continued to appoint mayors rather than hold elections for these positions (Sherwood, 1967: 36). Under the prevailing system of *coronelismo,* governors brokered fiscal and other services for local political chiefs (*coroneis*) in exchange for votes in state elections. According to Nunes Leal, this political system depended on fiscally weak municipalities (1976: 45). Unsurprisingly, no politically significant demands for stronger municipalities were issued in this period.

The coup in 1930 that brought Getúlio Vargas to the presidency marks the beginning of a fifteen-year period that partially reversed Brazil's previous experiences with political and fiscal decentralization. Vargas's central project involved the strengthening of the federal government through the weakening of the traditional oligarchies that dominated the states. After federal troops put down the São Paulo rebellion of 1932, regional elites successfully pushed for a new constitution in 1934 that would regularize Vargas's provisional government (Abrucio, 1998: 44). Though the 1934 document incorporated some decentralizing measures, Vargas used these measures to weaken the states by strengthening municipalities. The 1934 constitution reduced the states' fiscal powers by preventing them from taxing goods shipped between states and by forcing the states to share with the municipalities proceeds from an important tax on industry and professions (Nickson, 1995: 119; Skidmore and Smith, 1997: 168). Municipalities, in contrast, were empowered by the constitution, which gave them the right to levy their own taxes and elect all officeholders (Mahar and Dillinger, 1983: 3).[7] These measures proved short-lived, however, with the 1937 transition to authoritarian rule under the *Estado Novo*. Though the 1937 constitution did not formally reverse municipal decentralization, between 1937 and 1945 all municipal executives were appointed by the state intervenors who were in turn appointed by Vargas (Sherwood, 1967: 120).

The nearly twenty years that constitute the Second Republic (1945–64) are an important period for the democratization hypothesis. The collapse of authoritarian rule in 1945 and the holding of elections for a constituent assembly that were Brazil's freest up to that point generated significant pressures for decentralization to both the state and municipal levels. At the state level, the 1946 constitution devolved responsibility for important taxes to the states. In addition to the sales taxes that compromised nearly 90 percent of all state tax revenues in this period, governors were given the right to collect taxes on exports from their states (Sherwood, 1967: 118). This devolution of authority over trade taxes to the subnational level is rare in the developing and developed world alike. In addition, the 1946 constitution reserved for the states 50 percent of electric tax collections and 48 percent of the National Highway Fund, which was generated by a petroleum tax (Cann, 1970: 14). By emphasizing population and consumption, the criteria used to distribute these revenues among the states rewarded the highly urbanized ones. According to observers, the federal government was more diligent about transferring revenues to the states in a timely manner than it was in implementing the municipal revenue sharing system, discussed below (Mahar, 1971: 79; Sherwood, 1967: 127).

Turning from the state to municipal governments, the 1946 constitution also represented significant improvements in the fiscal status of municipalities. Given the political power of the governors and the extent to which the fiscal weakness of municipal governments was a political asset for governors, evidence of changes that benefited the municipalities is problematic for the hypothesis under review here. In response to the "municipalist" sentiment prevalent in the constituent assembly, the 1946 constitution provided the municipalities with two new tax bases, a stamp tax and a business and industry tax (Sherwood, 1967). The constitution also established revenue sharing mechanisms from both the federal and state governments. According to Article 15, the federal government was obligated to share 10 percent of income tax revenues with the municipalities, in addition to shares in excise taxes and taxes on fuels, electric energy, and minerals (Cann, 1970: 15). The municipalities received equal shares of these transfers, despite differences in size, population, and local tax-raising capacity, which was a considerable advantage to the many poor municipalities located in the north and northeast.[8] Municipalities were expected to spend half of their transfers on projects in rural areas (Sherwood, 1967: 116). The 1946 constitution also obliged state governments to share with the municipalities 30 percent of their excess tax revenues and 40 percent of the revenues from any new state taxes (Mahar and Dillinger, 1983: 3).

Fifteen years into this democratic period in Brazil, further changes were made that increased fiscal decentralization to the municipalities. In 1961, a constitutional amendment increased revenue sharing with the municipalities by giving them a 15 percent share in federal consumption tax revenues (Cann, 1970: 15). Unlike the 1946 sharing of income tax revenues, the 1961 change did not exclude state capitals from participating and placed no restrictions on the use of revenue transfers. The 1961 amendments also devolved authority over two additional taxes that were previously collected by the states to municipalities: the rural property tax and the real-estate transfer tax (Sherwood, 1967: 121).[9]

For a number of reasons, however, revenue transfers to municipalities did not fully deliver on their promise, and one should not exaggerate the extent of fiscal decentralization to municipalities that occurred in this period. According to observers, there was a serious gap between constitutional language and actual outcomes. First, the escalation of inflation after the mid-1950s reduced the real size of federal revenue transfers to both states and municipalities (Mahar, 1971). The benefits of the inflation tax accrued solely to the federal government. Second, the fact that all municipalities shared equally in federal revenue transfers triggered an explosion in the number of municipalities. The doubling in the number of municipalities that occurred between 1945 and 1966 led to a reduction in the size of fiscal transfers to each one (Cann, 1970: 22). Third, and most importantly, the federal and state governments often failed to transfer the revenues they were obligated by law to share with the municipalities. According to Mahar, because revenue shares for subnational governments constituted line items in federal budgets, they were subject to much political manipulation. Political leverage by local officials was important in getting shares released (Mahar, 1971: 76; Mahar and Dillinger, 1983). Most municipalities remained powerless to demand that their revenues be transferred, and those larger cities that had greater political power had less reason to lobby for transfers because they constituted much smaller percentages of their overall revenues (Sherwood, 1967: 124). According to one mayor writing at the end of the Second Republic, eighteen of the states failed to make any payment at all to the municipalities, in contradiction to revenue-sharing procedures (Ferreira, 1965: 423). Thus, though elections were held at both the state and municipal level during the Second Republic, the general conclusion about this period is that the former experienced much stronger gains in fiscal terms than did the latter. This difference reflects the reality that governors wielded more political power within the country's national political system.

Political and fiscal decentralization suffered important reversals with the coup of 1964, particularly during the first ten years of the military government that ensued. Unlike the earlier *Estado Novo,* the military leaders went to great lengths to preserve some role for elections, though they were forced to shift from direct to indirect gubernatorial elections when it became clear that they would be unable to control directly elected governors (Samuels and Abrucio, 1997). Elections were held in all but 201 municipalities, though the effective autonomy of mayors was limited (Nickson, 1995). Despite the holding of elections, political authority in the first half of the military government was highly centralized with respect to earlier and subsequent periods of democratic rule. The centralizing content of changes in fiscal arrangements is less clear, even in the first half of the military government. On the one hand, the military government actually made revenue sharing more automatic (Oliveira, 1995: 85; Mahar, 1971). On the other hand, the military imposed new earmarks on revenue transfers and decreased the size of municipal transfers by half (Nickson, 1995; Samuels and Abrucio, 1997).[10] More importantly, perhaps, the military government recentralized authority over tax bases that had previously been devolved. A new value-added tax (ICM) at the state level was one exception, though the federal government reserved the right to set the rate of this tax (Oliveira, 1995). On balance, fiscal authority became more centralized, and restrictions on democracy at the subnational level clearly facilitated these centralizing changes.

The centralizing dynamic set into motion in the 1960s, however, was arrested by the victory of the opposition party in legislative elections at both the state and national levels in 1974. In response to the defeat of candidates of the governing ARENA party (National Renewal Alliance), the military began to cede powers to state governors beginning in the mid-1970s (Samuels and Abrucio, 1997). According to Samuels and Abrucio, this change in the political environment led to important decentralizing reforms. First, in an attempt to court the governors, the military doubled the tax shares of the states and municipalities in 1975. Second, it reduced the extent of earmarking in 1979. Third, the Passos Porto amendment further increased the states' and municipalities' shares in federal tax revenue in 1983 (Samuels and Abrucio, 1997: 30–31). Finally, in support of the hypothesis evaluated here, direct gubernatorial elections in 1982 set the stage for a return to democracy in which subnational fiscal powers have been increased to historic highs. The political power of governors over the deputies who participated in the 1988 Constituent Assembly is reflected in increased taxing powers for subnational governments, further limits on earmarking, and five constitutionally mandated revenue-sharing schemes (Samuels and Abrucio, 1997; Shah, 1991b).

Chile

In contrast to Argentina and Brazil, the election of subnational officials in Chile has not translated into significant pressures from below for fiscal decentralization. The leaders of local government, including mayors and municipal councilors, were first elected under the country's thirty-year Parliamentary Republic between 1891 and 1924. After being suspended during a period of political turbulence between 1924 and 1935, local elections were held once again between 1935 and 1973. After the military coup in 1973, the Pinochet government appointed all subnational officials, until a constitutional reform in 1992 reinstated elections for local office. Thus, Chile has nearly eighty years of experience with municipal elections. Despite this long history, however, Chile remains one of the most fiscally centralized countries in Latin America (Garman, Haggard, and Willis, 1996; Yáñez and Letelier, 1995). Furthermore, the limited fiscal decentralization that did occur in the context of the transition to democracy in the 1990s was initiated by political elites at the center rather than resulting from demands by local officials (see Bland, this volume). Why have local elections failed to generate greater pressures for fiscal decentralization in Chile? Have local officials failed to demand greater authority, or have they done so unsuccessfully?

Evidence from the Parliamentary Republic offers a powerful challenge to the argument that elections necessarily transform local officials into protagonists of decentralization. Before 1891, the national executive played the dominant role in Chilean political life, to the detriment of both the national legislature and local governments (Blakemore, 1964; A. Valenzuela, 1977: 190). Frustration with the statist agenda of Liberal president Balmaceda led Conservative Party legislators in the late 1880s to propose political decentralization as a means of checking the president. Though Liberal Party legislators feared that the Conservatives' core constituents, including local oligarchs, landowners, and the clergy, would dominate in local elections, they supported decentralizing legislation as a way of opposing attempts by Balmaceda to circumvent Liberal Party input into the choice of his successor as the party's presidential candidate. When the president refused to endorse Congress's attempt to legislate municipal autonomy, conflict between the branches ultimately led to a breakdown in constitutional rule. The ensuing civil war between Congress and the president was fought largely over the issue of municipal autonomy from the national executive branch, with the forces of Congress victorious (A. Valenzuela, 1977: 191).

One of the principal consequences of the civil war was the 1891 Municipal Law, which granted both political autonomy and considerable fiscal resources to local governments. Specifically, the law transferred to municipalities authority over the collection of property taxes, personal taxes, taxes on tobacco and alcoholic beverages, and taxes on industries and professions (A. Valenzuela, 1977: 197). In this first instance, then, political and fiscal decentralization came together as the result of conflict between national forces. Local officials were endowed with augmented fiscal powers not because they demanded them, but because this was a means by which the president's opponents in the national congress could check his power.

More important for the hypothesis under review here, once taxing authority was devolved in 1891, independently elected local officials declined to use these new fiscal powers. Instead, by not acting to collect the taxes that were now within their power, they chose to remain dependent on revenues they could extract from the center. Valenzuela evaluates a number of explanations for this response by local officials to fiscal decentralization. First, his research suggests that career paths alone cannot account for the disinterest in collecting taxes. Valenzuela finds that few of those who served in these local positions went on to run for and hold national office, which makes it difficult to attribute their tax preferences to their disinterest in remaining at the local level and their interest in pursuing national office. Second, political resistance by local elites to more aggressive taxation by municipal leaders represented a serious constraint on local taxation (A. Valenzuela, 1977).

A third explanation may be found in the nature of the political system. As Valenzuela concludes, "It is clear that the political system of Chile at the time made it unnecessary for the local communities of the country to become financially autonomous" (A. Valenzuela, 1977: 199). Of particular importance is the relationship between local officials and members of the national congress. Throughout the Parliamentary Republic, members of Congress transferred resources and brokered favors for local officials in exchange for their support in congressional elections (A. Valenzuela, 1977: 132–33). By controlling the local bases that members of Congress needed in order to win elections, local officials had a powerful resource at their disposal. Mayors and municipal councilors remained confident that this political resource would be sufficient in demanding the fiscal resources they needed from the central government.

This line of argument raises important comparative questions, however. The Argentine and Brazilian party systems were also infused with the type of clientelism that enabled local leaders to condition their support for national politicians on the fiscal goods delivered by the latter. Why did subnational officials in Argentina and Brazil remain unsatisfied with their ability to lobby the center for these resources and seek instead to secure independent access to fiscal revenues? There are a number of possible explanations for this variation. First, the Chilean nitrate boom in the late nineteenth century significantly increased the national government's proceeds from export taxes and may have encouraged local leaders to expect that buoyant revenues would facilitate their lobbying efforts for fiscal transfers. Whereas key commodity exports in Argentina and Brazil were privately owned and hard to tax, the dominance of minerals in Chile's export structure may have convinced subnational officials that collecting their own taxes or demanding automatic transfers was unnecessary. Second, much time elapsed between the period in which Chilean subnational officials proved themselves to be uninterested in fiscal powers (the late nineteenth and early twentieth centuries) and the transitions to democracy in Argentina and Brazil in the 1940s, when subnational officials began to press for fiscal powers. As suggested in the introductory chapter to this volume, sociostructural factors such as urbanization may have altered the preferences of subnational actors in the interim, increasing the perceived need for greater powers in a way that can be considered independent of party system incentives.

The Parliamentary Republic came to an end with the military coup of 1924 and the suspension of local elections. This marked the return to a period of presidential dominance over the national legislature. The 1925 constitution revoked most of the fiscal powers that had been devolved in 1891 but never used by local officials (Abalos, 1994: 6). When municipal elections were held again in 1935, revenue authority remained centralized at the national level. The next forty years are conspicuous for the absence of serious demands by local officials for expanded fiscal powers. As in the Parliamentary Republic, local officials were able to exchange their electoral support for members of Congress for the deliverance of fiscal transfers and resources from the center. For their part, members of Congress in the 1935–73 period had their own good reasons to oppose revenue decentralization. If local officials were to collect their own revenues or receive automatic shares from the center, they would not be as dependent on the brokerage services of legislators, and legislators in turn would have no way of encouraging mayors to deliver their political bases. A critical difference with Argentina and Brazil is that while local officials had considerable leverage over national legislators in Chile, they did not exert influence over candidate selection in legislative races.

Like the Argentine and Brazilian military regimes discussed above, Pinochet's government reversed the previous decentralization of political authority. Unlike in Argentina and Brazil, however, Pinochet did not have to reverse fiscal decentralization because this had not happened in Chile to any significant degree. Control over fiscal authority remained highly centralized throughout the Pinochet era, but his government did devolve significant expenditure responsibilities to the municipalities, particularly in the areas of education and health care (Burki, Perry, and

Dillinger, 2003: 13; Yáñez and Letelier, 1995). According to Marcel, the Pinochet government saw municipalities as agents of the central government in its attack on statism rather than as autonomous entities with the power to make decisions and allocate resources independent of the center (Marcel, 1994: 104).[11] Since municipal revenues were insufficient to pay for the services that were devolved, the central government financed them through ad hoc transfers, which gave ultimate control to the national executive (Garman, Haggard, and Willis, 1996).

The most recent and ongoing experience with subnational elections in Chile likewise offers little support for the argument that local elections are the dominating force leading to fiscal decentralization. When Chile returned to democracy at the national level in 1990, subnational elections were not held immediately. Instead, President Aylwin's *Concertación* government was forced to bargain with the rightist opposition in the Senate over the structure of subnational government. According to this agreement, elections for municipal office would be held as Aylwin had proposed, but a new regional level of government would be created along the lines proposed by the opposition (see Bland, this volume). The 1992 constitutional reform that approved this new system of subnational government also made changes to municipal revenue systems that were designed to augment municipal tax revenues, though in general fiscal authority remained highly centralized (Garman, Haggard, and Willis, 1996; Marcel, 1994: 93). Because of the simultaneous timing of this limited fiscal decentralization and political decentralization, the former cannot be attributed to the latter. Instead, decentralization in Chile has been characterized by a clear top-down logic (see Bland, this volume).

Because the executive branches of Chile's new regional governments are controlled by *intendentes* who are appointed by the president and regional councilors who are indirectly elected by municipal councils, it is not surprising that regional governments have not demanded greater independent fiscal powers. In the years since the establishment of municipal elections, mayors have begun to articulate demands for greater revenues in order to provide the governmental services that were devolved by Pinochet. In pressing these demands, mayors are better organized than ever before, as seen in the establishment in the 1990s of the *Asociación Chilena de Municipalidades* (Chilean Association of Municipalities) (Martelli, 1998). As in earlier periods, however, mayors still do not enjoy the political leverage that would enable them to translate their claims into actual increases in revenue authority.

Uruguay

As in Chile, the first instance of political decentralization in Uruguay resulted from power struggles at the national level. Whereas in Chile these struggles took the form of interbranch conflict between the president and the legislature that cut across partisan lines, in Uruguay the conflict was centered between the two traditional parties, the Colorados and the Blancos. Historically, the Colorados received most of their electoral support from the professional and commercial classes in Montevideo in the south, while the rural interests centered around the agro-export sector in the interior formed the political base of the Blancos. That the Blancos have consistently articulated a more aggressive case for decentralization than the Colorados may offer additional support for O'Neill's thesis (see O'Neill, this volume).

In the latter half of the nineteenth century, the Colorados came to dominate the increasingly consolidated central state apparatus, with the Blancos largely excluded from patronage and power (de Posadas, 1988). This exclusion led to an uprising by the Blancos in the 1897 revolution, which demanded electoral guarantees and the representation of opposition parties in government (*representación de minorías*). In the Pacto de la Cruz, which brought an end to the uprising, the Colorados agreed to reserve one-third of the seats of the lower chamber for the minority party and to increase the power of the Blanco Party over Uruguay's only subnational level of government, the departments (Faig, 1999: 13). Specifically, the Colorados agreed that the executive offices (*jefaturas políticas*) in six of the nineteen departments would be handed over to Blanco individuals selected by the national Blanco Party (de Posadas, 1988: 55, 85). The pact also put an end to the majoritarian system used to constitute the legislative branch of the departments (*Juntas Económico Administrativas*) by granting three seats in these bodies to the minority party (Tourreilles, 1999: 103; Lindahl, 1962).

The political decentralization achieved in the 1897 pact did not lead to any real fiscal decentralization. The departments continued to play an insignificant role in the provision of education, public health, police, and social assistance (de Posadas, 1988: 88; Fitzgibbon, 1954: 143). The Blancos strategized, however, that political control over the six departments would give them a sufficient base to defend themselves from the hegemonic pretensions of the Colorado Party (de Posadas, 1988: 56). In 1903 and 1904, the Blancos took up arms to defend the terms of the pact when the Colorados partially reneged on their right to name subnational officials and when the Colorados sent national soliders to one of the departments, which the Blancos took as a violation of the pact (Tourreilles, 1999: 56). The Pacto de la Cruz should be considered a potentially decentralizing reform even though it did not lead to direct elections for subnational offices and even though these positions were filled via the decisions of national Blanco Party leaders. Because the Blancos were locked out of power at the national level, the pact effectively increased the autonomy of subnational governments from the Colorado-dominated national government.

Political decentralization after 1897 was short-lived. The year 1903 marked the election of the legendary Colorado president José Batlle y Ordoñez, who dramatically expanded the powers of the central government and laid the foundations of the Uruguayan welfare state, Latin America's first (Collier and Collier, 1991; Vanger, 1963). Though Batlle had to agree to continue the policy of power sharing with the Blancos in order to get the nomination in 1903 (Lindahl, 1962: 21), by 1908 he had sufficient power to reverse the political decentralization granted in 1897. Law 1417 of 1908 reversed the 1897 power sharing agreement by replacing all *jefaturas políticas* with *intendentes* named by the president (Nickson, 1995: 252). The legislative bodies (*Juntas Económico Administrativas*) were in turn placed under the control of the *intendentes*. Though it opposed both political recentralization and the expansion of the state's role in the economy, the Blanco Party was powerless to resist these changes.

By 1916, however, the dynamic between the two parties changed in a way that ultimately led to political and fiscal decentralization. A pivotal event was the defeat of Batlle supporters in the 1916 elections for representatives to a constituent assembly that would consider the president's proposal to replace the country's unipersonal executive with a collegial executive body. Due to the winner-take-all elections Batlle proposed for this collegial body, most political actors attributed the president's proposal to his desire to retain Colorado control over the executive branch and his own control over the Colorado Party (Lindahl, 1962).[12] In an interparty agreement sealed in the constituent assembly, the Blancos agreed to Batlle's collegial executive in exchange for the political autonomy of the departments and fiscal decentralization (Martins, 1978: 147). The

1918 constitution thus allowed for the direct election of departmental legislators (*Asambleas Representativas*) and a collegial executive branch at the departmental level (*Consejos de Administración Departamentales*), which would be filled by proportional representation (Tourreilles, 1999: 99–104).

The 1918 constitution also granted significant fiscal powers to the departments (Fitzgibbon, 1954: 144; Lindahl, 1962: 37; Martins, 1978: 147).[13] Shifting taxing powers to the departments was a significant victory for the Blanco Party, whose land-owning constituents had vociferously but unsuccessfully resisted Batlle's attempts to increase the tax burden on *estancieros* in the interior (Rilla, 1985: 76, 93). The 1918 reforms in Uruguay, like the 1891 reforms in Chile, represent simultaneous political and fiscal decentralization from above and thus do not support the argument that fiscal authority follows subnational elections. Unlike the Chilean case, where local officials declined to use their augmented fiscal powers, subnational officials in Uruguay were apparently quick to use their new powers (Cagnoni, 1979: 177). According to Nickson, "the severe fiscal crisis of the state that erupted in 1929 was blamed on the financial profligacy of departmental governments" (1995: 252). When President Gabriel Terra ended democracy by closing Congress in 1934, he cited the economic crisis provoked by fiscal decentralization: "We can no longer continue with a regime that lets 19 different governmental authorities decree all manner of taxes" (Martins, 1978: 153). Such arguments were strengthened when the outbreak of the world economic crisis in the early 1930s placed further strains on national budget deficits.[14]

Political and fiscal decentralization were both reversed with the coup that took place in 1934. As a result of the new constitution that was written in this period, the departments were denied the right to collect taxes and issue debt (Jacob, 1983: 60). In order to impose taxes, *intendentes* had to get the approval of a national executive body (the *Tribunal de Cuentas*) and national legislators (Martins, 1978: 155). Imposed under nondemocratic auspices, the 1935 municipal law tightened control by the central government over departmental finances. The year 1935 also marked the recentralization of services such as hygiene, pasteurization, and a variety of activities associated with the meat industry (Cagnoni, 1979: 168). The 1966 reform of the constitution further diminished departmental autonomy in the fiscal sphere, largely through the introduction of planning that reduced departments to bodies implementing centrally devised plans (Cagnoni, 1979: 177).[15]

Though elections were held for departmental offices between 1938 and 1973, no significant fiscal decentralization was forthcoming (Martins, 1978: 158). Why did departmental officials not demand the sort of fiscal powers they enjoyed under the previous period of democratic rule? First, it should be remembered that departmental officials did not demand fiscal powers in the earlier period. Second, a deeper answer can be found in the nature of the Uruguayan party system. Though national parties are highly factionalized, factional lists within each party are organized around national as opposed to subnational candidates. Uruguayan senators, like the president, are elected in a single nationwide district, and factions group themselves into *sublemas* that support a single candidate for president or senator (Gillespie, 1991: 20–21). Departmental chief executives in Uruguay do not play the roles played by their counterparts in Argentina, much less Brazil. Reflecting this political reality, de Posadas has proposed making the departments more important in the election of deputies as a certain means of promoting decentralization (de Posadas, 1988: 219). In addition to electoral laws, the timing of elections might help account for this outcome. National and subnational elections are always held concurrently and ballots cannot be split, which leads to the nationalizing of departmental electoral contests and the downplaying of subnational interests (González Block, 1991: 31; Nickson, 1995: 253).

With the 1973 coup, the military government disbanded departmental assemblies, dismissed democratically elected *intendentes,* and revoked what limited taxing powers departments had enjoyed in the previous period (Cagnoni, 1979: 187). Given the absence of significant decentralizing measures in the previous democratic period, the Uruguayan experience with extended military rule from 1973 to 1984 resembles the Chilean rather than Argentine and Brazilian cases. Another parallel with the Chilean case is that the Uruguayan generals also considered regionalization, arguing that it would be more efficient to replace the nineteen traditional departments with eight regions (Cagnoni, 1979: 190). By the end of the military period, subnational governments in Uruguay collected only 6.9 percent of the total tax revenues, with the national level collecting the remaining 93.1 percent. Montevideo collected nearly half of the departments' share in tax revenue, with the remaining eighteen departments controlling only 3.7 percent of the total tax revenue in the country (Partido Nacional, 1989: 58).

Subsequent to the transition to democracy in 1984, which reverted to the electoral system described above, fiscal decentralization has been limited. In the current period, as before in Uruguay's history, the Blanco party has expressed more interest in decentralization than the Colorado Party. In 1985, opposition Blanco Party leader Wilson Ferreira Aldunate invoked the 1897 rebellion led by Aparicio Saravia in his call for fiscal decentralization. Ferreira criticized the current system according to which *intendentes* "have to go begging for resources, and obtain them or not based on the whims of the Economic Ministry" (Partido Nacional, 1989: 94). Unlike earlier periods, the emergence of the nontraditional, center-left Frente Amplio Party has added an additional voice for decentralization, with the Frente controlling the important departmental government of Montevideo since 1989 (Quintana, 1992). The construction of Mercosur has undercut the claims of decentralization's many critics, who traditionally have defended centralism as necessary given the country's status as a buffer state between much larger Argentina and Brazil. Despite these developments, there are striking continuities from earlier periods in the distribution of fiscal authority. Though some services have been devolved in the contemporary period, fiscal authority has remained highly centralized, with the central government reserving for itself the right to introduce all new taxes (Nickson, 1995: 255). The Frente Amplio government led by Tabaré Vázquez in the department of Montevideo endorsed administrative deconcentration within that department, but has not been able to bring about the greater decentralization of fiscal authority from above (Quintana, 1992: 17).

CONCLUSION

According to a recent survey of the shift toward more decentralized patterns of government in the developing world, there were few genuine cases of decentralization before the mid-1980s (Manor, 1999: 35–36). Furthermore, earlier experience with decentralization has not been very useful as a predictor of decentralization in the contemporary period; most countries are now experiencing decentralization for the first time ever (Manor, 1999: 34). Nevertheless, decisions to decentralize and recentralize fiscal authority that predate the contemporary period can be mined for insights into the causes and consequences of decentralization.

As in the contemporary period, the balance of power between national and subnational officials is a critical factor in understanding past experiences with decentralization. Of particular importance are the types and amounts of leverage that actors at one level of government enjoy relative to actors at the other level. In Argentina and Brazil, governors exert influence over the careers of the national legislators who represent their districts and who must endorse decentralizing policies for them to become law. Through this means, governors can also exert influence over presidents who routinely feel the need to negotiate with governors to facilitate their policy agendas in Congress. Thus, as in all countries, national politicians in Argentina and Brazil have controlled the decision to decentralize, but governors have exerted sufficient authority relative to these national actors to make decentralization a reality. Brazilian governors enjoy much more power than their Argentine counterparts, and this disparity is reflected in the fact that national politicians in the 1990s had much greater success in curbing some of decentralization's excesses in Argentina than in Brazil (Dillinger and Webb, 1999).

Because national political systems deny subnational chief executives equivalent powers over national politicians in Chile and Uruguay, an important impetus for decentralization is absent in these countries. In Chile, as Valenzuela's work shows, the behavior of local officials mattered enormously to national legislators because the former controlled local political bases that legislators needed to succeed in their careers. Unlike governors in Argentina and Brazil, however, elected subnational officials in Chile and Uruguay did not serve as gatekeepers who control candidate selection and appointment procedures for the positions to which legislators aspire. Chile's two most significant episodes of fiscal decentralization—after the 1891 civil war and one hundred years later during the most recent democratic transition—were both initiated from Santiago as a solution to national problems. Likewise, decentralization in Uruguay was adopted in various forms in 1897 and 1918 as the result of agreements between national actors from which subnational officials were absent. As this chapter has shown, decentralization in Argentina and Brazil can only be understood as a response to national conflicts in the sense that subnational officials successfully inserted their demands for greater authority into the national policy agenda.

The findings from Argentina, Brazil, and Chile support the argument made by Manor that regional officials (e.g., governors) are more able to secure decentralization than are local officials due to their greater importance in national politics. According to Manor, when decentralization occurs to the intermediate level of government rather than the local level, regional elites have been better able to resist subsequent attempts by national-level politicians to reclaim powers (Manor, 1999: 82). Uruguay is a confounding case for this argument, however, because the chief executives in the departments, Uruguay's only subnational level of government, resemble regional officials, and yet they have not successfully pressed decentralizing claims. The Uruguayan case suggests that the structural position of regional officials is perhaps less important than how they are inserted into the political system and whether they can influence the careers of national decision-makers.

By uncovering the significance of the political relationships that connect subnational politicians to their national counterparts, the historical experiences evaluated here illuminate the conditions under which decentralizing pressures from below are successful. Apart from the specific question of whether pressure from subnational politicians leads to decentralization, the four cases offer much evidence for the conclusion that decentralization tends to follow democratization, while recentralization is a common occurrence under authoritarian government. Though decentralization in Chile and Uruguay has resulted from top-down rather than bottom-up pressures and lagged far behind Argentina and Brazil, such moves toward decentralization as have occurred in the former are unique to periods of democratic rule. A final insight offered by these cases is that decentralization has proved historically to be a quite volatile policy area, sounding a note of caution for those who consider the latest wave of decentralization to be its last.

Notes

For their helpful comments on this chapter, I thank Lisa Baldez, John Carey, Tulia Faletti, Vanya Krieckhaus, Al Montero, Tim Power, David Samuels, Mathew Shugart, Kathryn Sikkink, Eliza Willis, and the participants of the conference on causes and consequences of decentralization in Latin America held at the University of Minnesota, February 2000. Rebecca Weitz provided valuable research assistance. This research was made possible by grants from the Fulbright Foundation, the Woodrow Wilson International Center for Scholars, and the Center for International Studies at Princeton University.

1. In Bolivia, a municipal code was enacted in 1942 but no direct elections for local government were held until after 1987 (Nickson, 1995: 108). In Colom-

bia, elections for mayor in 1988 were the first in one hundred years. In Ecuador, a municipal code was passed in 1966 but not implemented until the 1980s (Nickson, 1995: 169). Panama and Paraguay held local elections for the first time in 1994 and 1991 respectively. In Peru, though direct elections for municipal office were supposed to begin in 1892, well before the current democratic period, local elections took place only in 1963 and 1968 (Nickson, 1995: 238). In Venezuela, governors and municipal leaders were appointed until 1989 (Willis, Garman, and Haggard, 1999: 36; Penfold-Becerra, this volume).

2. Given the centralist tradition in Latin America, a more dramatic departure from the policy status quo than decentralization would be hard to find.

3. Contemporary Chile is a case in point where the two parties that most consistently support decentralization, *Renovación Nacional* and the *Partido por la Democracia*, come from the rightist and the leftist blocs, respectively. Opposition to decentralization by the center-left *Demócrata Cristiano* and far-right *Unión Demócrata Independiente* similarly cuts across ideological lines.

4. For contrasting views in the debate over whether revenue transfers should be taken as a form of decentralization, see Manor (1999: 13) and Rondinelli, Nellis, and Cheema (1984: 44).

5. Subprovincial governments were not included in the arrangement, though in recent times some provinces have adopted provincial coparticipation systems with municipalities.

6. Though it helped the president in a variety of ways, in the absence of a revenue-sharing law, provincial governments under Peronist control were able to extract large transfers from the federal treasury by running up debts they could not pay. Thus the absence of a revenue-sharing law did not unambiguously promote the president's interests. See Sanguinetti (1994).

7. The 1934 constitution also stipulated that 20 percent of any new taxes collected by national and state governments would be shared with municipalities (Sherwood, 1967: 122).

8. Thus, the design of fiscal institutions in the 1946 constitution reflects the same bargain that characterizes the 1988 constitution: in both, the wealthier states of the south are given important revenue powers in exchange for revenue transfers that benefit the north disproportionately.

9. The tax on rural property was returned to the federal government in 1964 as part of the agrarian reform. This should not be considered a recentralizing reform, however, but one that was designed to facilitate agrarian reform. Proceeds from the tax were automatically shared with municipalities (Cann, 1970).

10. See Mahar (1971) for the opposite argument that revenue sharing increased fivefold between 1966 and 1969.

11. See Bland (this volume) for a more complete discussion of Pinochet's "regionalization" strategy.

12. According to Batlle's proposal, the Blanco Party would have to win several consecutive elections in order to gain a majority in the collegial body (de Posadas, 1988: 95).

13. It also allowed for the creation of a parastatal sector (*entes autónomos*), which is a form of decentralization (de Posadas, 1988: 95; Rondinelli, Nellis, and Cheema, 1984).

14. Interestingly, the Great Depression triggered centralizing moves in three of the four countries discussed here: Argentina, Brazil (at the state but not the municipal level), and Uruguay.

15. Planning in Uruguay had a strong sectoral as opposed to territorial component.

CHAPTER 6

Electoral Dynamics and Decentralization in Venezuela

MICHAEL PENFOLD-BECERRA

The scope and extent of decentralization in Latin America has varied widely. As the introduction to this volume argues, institutional and electoralist approaches have most successfully explained this diversity. However, these approaches struggle to explain change in the patterns of decentralization within countries over time. By stressing how electoral and party systems distribute power brokers in national and subnational office, electoralist approaches explain decentralization cross-nationally as a product of a given institutional structure.[1] Thus, for example, a party system that tends to reinforce the power of national-level power brokers ought to limit decentralization or even avoid it altogether. Following this logic, one might suppose that Venezuela should not have decentralized at all during the 1990s given the dominance of two highly centralized political parties: *Acción Democrática* (Democratic Action, or AD) and the *Comité de Organización Política Electoral Independiente* (Organized Political Committee for Independent Elections, or COPEI).[2] Nevertheless, these parties agreed to implement both political and policy decentralization beginning in the late 1980s.

A "comparative statics" approach that might work well for explaining cross-national variation at a given point in time cannot explain this outcome. Instead, we must look at the *evolution* of power relations within Venezuela's hegemonic parties. This chapter explains decentralization by focusing on two factors that ultimately *changed* the interests of party brokers in Venezuela. The first factor was a generalized legitimacy crisis within the hegemonic parties. This problem had deep roots. From 1958 to 1988, AD and COPEI national elites maintained strict controls over legislators and gubernatorial appointments through a system of self-serving patronage known as *cogollismo*. During the 1980s, *cogollismo* became the target of increasing public derision because of pervasive corruption and because neither party appeared capable of resolving the country's increasing economic problems or of improving public services. Despite Venezuela's tremendous oil resources, in the 1980s the government experienced a dramatic fiscal crisis. In addition, threats of military intervention and a pervasive sense of social discontent weakened the centralized two-party system throughout the 1980s and into the 1990s.

The widespread political crisis initially motivated national party leaders to propose and enact political decentralization in 1989 without any antecedent change in the party system structure. Yet even this attempt at moderate reforms was insufficient to prevent antisystemic political action (Navarro, 1995). Mass riots protesting transport and gasoline price hikes in February 1989 subsequently pushed party elites to attempt to reinvigorate ties to disillusioned constituents by decentralizing authority and resources and allowing direct elections of governors and mayors for the first time. In short, the general crisis tended to weaken the authority, legitimacy, and power of the national political elites.

Politics abhors a vacuum, and the general weakening of the traditionally strong parties in Venezuela tended to concomitantly increase the power of new regional and local political actors. Thus, the second factor that changed the interests of party brokers is the flip side of the first: at a time when the national parties were rapidly losing popularity and legitimacy, the initial move toward decentralization altered the career incentives of politicians within the dominant parties because subnational offices became relatively more attractive. The new governors rapidly developed an interest in increasing the fiscal and policy resources of their office, and once the process of decentralization began, they organized to demand further transfers of revenues and responsibilities from the central government. Acting as political entrepreneurs, the governors lobbied the central government through the nonpartisan Association of Venezuelan Governors (AGV). Governors aimed to speed up and broaden the decentralization process because they understood that they could benefit from providing the public services that voters demanded and that the national parties either would not or could not provide. These subnational leaders, acting together and in a suprapartisan fashion, thus gained increasing legitimacy at the same time that national political leaders were rapidly losing legitimacy. Winning subnational political office quickly became much more desirable for a career-minded politician. In short, macro political dynamics surrounding the breakdown of Venezuela's traditional party system encouraged a new micro logic that was reshaping power relations within Venezuela's parties and was encouraging additional decentralization.

However, although the governors succeeded in deepening decentralization to a degree that a focus on purely party-system variables would not have predicted, their ability to transform Venezuela into a far more decentralized system was ultimately hampered by the precipitous decomposition of the very same party system that they were helping to transform. Unable to exert continuous leverage on national party leaders in a highly uncertain political context, the pattern of decentralization in Venezuela remained uneven and limited when compared to other countries in Latin America. In addition, the rise of Hugo Chávez to the presidency in 1998 and the approval of his constitution in late 1999, which grants the president extraordinary decree authority and a prolonged mandate, cleared the way for recentralization.

In summary, the case of Venezuela is one of (1) initial decentralization without preceding electoral-institutional change; (2) an uneven pattern of decentralization shaped by the dynamic expectations of political entrepreneurs and emerging intergovernmental conflicts between governors and national party elites; and (3) sudden recentralization in response to a generalized crisis of governability. Venezuela thus illustrates the fact that a "comparative statics" approach that maps institutions onto outcomes may fall short of providing a full explanation; these institutions are often not the sources of change but are subject to change themselves, and the change in the institutional structure may be what is driving the decentralization or recentralization process. Decentralization in Venezuela does support the hypotheses that the linkages between national and subnational politicians affect the relative leverage of both, and that *changes* in this relative balance of power subsequently affect the scope and form of decentralization. However, the Venezuelan case also shows that when these linkages—which comprise the sinews of the party system—rapidly decompose, a process of decentralization pushed by subnational political pressures (i.e., bottom-up decentralization) can be short-circuited. In the next section, I discuss the origins of the decision to politically decentralize in 1989 and the implications this decision had for fiscal and policy decentralization during the 1990s. In the subsequent section I examine how political decentralization reshaped career patterns and, combined with escalating systemic crises in the party system and the economy, created opportunities for altering the electoral order and the pattern of fiscal and policy decentralization through coordination among the governors. I then discuss how the collapse of the existing system ultimately stalled the decentralization process.

INITIATING POLITICAL DECENTRALIZATION IN VENEZUELA

The initial phase of decentralization in Venezuela follows the argument of Willis, Garman, and Haggard (1999), which suggests that decentralization, if it happened at all in a system like Venezuela's, would follow a top-down logic and remain a highly centralized process. Beginning in the early 1980s several social actors, minority parties, intellectuals, economic groups, and civic associations initiated demands for political decentralization as a means to promote greater government accountability. These demands were a natural reaction against a regime that began as a pacted transition to democracy in 1958 but became increasingly controlled by AD and COPEI elites. Democratic procedures in Venezuela were virtually reduced to the election of the president. AD's and COPEI's national party leaders determined the nomination of candidates to both houses of Congress as well as to the state legislature and municipal councils.[3] The parties appointed judges based on their party loyalty, and the president appointed governors and the mayor of Caracas.[4] Governorships were commonly assigned to members of the political party in power and became instruments of political patronage. Bureaucratic overstaffing and the distribution of public contracts functioned as effective mechanisms for feeding political machines capable of winning national elections.

Under the patronage regime of *cogollismo*, national party leaders exercised strong discipline over their members and appointees.

The *cogollo* system, lubricated by oil wealth, functioned well until the 1980s, when low growth, declining wages, and increasing popular demands for greater political accountability led to a series of reform efforts (Navarro, 1995). In December 1984, AD president Jaime Lusinchi (1983–89) first acknowledged the need for reform. Urged on by a group of political, intellectual, and business elites led by the minister of the presidency, Simón Alberto Consalvi, Lusinchi issued a presidential decree creating the Presidential Commission for Reform of the State (*Comisión Presidencial para la Reforma del Estado*, or COPRE). He appointed as members of this commission nonpartisan intellectuals, who were assisted by a staff of experts on state reform, as well as individuals linked to the most important political parties. After a series of meetings, COPRE recommended political and administrative reforms in six areas: (1) internal reform of the political parties to promote their democratization; (2) reform of the electoral system to encourage a more personal vote; (3) the direct election of governors and mayors to improve political accountability; (4) reforms to make the judicial system autonomous from politics; (5) civil service reform; and (6) the transfer of central government administrative responsibilities to regional and local governments.[5] Although public opinion may have favored some form of political change, the elitist composition of COPRE meant that this initial proposal for decentralization was not the product of organized social mobilization but of the calculations of the Venezuelan political, academic, and business elite (Grindle, 2000: 54–57).

AD held an absolute majority in both houses of Congress at the time, and COPRE's reform proposals met with immediate resistance from AD's National Executive Committee (CEN). AD's national party leaders considered COPRE's recommendations too radical to be implemented. AD's president, Gonzalo Barrios, publicly rejected these reforms, especially the direct election of governors, stating that "the country is not historically prepared for these reforms."[6] AD's General Secretary Manuel Peñalver, suggesting that the reforms were too "modern" for Venezuela, commented that "we are not the Swiss."[7] Even Lusinchi, who had reluctantly accepted Consalvi's ideas for the commission, opposed the direct election of governors as a threat to the position of the dominant parties (Grindle, 2000: 59). Not surprisingly, the proposed reforms were defeated in Congress without even being discussed. National legislators decided to postpone discussions until the country could reach a "consensus" about the viability of the reforms.

The presidential campaign of 1988 created an opportunity to reconsider COPRE's proposals. For the leftist opposition parties, Lusinchi's reticence toward COPRE presented an opportunity to attack both AD and COPEI's apparent indifference to a deepening economic crisis and a legitimacy crisis in the political system. Intent on muting the left's arguments, AD's nominee Carlos Andrés Pérez and COPEI's nominee Eduardo Fernández both distanced themselves from Lusinchi's position and called for political reforms. Fernández proposed that COPRE's propositions be passed in Congress, essentially as an agreement between AD and COPEI. Pérez rejected this proposal and instead suggested that these reforms should only be passed through a political pact that would include AD and COPEI, as well as other political parties. Pérez knew that the CEN would only cooperate if he could muster truly broad public support for a political pact. This was not a difficult task given escalating public antipathy toward the political system and concerns that the weakness of political leadership was imperiling the economy. More important for Pérez, simply proposing COPRE's reforms for democratizing the parties, reforming the electoral system, and instituting direct elections for governor and mayor would greatly enhance his own support among local elites and marginalize the traditional AD *cogollos* who favored Lusinchi's more modest reform proposal. Thus, the CEN was forced by Pérez's campaign to abandon its opposition to political reform.

COPRE mediated between all the political parties—AD, COPEI, *Movimiento al Socialismo* (MAS), *Unión Republicana Democrática* (URD), and *Movimiento Electoral del Pueblo* (MEP)—to reach agreement regarding the content of the reform proposals to be included in the pact. Once the broad support for the pact was assured, AD's CEN supported the reforms in Congress. Thus, in June 1988 the national legislature approved three reforms: (1) the direct election of mayors; (2) the reform of the electoral system from a system of proportional representation (PR) with closed lists to a mixed-member system (although implementation of this proposal would be delayed);[8] and (3) the approval of a law to initiate administrative and fiscal decentralization. However, AD's control of the legislature still permitted its centralized leadership to restrict the scope of the reforms, in an attempt to minimize the expected loss of central political control. The direct election of governors was postponed, the process of administrative and fiscal decentralization was limited to municipal governments, and the implementation of the new electoral system was postponed until the 1993–94 presidential and congressional elections.

The massive rioting known as the *Caracazo* that erupted one month after Pérez's inauguration was the event that finally prompted AD to support broader reforms such as the direct election of governors and the transfer of policy responsibilities and fiscal resources to the subnational level. The spontaneous protests of the *Caracazo*, which erupted after an increase in public transportation fares triggered by an increase in the price of gasoline, lasted more than two days, and the violence spread to eight major cities.[9] After the first day of protest, poor inhabitants of the *barrios* started to loot commercial establishments in almost all areas of Caracas. The magnitude of the riots and the limited capacity of police to deal with these disturbances forced the government to call out the army, and in the end more than three hundred people died and more than one thousand were injured.

This social upheaval revealed the profound depth of Venezuela's political crises to all political parties. The political class could no longer ignore the connection between increasing abstention in national elections and the widespread and convulsive animus exhibited during the *Caracazo* (Grindle, 2000: 64–65). Although many politicians suggested that the riots were a direct response to the neoliberal reforms Pérez announced shortly following his inauguration, it was apparent that the majority of the population had become disconnected from the political system. These events pushed the traditional parties to abandon their resistance to COPRE's broader reform proposals. Thus, on April 13, 1989, Congress approved a revised law opening the way for direct elections of governors and mayors in December of that year. Other laws provided that the new governors and mayors would also receive expanded fiscal resources and policy authority.

Although these proposals moved Venezuela away from its highly centralized political system, national party elites retained an extraordinary amount of control over the process of decentralization, and the degree of decentralization was quite limited. That is, the process initially had a strong top-down element. Under the laws regulating fiscal and administrative decentralization, states gained some autonomy to collect taxes, but they still depended on transfers from the central government for nearly all of their income. (Municipal fiscal autonomy was also highly limited.) Table 6.1 reveals the high degree of subnational dependence on national-government transfers even after the limited fiscal decentralization. Fiscal transfers were allotted under a system known as the *Situado Constitucional*, implemented with the 1961 constitution, which allotted a portion of central-government revenue to transfers to state governments (states subsequently had to transfer a portion of this revenue to municipalities). The constitution restricted the capacity of the states to raise their own revenue by limiting their control of taxes to levies on transportation and stamps. As Table 6.1 demonstrates, fiscal transfers as a portion of states' revenue fell from 1989 to 1993 by only 3.2 percent and still dominated subnational government financing.

The top-down nature of the initial decision to decentralize is also reflected in the Organic Law of Decentralization (*Ley Orgánica de Descentralización*), which Congress passed in 1990 and which immediately devolved certain policy domains to the states (e.g., regulation of ports, airports, and mines). This law also established the procedure for devolv-

Table 6.1.   *Situado Constitucional* and Venezuelan States' Revenues, 1989–93

	1989	*1990*	*1991*	*1992*	*1993*
Situado Constitutional, Funds	25,554,718 97.05%	66,562,013 98.47%	106,216,501 95.20%	133,997,488 94.84%	161,561,942 93.85%
Own Revenues	233,959 0.89%	290,173 0.43%	4,616,752 4.14%	4,211,057 2.98%	7,129,607 4.14%
Other	542,181 2.06%	741,546 1.10%	740,576 0.66%	3,072,333 2.18%	3,463,156 2.01%
Total	26,330,858 100%	67,593,732 100%	111,573,829 100%	141,280,878 100%	172,154,705 100%

Source: Oficina Central de Presupuesto.
Note: Revenues in thousands of Bolivares.

ing other policy responsibilities in areas such as health and education. Yet the new rules also allowed the national government to control the decentralization process. The new law did not oblige the national government to provide revenues or devolve policy responsibilities in any broad area of public services; states would need to individually and formally petition the Senate for the transfer of public services, and the petition could only be approved after the state had reached an agreement with the relevant national ministry on the specific terms governing the distribution of personnel, budgetary resources, and equipment.

Moreover, petitions to transfer services could only be assessed by the Senate on a case-by-case basis, thereby slowing the process.[10] Finally, financing of newly devolved services remained a prerogative of the designers of the national budget, i.e., national legislators loyal to the traditional parties. After a state petition, the national legislature retained the authority to decide whether or not to include the requested amount in the national budget. Outcomes, then, were highly contingent on the governor's ability to negotiate and his political affiliation.

In summary, the new law essentially gave the Senate the prerogative to determine the manner in which the decentralization of services such as health care or education would proceed. Thus, the initial pattern of decentralization conforms to the predictions of "static" electoralist arguments such as those of Willis, Garman, and Haggard (1999). However, the process of decentralization would change in Venezuela after these initial reforms were passed. Decentralization, the precipitous decline of the national parties, and the crisis of the presidency would greatly alter political "linkages" in ways that would enhance the position of the governors. Their capacity to coordinate their interests would shift bargaining leverage away from national organs such as the legislature and ministries of the executive branch.

THE SECOND PHASE OF DECENTRALIZATION

The transfer of revenues and responsibilities after the first direct gubernatorial elections in 1989 was not immediate. Between 1990 and 1992 governors did not succeed in their efforts to push the Senate and the national party leaders who controlled Congress to accept the regional administration of public services. National party leaders remained very reluctant to initiate a process of decentralization that would undermine their patronage networks, which depended in part on the centralized (mis)allocation of resources in areas such as health care and education. Yet several sudden changes in Venezuelan politics altered the rules of the game and created opportunities for further decentralization. First, the crisis of the presidency under Carlos Andrés Pérez exacerbated the political crisis of the party system to new heights during the early 1990s. The crisis deepened the fragmentation of the party system, accelerated the decline of popular support for AD and COPEI in particular, and expanded personal (as opposed to party) voting.

Second, the political crisis itself encouraged renewed efforts to decentralize. The crisis at the national level and decomposition of the dominant party system motivated subnational political entrepreneurs to challenge the *cogollo* system within AD and COPEI. The increased value of holding subnational office, especially relative to the uncertain future facing national party elites and legislators, along with the possibility that subnational politicians could cultivate personal votes for subnational executive positions independently of national party *cogollo* structures or dictates of the national executive committee, altered politicians' career strategies. Third, the creation of the AGV dramatically increased the governors' capacity to coordinate their interests. Given the crisis of national institutions and the enhanced political position of the governors, the AGV was able to mobilize a bottom-up deepening of decentralization. However, the ability of the AGV to sustain these bottom-up pressures was short-circuited by the total collapse of the partisan system and the rise of Hugo Chávez to the presidency in 1998. I examine each of these points below.

The Deepening Political Crisis

Having campaigned on COPRE's proposals for reform but facing a reluctant Congress, Carlos Andrés Pérez struggled to address the political crisis first punctuated by the *Caracazo*. During the first two years of the new administration, COPRE provided direct technical support to the newly elected governors as a way of getting past legislative intransigence. COPRE opened branch offices in each state with the explicit purpose of assisting governors in the formation of their administrations and in formulating their petitions to national ministries and the Senate. Pérez had faith that this technical assistance would speed the process of decentralization. Interestingly, the executive branch actually played a crucial role in encouraging the governors to coordinate their efforts. In 1990 the president convinced governors from four different political parties (AD, COPEI, MAS, and La Causa R) to meet informally every six months to coordinate their efforts to pressure Congress to approve legislation decentralizing health and education services.[11]

Congressional leaders in AD and COPEI especially blocked these efforts. For example, in 1991 the Senate postponed consideration of petitions requesting decentralization of the health care system in the states of Aragua, Anzoategui, Bolívar, Carabobo, and Falcón. The governors of these states, most of whom were elected on the party label of AD or COPEI, blamed the *cogollista* interests of the traditional parties for these delays. Aldo Cermeño, the governor of Falcón, an important state in the northwest, argued publicly that "there is no reason why, more than a year after the process of decentralization has been initiated, that the transfer of services such as health care and education should still be hindered by old patronage networks at the national level."[12] Between 1989 and 1992 not a single transfer of administrative responsibilities was approved.

In 1992, however, the fate of decentralization changed dramatically. In February, a failed coup d'etat led by midranking and junior officers took most politicians by surprise. The rebels justified their behavior by claiming that the army was being "transformed into a praetorian guard to protect a government that serves the interests of a small group of individuals" (Cabellero, 1996: 7). Their disapproval of the market-oriented policies being implemented by the Pérez administration and their discontent with the corrupt practices that characterized Venezuela's political and economic elites motivated this group of officers to plot a coup. In November, another failed coup, led this time by high-ranking naval and air force officers, convinced most Venezuelans that Pérez and the traditional parties simply could not be rescued (Romero, 1997). The percentage of the electorate identifying itself with AD and COPEI fell precipitously in the months following the second coup (Grindle, 2000: 74). Feeling the pressure, the parties reacted by blaming Pérez. The CEN sought its revenge on a president who had appointed technocrats instead of co-partisans to his cabinet, who was unwilling to distribute patronage according to the old rules, and who was apparently willing to promote political reforms against the will of the party. AD thus joined opposition voices and called for Pérez's impeachment. In May 1993, the president was forced to resign under charges of malfeasance. An interim government then prepared for presidential elections that December.

In June 1993, Ramón J. Velásquez, a well-known Venezuelan historian and senator who presided over COPRE from 1984 to 1986, was elected president of Venezuela by the national legislature following the impeachment proceeding against Carlos Andrés Pérez.[13] Although he was only meant to be an interim president until the elections scheduled for December 1993, Velásquez's short tenure proved important for the process of decentralization. His very first administrative decision was to create a Ministry of State for Decentralization as well as an Intergovernmental Decentralization Fund (FIDES). Both greatly expanded the authorities and resources available to the governors. FIDES provided funds to the state governments for investment projects not funded by the *Situado Constitucional*. In addition, the *Situado* was expanded from 15 percent of national government revenues to 20 percent by 1994. Armed with new authorities and resources and facing a decaying traditional party system and a power vacuum in the presidency, the governors reconfigured their political interests and mobilized on behalf of deepening the decentralization process.

Partisan Decomposition and Changing Career Paths

Prior to Velásquez's appointment, the unprecedented direct elections for governors and mayors in 1989 began a process of reconfiguring political careers in Venezuela. First, the 1989 elections created new degrees of subnational *political* autonomy that made gaining gubernatorial and mayoral seats valuable in the career trajectory of politicians (Kornblith and Levine, 1995: 63–67). This also meant that political aspirants had to pay attention to state and local issues, which led to a remarkable shift in political campaigning that focused more attention on issues involving subnational public services (Grindle, 2000: 87). Second, the extended crisis of 1989–93 that resulted in declining voter identification with the traditional parties caused both AD and COPEI to decentralize their own party structures to some degree, favoring popular local leaders and demoting unpopular party bureaucrats (Kornblith, 1996). Such changes in strategy kept AD and COPEI dominant at the subnational level. The two major parties captured 17 of 20 governorships in 1989, 16 of 22 in 1993, and 15 of 22 in 1995. They also retained political control over 87 percent of the municipalities throughout the 1990s (Crisp and Levine, 1998: 35–37). However, this success was chimerical, since the new generation of subnational politicians challenged the *cogollo* structure of the party hierarchy (Coppedge, 1994: 52). Thus, the resistance of the national leaders of AD and COPEI to decentralizing during the 1989–92 period deepened intergovernmental cleavages *within* the traditional parties less than it deepened differences *between* them (Kornblith and Levine, 1995: 67; Ellner, 1996: 92).

The subnational career path was also strengthened directly by the crisis of the Pérez presidency. National polls in the wake of the two failed coup attempts in 1992 indicated that Venezuelans believed that subnational government functioned best and that future presidents would need to first demonstrate their worth in state government (Grindle, 2000: 74–75). Three of the four major candidates for the presidency in 1993 hailed from gubernatorial or mayoral seats as opposed to emerging from the national hierarchy. Sensing the importance of this precedent, an increasing number of politicians in Congress ran for governor or mayor in 1993 and 1995. In a short period of time, politicians in Venezuela realized that having a viable political career in national politics required proving oneself in subnational office first.

It was the rapid decline in the dominance of AD and COPEI and the *cogollo* system, coupled with an increasing fragmentation in the party system as a whole, that reduced the relative attractiveness of pursuing a political career in Congress. In 1993, the 1988 pact allowing for plurality ballots in the Chamber of Deputies was finally implemented. Evidence that this reform itself eroded party loyalty and enhanced personal voting is mixed, but its implementation confirmed the growing influence of individuals and small parties. First, the effective number of parties more than doubled from 2.24 to 4.8, and opposition parties such as La Causa R, MAS, and *Convergencia Nacional* (CN) made headway in national and subnational elections. Second, AD and COPEI's share of the vote eroded rapidly, falling for the presidency from 92.9 percent in 1988 to 46.3 percent in 1993 and for legislative office from 78.4 percent in 1988 to 46 percent in 1993 (Crisp and Levine, 1998: 35).

The opposition parties, however, could not step in and secure for themselves the dominant position AD and COPEI once held. Endemic discontent led to system-wide party dealignment (Molina and Pérez,

1998). The result was fragmented party rule in Congress. In the 1993 congressional elections, AD won only 23.34 percent of the seats, COPEI gained 22.82 percent, La Causa R, 20.68 percent, MAS, 10.81 percent, CN, 13.84 percent, and the rest of the parties, 8.12 percent. The chief implication of partisan dealignment for the presidency was that potentially unstable alliances were necessary to implement reform. In December 1993, a coalition of MAS, CN, and other smaller parties elected former president and COPEI founder Rafael Caldera to the presidency. COPEI and AD had lost the presidency for the first time under the post-1958 democracy, yet Caldera's attempts to restore the old pacts among the major parties failed (Romero, 1997). Tables 6.2, 6.3, and 6.4 illustrate these transformations.

The fragmentation of the party system between 1993 and 1998, along with the changes in the electoral system, weakened national party leaders and gutted the old, centralized *cogollo* system. Volatility among the electorate's partisan loyalties increased markedly during this period. Surveys in 1983 showed 35.3 percent of respondents favored AD, COPEI, or MAS, but by 1993 that figure had fallen to 27.8 percent and in 1998 to 14 percent (J. Molina, 2000: 6–7). This trend and the new mixed-member electoral system in 1993 created incentives for politicians

Table 6.2.   Decline of the Traditional Parties in Venezuela, 1984–99

	Seats in the Senate		Seats in the Chamber of Deputies	
Lusinchi (AD)	AD	64%	AD	56%
1984–89	COPEI	32%	COPEI	30%
Perez (AD)[a]	AD	48%	AD	48%
1989–93	COPEI	43%	COPEI	33%
Caldera	AD	32%	AD	27%
(Conv/MAS)	COPEI	28%	COPEI	26%
1994–99				

[a] Perez was impeached before the end of his presidential term.

Table 6.3. Percentage of Seats Controlled by AD-COPEI in the Legislature, 1973–93

Election	Percentage
1973	74.68
1978	79.48
1983	78.58
1988	74.30
1993	45.96

Source: Consejo Nacional Electoral.

Table 6.4. Results of the 1993 Elections for Congress in Venezuela

Political Party	Percentage of Seats
AD	23.34
COPEI	22.62
La Causa R	20.68
MAS	10.81
CN	13.84
Others	8.12

Source: Consejo Supremo Electoral.

to cultivate personal votes, especially in local constituencies. As a result, and in significant contrast to the way things had worked for decades, subnational politicans' loyalty to party elites dwindled. As Merilee Grindle puts it, "[T]he relationship [of governors and mayors] with the party leadership in Caracas became more one of bargaining and negotiation than one of submission" (1996: 83). Additionally, some of the new political parties that challenged AD and COPEI, particularly La Causa R and to a lesser extent MAS, focused on gaining subnational positions as a means of increasing their electability nationally (López-Maya, 1997); compare with O'Neill's analysis of Bolivia in this volume. These parties, therefore, embraced the decentralization of public services and the expansion of intergovernmental fiscal transfers as a way to gain power. In short, the changes in both the established as well as emerging parties enhanced the relative power and legitimacy of subnational political officials.

The Coordination Politics of the Governors

Deepening decentralization, however, would require coordination among the governors. Given the new resources and policy authorities that were decentralized during the interim government of Ramón J. Velásquez, the governors merely needed to coordinate their support for more systematic decentralization. In the early 1990s the governors proved that they could speak as one. A collective statement by the governors, the *Declaración de Barquisimeto*, made the case for greater decentralization. The document condemned thirty-five years of national government ineptitude in providing efficient and effective administration of the most essential public services. The governors claimed that the centralist model of administration was exhausted (Brewer-Carias, 1994: 333). They argued that only the immediate transfer of budgetary revenues, fiscal authority, and administrative responsibilities to the regions would help solve the serious social, political, and administrative problems that Venezuela's democratic regime was confronting.

The new Ministry of Decentralization responded by creating an institutional mechanism for the governors to organize around their common interests. The ministry created the Association of Venezuelan Governors in 1993, which met formally every three months and elected its own president every six months. Governors started to use this organization as a forum to discuss and present a united position in relation to national issues. In numerous joint statements such as the *Declaración de Carabobo*, the *Declaración de Maracay*, and the *Declaración de Valencia*, the governors presented themselves as the "vanguard movement" of political change in Venezuela (Brewer-Carias, 1994: 336–44). The AGV's joint statements became the most influential source of pressure for decentralization. In the midst of the crisis of the traditional party system in 1993 and 1994, the governors could claim (and they did) that the AGV was a more legitimate representative of the Venezuelan people than the parties. With such arguments, the AGV extracted a series of important concessions from Congress, including electoral reform and extensive decentralization of fiscal resources and policy authority. For example, in 1993 and 1994 a total of $4.5 billion in national investment funds were decentralized to the states.

The AGV was most successful in expanding the governors' share of new revenue sources. Under the Velásquez interim government, the AGV lobbied for a share of the new value-added tax (VAT). Velásquez agreed and in 1996 Congress approved the law that defined the revenue share for regional and local governments, setting it at 18 percent in 1996 and gradually increasing it to a maximum of 30 percent by 2000.[14] FIDES administered these funds in response to state and municipal petitions.[15] The introduction of FIDES transfers and the initiation in 1997 of the transfer of a portion of fiscal revenues to the states caused the total amount of transfers to increase in the post-1994 period, as Figure 6.1 indicates. This upward trend started immediately after changes in the electoral system were implemented.

Gubernatorial coordination also reinforced bottom-up pressures to expand policy decentralization in meaningful ways in the post-1993 period. Less resistant to approving administrative transfers, legislators in this period approved a series of state petitions. A snapshot of administrative decentralization in 1996, as revealed in Table 6.5, illustrates a spate of new activity in contrast to the absence of petition approvals during the Pérez administration. Three states received policy responsibility over education. Three more states petitioned for decentralization in this service area. Health care was decentralized to thirteen of twenty-two

Figure 6.1. Intergovernmental Financial Transfers (%GDP) in Venezuela, 1989–97

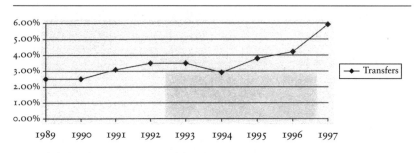

Source: Oficina Central de Presupuesto.

states, and five more states submitted petitions in this area. Public services dealing with child care were decentralized to six states, and the same number of states submitted petitions. Agricultural policies were decentralized to two states while other services such as housing and nutrition were devolved to one state in each of these areas. Such examples are evidence of the effectiveness of gubernatorial cooperation in the context of a demoralized partisan system.

This process highlights the importance of subnational actors' political coordination for decentralization. Directly elected governors and mayors have incentives to protect or expand fiscal and administrative decentralization. Their best opportunity to act on their incentives comes when a political crisis at the national level affects the central government's bargaining power (a good comparison is Brazil in the late 1980s, which had a very different party-system structure).[16] However, political crises are not a sufficient condition for governors and mayors to successfully gain increased decentralization. Subnational officials need some institutional mechanism (political pacts, the creation of a political association, etc.) to coordinate their activities, present a unified front, and help them reduce uncertainty and sustain collective action.

The Limits of Bottom-Up Decentralization in a Decomposing Party System

In the mid-1990s, decentralization had begun to gain momentum in Venezuela. Yet decentralization did not continue at the same pace, and it ultimately was reversed. Decentralization did not continue in Venezuela because the Caldera administration (1994–99) opposed further decentralization and because Caldera's administration heralded the final and complete collapse of Venezuela's party system. This prevented a potential consolidation of subnational authority. The decline of the party system disabled potentially valuable mechanisms of bottom-up pressure such as the ability of governors and mayors to shape the political career interests of legislators (see Samuels, this volume).[17] The complete collapse of the center, including the failed Caldera presidency, led to Hugo Chávez's rise to power. The result was a dramatic recentralization of public administration.

Caldera did not favor continuing the decentralization process. Having campaigned against Pérez's neoliberal reforms, Caldera was hesitant to pursue further decentralization because decentralization could be in-

Table 6.5. Decentralization of Public Services in Venezuela as of 1996

Sector	Approved	Petitions
Education	Lara, Aragua, Mérida	Monagas, Trujillo, Bolívar
Health Care	Aragua, Carabobo, Sucre, Zulia, Monagas, Bolívar, Trujillo, Táchira, Falcon, Anzoategui, Lara, Mérida, Miranda	Nueva Esparta, Yaracuy, Apure, Guárico, Portuguesa
Child Care	Aragua, Carabobo, Monagas, Táchira, Lara	Sucre, Zulia, Trujillo, Guárico, Yaracuy
Agriculture	Aragua, Lara	Carabobo, Sucre, Monagas, Bolívar, Trujillo, Falcón, Yaracuy, Guárico, Apure
Nutrition	Aragua	Carabobo, Sucre, Monagas, Bolívar, Guarico
Housing	Carabobo	Miranda, Sucre, Lara, Zulia, Monagas, Trujillo, Yaracuy

Source: Ministério de Relaciones Interiores.
Note: As of 1996, Venezuela had twenty-two regional governments.

terpreted as a dismantling of the central-government apparatus. The president reduced the Ministry of Decentralization to an office of the Ministry of Internal Relations, and he opposed efforts to transfer a portion of oil royalties to subnational governments.[18] Thus, even though administrative decentralization proceeded (Table 6.5), Caldera slowed down the process during the first two years of his administration, approving only three state petitions (Grindle, 2000: 81). The president's reluctance to deepen decentralization did not halt the process, but his position created obstacles for the AGV's efforts to deepen it.

Subnational authorities were also unable to expand upon what they had already gained because the political system began to completely collapse. Caldera's administration was plagued by several factors that undermined the party system as a whole. First, the president lacked a congressional majority, and the alliance that had installed the ex-COPEI leader in the presidency was thus unable to give his reform proposals sufficient and sustained legislative support. Partisan fragmentation in Congress made passing any legislation an arduous and time-consuming task. Caldera had no more than 24 percent of seats in the lower house (CN and MAS), not even enough to block two-thirds votes to censure and remove cabinet ministers.[19] He attempted to create coalitions including AD, but all of these attempts failed. Fragmentation and unstable congressional alliances encouraged the president to attempt to rule by decree (Romero, 1997: 28–31).

This effort to bypass Congress exacerbated executive-legislative conflict and weakened party discipline even further. For example, during the first year of his presidency, Caldera used his decree powers to suspend constitutional guarantees that he argued impeded the sweeping reforms the country needed. When the major parties in Congress attempted to trim Caldera's expanded authorities, he threatened to appeal to the public to override the legislators' objections. This game of chicken ended when Congress acceded to the president's suspension of certain constitutional rules governing the exchange rate, prices, and the banking system. This move institutionalized presidential discretion over future suspensions of constitutional rights and weakened party discipline by making the president more autonomous from partisan interests in Congress (Crisp, 1997: 195–98).

The ongoing political crisis, unfortunately, was coupled with escalating economic and social problems. The increasingly dramatic situation undermined the electorate's hopes that the president could implement meaningful reform. This combination of heightened executive-legislative tension, economic crisis, and antipolitical voter sentiment set the stage for the political system's total collapse in 1998. Although Caldera's decrees, which included substantial public intervention in the financial system, temporarily increased his popularity in 1994, the failure of the government's reforms to improve living standards led to widespread attacks on the president, Congress, and the party system after 1995 (Romero, 1997: 24). No existing institution would recapture the public's faith, and growing segments of the electorate placed their hopes on political outsiders, most prominently the ex-coup plotter Hugo Chávez, who was elected president in December 1998 by the largest margin in Venezuelan history.

Unlike Pérez and the COPRE reformers, Chávez believed that centralization and reorganization of the constitutional order from above was the key to taking Venezuela from the brink of political, economic, and social meltdown. He called a constituent assembly (dominated by his own supporters) and engineered a new constitution that extended the president's term from five to six years and allowed for reelection. This new constitution and the assembly's summary closing of a legitimately elected Congress were the clearest indicators of swift centralization during the first two years of Chávez's administration. A series of elections and referenda in 1999 and 2000 gave Chávez unprecedented authority over national institutions such as the legislative and judicial branches of government, as well as subnational governments. The new president also put the final nail in the coffin of the traditional parties. Chávez's constant theme of associating corruption, which is blamed for all of Venezuela's problems by the majority of the electorate, with AD and COPEI decimated what remained of party identity (Naím, 2001). Thus the collapse of *all* partisan and subnational political careers and the rise of a messianic, populist figure to an empowered presidency short-circuited the process of decentralization.

CONCLUSION

This chapter challenges Willis, Garman, and Haggard's (1999) treatment of the Venezuelan case on three levels. First, the decision to politically decentralize was unexpected given no *ex ante* change in the hegemonic party structure. Second, the degree of subsequent fiscal and policy decentralization, both quantitatively and qualitatively, was greater than these authors argued. Third, decentralization was not due to a *continuation* of disciplined national parties but to the *decomposition* of the party system and the collapse of the system of linkages that connected politicians at different levels of government. Ultimately, this very collapse limited bottom-up pressures for further decentralization and opened the way for the rise of a hyper-centralizing presidency.

Venezuela's initial political decentralization in 1989 resulted from the confluence of several macro political factors. The escalating governability crisis, which was caused by the increasing debility of the post-1958 democracy and the emerging economic contradictions of the petro-state, convinced all major political actors to embrace decentralization as a stopgap effort to attempt to relegitimize the political system. At that time, the traditional parties retained control of nominations to party lists, but the deepening political crisis, punctuated by two coup attempts in 1992 and the collapse of Carlos Andrés Pérez's presidency in 1993, reoriented politicians' career incentives away from the national parties, changing many politicians' "micro" incentives. Gaining and retaining subnational office became relatively more important, even for those ambitious politicians who planned to later seek national positions. The precipitous erosion of the *cogollo* system in the early 1990s along with voter disenchantment with AD and COPEI reduced the rewards of kow-towing to the leaders of the traditional parties and encouraged the emerging subnational elite to push for additional decentralization.

Fiscal and policy decentralization accelerated following Velásquez's interim presidency and the 1993 electoral reform. It deepened through the greater coordination of the governors.[20] Intergovernmental negotiations involving the governors, the president, and Congress resulted in victories for subnational governments such as increased fiscal transfers and policy decentralization. Thus bottom-up pressures played a decisive role, even in the face of a reluctant president (Caldera) and continuing efforts by the traditional party elite to retain control over scarce patronage resources.

It was not the continued existence of highly disciplined national parties that ultimately halted the process of decentralization in Venezuela, as one might interpret Willis, Garman, and Haggard (1999) as suggesting. The deepening crisis of the Venezuelan state and the decomposition of the party system became so extreme that it ultimately undermined the ability of the governors to engineer more decentralization. The erosion of the major parties and the instability of legislative alliances created incentives for president Caldera to rule by decree, and the collapse of the party system opened the way to Chávez's election. His rise to power signaled the institutionalization of both an antiparty and anti-

Congress center of authority that would recentralize the Venezuelan state after 1998.

The Venezuelan case suggests that bottom-up pressures for decentralization can be limited by several conditions. First, the president's view of decentralization as a solution to political problems is a relevant variable that should be a focus of future research. While Pérez and Velásquez viewed it as such, Caldera did not. Second, the support of legislative parties also matters. During the shortened Pérez administration, the traditional parties agreed to politically decentralize, but they successfully resisted fiscal and policy decentralization. Their view changed in the midst of the severe crisis of the 1992–93 period. The salience of pursuing subnational political careers changed the interests of national legislators in favor of fiscal and policy decentralization. Paradoxically, bottom-up pressure might not be possible without a preceding change of interests by national leaders to decentralize. The collapse of the center, then, can short-circuit the mechanisms of subnational leverage (i.e., the governors' control of legislative political careers).

The Venezuelan case tends to contradict the conventional hypotheses that link democracy and decentralization. First, unlike many of the other countries discussed in this volume, Venezuela is not an example of decentralization emerging during or directly following a process of democratization. Venezuela had been a (highly centralized) democracy for decades before any decentralization began. Moreover, it is not clear whether political decentralization in 1989 encouraged or helped undermine the democratization of this elite-dominated system. Decentralization did challenge the *cogollista* system and encourage politicians to be more accountable to local constituencies, but it failed to completely undo the centralizing tendencies of the presidency and the party system. The total collapse of this system in 1998 appears to have undermined the prospects for true decentralization in Venezuela's near future. The implications for democracy of Venezuela's sudden recentralization of authority under Chávez may not be fully known for some time. Chávez's brand of anti-institutional populism has already justified attacks against the independence of subnational governments, the judiciary, and the press. These actions led Brazilian president Fernando Henrique Cardoso to quip recently that the Venezuelan leader is an "unconscious authoritarian." If such evaluations continue to be confirmed by Chávez's actions, then the demise of democracy may become one of the unintended consequences of greater centralization.

Notes

The author thanks the editors and the reviewers for their comments on previous drafts of this chapter.

1. See Willis, Garman, and Haggard (1999), Garman, Haggard, and Willis (2001), and Eaton (this volume) for examples. For the classic argument that influences this work, see Riker (1964).

2. Between 1973 and 1988, AD and COPEI presidential candidates received 90 percent of the vote and congressional candidates received 80 percent.

3. Between 1958 and 1988 the electoral system in Venezuela was a proportional representation system with closed lists. Voters cast their ballots for a single slate determined by party leaders. These institutions allowed national party leaders, in particular those from the two largest political parties, AD and COPEI, to maintain tight controls over elected politicians in the national legislature. Politicians in Congress were so disciplined that roll calls were hardly necessary. See J. Molina (1991), Coppedge (1994), and Crisp (2000).

4. In other cities mayors were elected by city councils on closed lists and were usually members of the party with the largest block on the councils.

5. For a discussion of these reforms see Grindle (2000: 52–64) and COPRE (1986).

6. *El Universal,* June 26, 1986.

7. *El Nacional,* January 27, 1987.

8. The mixed-member system was implemented in 1993. Like the German model upon which it is based, half of the Chamber of Deputies (lower house) is elected in "first-past-the-post" fashion from single-member districts. The other half is elected by closed-list PR. Party allocation of seats in the Venezuelan chamber is based on the proportional party vote. Individual politicians can then be elected in single-member districts, but this has no effect on the proportion of seats for the politician's party. The Venezuelan Senate, as in the old system, is elected through closed-list PR. For more on the 1993 reform, see Carey (1996: 86–88) and Crisp (2000).

9. For an excellent overview of the impact of these riots and of Venezuela's political crisis in general, see McCoy and Smith (1995). Another useful source is the entire issue of the journal *Politeia* on the *caracazo* or "27-F," Universidad Central de Venezuela, Facultad de Ciencias Juridicas y Politicas, no. 15, 1990.

10. The new regulations did not commit any national ministry to comply with state petitions. States had the burden of proof to demonstrate that they could deliver the service previously administered at the national level. National ministries could either aid the state's proposal or not. The Senate would then decide, without time constraints, whether the transfer should be approved or denied. The Senate was also in a position to make a different bargain with each

state in relation to the decentralization of different public services like health care, education, sports, culture, technology, agriculture, housing, tourism, nutrition, and child care. According to the law, senators retained the discretion to quantify the financial resources to be transferred to a state once the decentralization of a specific service was approved.

11. The governors agreed to the president's proposal, which was reflected in the document, *La Declaración de la Casa de la Estrella.*

12. *El Universal,* March 5, 1992, pp. 1–15.

13. Although Velásquez was affiliated with AD, he was actually an independent, a condition that made him useful as a transitional figure. See Coppedge (1994: 51).

14. As part of Caldera's economic program, the law modified the agreed VAT's tax base to certain goods.

15. FIDES has separate funds for state and municipal governments, and each fund has a board of directors who approves and monitors all disbursements. For more on this process, see FIDES (1996).

16. Political crises are defined as events, economic or political, that are perceived as factors seriously diminishing the bargaining power of national politicians.

17. This is a point for future comparative research. Does the weakening of the center prevent subnational actors from decentralizing resources and policy authorities? To the extent that a national government suffers a crisis of legitimacy and Congress's authority is circumvented by the presidency, what mechanisms exist to engineer decentralization from below? The Venezuelan case suggests that bottom-up approaches are limited if the center is unwilling (Caldera) and if the center is in a process of complete collapse.

18. Under the oil royalties legislation, the national government would transfer at least 20 percent of its fiscal revenues in oil royalties to the states through FIDES projects beginning in 1997. This amount would increase to 30 percent by 2000. Distribution would be uneven. Over 70 percent of these funds would go to oil-producing states and 30 percent to the rest of the states. The policy was first implemented in 1997.

19. Minister of Health Carlos Walter was censured successfully (a rarity in contemporary Venezuelan politics) for his failure to handle a dengue fever epidemic. For a discussion of censure votes as a test of partisan discipline and legislative majorities in Venezuela, see Crisp (2000: 61–66).

20. In hindsight one might wonder if the coordination of the governors would have been possible but for Velásquez's willingness to decentralize. This is an important question beyond the scope of this chapter, but it should be an area for future research on the Venezuelan case.

CHAPTER 7

Electoral Competition and Fiscal Decentralization in Mexico

Caroline C. Beer

As electoral competition has taken root at the state and municipal level in many areas across Mexico, democratically elected mayors and governors have begun to demand more autonomy from the central government and more control over local fiscal policy. As a result, the federal government has increasingly ceded more power and resources to those governments. In what ways can the Mexican experience shed light on the causes of decentralization and the allocation of decision-making authority within a political system? Does increasing political competition influence the arenas in which policy is produced or the institutional actors who have control over particular policy spheres? Or do institutional arrangements and other forces such as neoliberal economic reform, international pressure, and sociostructural factors determine where policy decisions are made?

In order to explain decentralization and growing local autonomy, scholars have pointed to variables as diverse as shifts in the political economy (Morris, 1992), the rational calculations of vote-maximizing national leaders (O'Neill, 2000 and this volume), legitimacy crises (Grindle, 2000; Penfold-

Becerra, this volume; Rodríguez, 1997), and static institutions such as electoral laws and candidate selection processes (Linz and Stepan, 1992; Willis, Garman, and Haggard, 1999; Garman, Haggard, and Willis, 2001; Haggard and Webb, this volume). In this chapter, I assess the role of these variables in bringing about political decentralization, and I also examine the consequences of changing patterns of electoral competition on the distribution of decision-making authority between national and subnational governments. The research presented here suggests that to solve the puzzle of why politicians would voluntarily cede power to other political actors, a micro-level bottom-up analysis stressing the incentives and opportunities facing subnational actors is useful to supplement the dominant top-down approach examining the interests of national politicians. This is the case because, all else being equal, national governments are more likely to cede power to subnational governments when faced with growing demands from subnational governments to do so. While subnational actors operate within a larger system that they do not control, they are able to exert some influence over national actors.

The central argument of this chapter is that subnational electoral competition is a crucial variable for understanding decentralization. Political leaders in more competitive arenas will attempt to expand their control over less competitive arenas. This happens, I argue, because politicians selected in competitive elections face incentives to extend their influence over greater policy domains in order to meet the demands of their constituents. Strong electoral support, in turn, bolsters the ability of elected politicians to gain greater control over policy making. In Mexico during the 1990s many states and municipal governments were more competitive than the national government. This asymmetry in levels of political competition resulted in decentralization of power to those states and municipalities with greater electoral competition than the federal government. The central hypothesis of this chapter is that elected leaders in subnational governments with high levels of electoral competition are more likely to seek fiscal autonomy from the central government than their counterparts in subnational governments with low levels of electoral competition. I test this hypothesis against the expectations of other explanations of decentralization with a statistical analysis of patterns of local fiscal autonomy in the Mexican states. By focusing on subnational politics and the interests of subnational leaders, I emphasize the bottom-up dynamics and micro-level determinants of decentralization.

The Mexican states provide a good set of cases for examining these issues for a number of reasons. First, the study of decentralization in Mexico allows us to shed light on important issues regarding the relationship between democratization and decentralization. The slow, incremental transition to democracy in Mexico allows for disaggregating the components of democracy and examining the relationship between one key aspect of democracy, namely, electoral competition, and fiscal decentralization, thus permitting a clearer specification of the causal linkages between the two processes. Moreover, there is enormous variation in levels of political competition among the states and between some subnational political environments and the national government. Thus, the highly heterogeneous nature of the process of democratization across subnational units in Mexico makes the allocation of greater power and resources to subnational governments a central concern for the quality of democracy. Just as the process of democratization has been uneven across the Mexican states, so too has the process of decentralization, with some states gaining extensive control over multiple policy arenas and others remaining under the control of the federal government (Cabrero Mendoza, 1998; Díaz Cayeros, 1995). Additionally, because the Mexican constitution forbids consecutive reelection for all government positions, Mexico provides a least likely case for testing the consequences of electoral competition.

EXISTING RESEARCH

Neoliberal Reform, International Factors, and Sociostructural Causes

Some scholars have emphasized the links between decentralization and the shift in economic orientation from import substitution industrialization (ISI) to neoliberalism. Morris (1992), for example, argues that as production for the domestic market declines in favor of production for the international market, industries find new advantages to locating near borders and transportation hubs rather than in the capital city. The resulting redistribution of people and production fuels demands for local autonomy and leads to decentralization. Following a similar logic, Gwynne (1992) provides evidence that the shift to an open economy in Mexico led to a boom along the northern border, thereby decentralizing industrial production. Focusing on the Mexican car industry, Wong-Gonzalez (1992) shows that automobile manufacturers moved production out of the center of the country to the periphery as a result of Mexico's integration into the world economy. He predicts that as the standard of living increases at the border in comparison with the rest of the country, it will put strains on the centralized political system because the northern states will demand better public services.

David Fox (1992) similarly contends that the debt crisis combined with democratization brought about decentralization in South America. When neoliberalism replaced ISI economic policies during the 1980s, the open economy allowed industries largely located in the periphery, such as agriculture and mining, to compete in the world economy without the discriminating taxes and exchange rates that had hampered their growth during ISI. Furthermore, since ISI policies centralized power, resources, and government subsidies in and near the capital cities at the cost of the peripheral areas, reductions in government spending under neoliberalism had more severe consequences in the center than in the periphery. As a result, people and production moved from the center to the periphery. At the same time, in many countries elections took on more importance as a consequence of democratization. Political decentralization followed because leaders had to court votes from the peripheral areas and could no longer depend solely on support from elites in the center as they had during authoritarian and military rule. Regional development gained importance because once democratization began to take place, leaders became accountable to areas outside of the capital. Furthermore, borders became increasingly important as economies lowered trade barriers throughout the region. In Fox's words, "Frontier regions have ceased to be national cul-de-sacs and are increasingly viewed as international crossroads" (Fox, 1992: 37).

Also focusing on the relationship between neoliberalism and decentralization, Doner and Hershberg (1996) argue that there is an elective affinity between the globalization of the world economy and decentralization because producers require increased flexibility and efficiency to compete successfully in the world market. Therefore, regional economic actors will demand political decentralization in order to increase the efficiency of public sector service delivery. Central governments concerned with economic development will respond to the demands of regional economic interests.

Alternatively, the general coincidence between neoliberal reform and decentralization may be the result of pressure from international financial institutions (IFIs) rather than a direct outcome of shifts in the political economy. During the extensive economic crises in Latin America during the 1980s and 1990s, these governments became increasingly subject to the conditionality requirements of international lenders. As a result of a general euphoria about the potential of decentralization, IFIs began to prescribe decentralization to developing countries as a cure-all for their many political and economic problems (IDB, 1997).

A related set of rationales focuses on the sociostructural factors of modernization as a cause of decentralization. The inefficiencies associated with the overconcentration and diseconomies of scale involved in Latin America's megacities may have motivated decentralization in some cases. In Mexico City, for example, urban problems such as overcrowding, pollution, and dwindling supplies of drinking water provide substantial incentives for decentralization (Aguilar-Barajas and Spence, 1988; Stansfield, 1992). Regional economic development projects that decentralize production may help relieve some of the problems of congestion in the capital cities.

These structural and economic explanations of decentralization shed light on how the macropolitical and economic contexts provide an impetus for decentralization. They tell us how and why decentralization may be beneficial for a country, and they explain a general affinity between decentralization and neoliberal reform. And, implicitly, they explain the incentives of politicians. If decentralization does lead to more efficient service delivery, then politicians interested in attracting investment will face pressure to decentralize in order to meet the demands of investors for an improved local investment climate and better infrastructure. Yet, available evidence has not conclusively demonstrated that decentralization actually leads to better service provision (see the introductory chapter in this volume). Consideration of macro and sociostructural factors alone cannot explain the micro-level motivations for decentralization that are the proximate causes of *diverse outcomes* in subnational policy performance.

Rational Choice and Elite Decisions

Much of the policy-oriented rational choice literature on decentralization builds upon economic models of fiscal federalism that provide theoretical justifications for the benefits of decentralization, but they provide few explanations for why individual politicians would choose to implement these policies. In general this research tends to be prescriptive rather than explanatory (see Haggard and Webb, this volume). According to Oates (1972), decentralization enhances economic efficiency because local governments are more capable of producing policy outputs that take local tastes into consideration. In the words of the Inter-American Development Bank (1997: 160), "The basic gain from decentralization comes from its potential to improve the match between public goods offered by local governments and preferences of the population." Bird (1993) maintains that services should only be provided centrally when tastes do not vary and when the costs of local administration outweigh the gains in efficiency. Other theorists argue that local autonomy improves economic development because competition between subnational units leads to better public service provision at lower tax rates. The Tiebout (1956) model holds that households "vote with their feet" and choose to live in areas where local governments provide the best services with the lowest taxes. The Organization for Economic Cooperation and Development (1998) contends that decentralization allows public and private resources to be put to better use in providing infrastructure to facilitate economic development and reduce inequalities.[1]

While the prescriptive rational choice theories of decentralization imply that decentralization will happen naturally because it is the most efficient way to allocate public resources, decentralization presents a fundamental anomaly for explanatory rational choice models. Why would power-maximizing politicians voluntarily cede power and resources to subnational governments? To explain this apparent anomaly, rational choice theorists might argue that politicians would give up some of their power and resources in order to strengthen their electoral support and ensure future electoral victory. O'Neill (2000; this volume), for example, argues that national leaders may implement decentralization policies when their party is likely to lose national elections in the near future but has strong electoral prospects in subnational elections. Conversely, O'Neill argues, politicians who believe that they will continue to win national elections are unlikely to implement decentralizing reforms.

Employing a softer, more nuanced sense of rationality, others have explained decentralization as a response to crisis and a means of maintaining the stability and legitimacy of the political system. Grindle (2000), for example, argues against the explanations derived from a narrow vision of rationality that would suggest politicians decentralize in order to gain electoral support. Rather, she contends that decentralization efforts in Venezuela, Argentina, and Bolivia were elite projects motivated by institutional crises. In these cases, politicians were willing to give up power in order to protect the long-term stability of the government.

Similarly, for the case of Mexico, Rodríguez (1993, 1997) argues that the economic crisis of the early 1980s led to declining legitimacy for the PRI (Institutional Revolutionary Party) and forced the party leadership to decentralize some policy-making power to state and local governments in order to placate demands for democracy, regain legitimacy, and hold onto power. She further argues that the PRI ceded control of non-vital functions in order to maintain control of the most important state powers. Rodríguez's explanation of decentralization stresses the top-down dynamics of the process. She asserts that the prospects for decentralization ultimately reside with the willingness of the ruling elite to relinquish power: "The central government, after all, decides why, where, what, and how to decentralize" (1997: 8). More substantial decentralization did not take place, Rodríguez contends, because "the willingness to decentralize political power still did not exist" (1997: 141).

Other work on decentralization in Mexico has also placed primary emphasis on the interests of the national ruling party. Kathleen Bruhn (1999) argues that the PRI allowed the opposition some control at the local and state level in order to distract its attention and undermine its ability to compete for control at the national level. Foweraker (1993) and Stansfield (1992) make a related argument about the decentralization of the education system in Mexico. They contend that education policy was decentralized to undermine the power of the national teachers' union. Decentralization has also been portrayed as an attempt to shift blame away from central authorities and maintain legitimacy for the government during a period of economic crisis and shrinking federal budgets (e.g., Trejo and Jones, 1998). González Block (1991) argues that the Mexican health care system was decentralized in the hopes of shifting blame away from the president for the declining health care expenditures. Grindle (1996) similarly sees the decentralization of the education and health care systems in Mexico as a response to economic crisis and shrinking resources allocated to social spending.

The most systematic evidence of how decentralization has served the interests of the PRI is presented by Molinar and Weldon (1994). In an examination of the determinants of PRONASOL funding, a poverty alleviation project that funneled resources through subnational actors, they find that political considerations played an important role in the allocation of resources. They demonstrate that the decentralization policy embodied in PRONASOL was driven not only by technical or economic motivations, but also by a definite political logic. Moreover, they find that PRONASOL's decentralized social spending was effective in regaining electoral support for the ruling party.

Institutional and Electoral Factors

The literature focusing on institutions provides various explanations for the causes of decentralization. Linz and Stepan (1992, 1996) contend that the sequence of elections is the key explanatory variable. Willis, Garman, and Haggard (1999) also place central importance on the timing of elections, but they also focus on the rules of candidate selection. In contrast to these more static institutional approaches, Stoner-Weiss (1997) emphasizes the dynamic impact of competitive elections on generating demands for policy autonomy.

Linz and Stepan's (1992, 1996) central thesis is that the sequence of elections during democratization determines whether political identities are constructed around regional or national interests. If the first competitive elections in a democratizing country are national elections, as was the case in Spain in 1977, then national political parties are likely to form and generate political identities based on nationwide interests. Conversely, if the founding elections of a new democratic regime are subnational elections, politicians are likely to focus on subnational issues, and parties representing local interests are likely to emerge. A party system formed around local interests and local political identities is much more likely to generate demands for local autonomy.

Willis, Garman, and Haggard (1999) argue that variations in patterns of decentralization can best be explained by the static institutions that influence the structure of the party system and the sensitivity of national politicians to subnational interests. They argue that the timing of national and subnational elections and the party rules of nomination are the main explanatory variables for decentralization. They hypothesize that when national legislators are elected at the same time as governors and mayors, national politics will be more sensitive to local political interests than if national legislators are elected at the same time as the president. This is the case, they argue, because legislators elected at the same time as local leaders arrive in office on the coattails of governors and mayors. If, however, national legislators are elected at the same time as the president, then they arrive in office on presidential coattails, thus diminishing the sensitivity of national politics to subnational actors. Alternatively, Turner (1998) argues that subnational politicians elected at the same time as national leaders tend to be less autonomous because they are elected on the coattails of the national politicians. Nonconcurrent national and subnational elections, he posits, encourage decentralization because subnational elections are dominated by local rather than national issues. Garman, Haggard, and Willis (2001) further posit that decentralization is more likely when candidate nominations are controlled by local elites rather than national party leaders and in open-list proportional representation systems rather than closed-list systems.[2] In essence they argue that countries with institutions favoring decentralized party systems are more likely to have greater levels of political decentralization than countries where the electoral institutions favor centralized parties.

The main weakness with the static institutional approach is the underlying assumption that institutions are the driving force of politics without acknowledging the fact that institutional characteristics such as the centralization of the party system and electoral laws tend to reflect deeper distributions of power within the political system. Institutional factors such as the type of proportional representation (PR) system, candidate selection processes, and the timing of elections should be thought of as *intervening variables* because they are the outcome of struggles between contending forces and thus both reflect and enforce an enduring distribution of power.

Willis, Garman, and Haggard (1999) imply that the incentives of subnational politicians are constant and that the process of decentralization is even across subnational units. They also assume that candidate selection processes vary among countries but not within countries. A brief comparison of the candidate selection processes of the PRI, PRD (Democratic Revolutionary Party), and PAN (National Action Party) in Mexico demonstrates substantial intracountry variation along this variable. The differences in decentralization, they argue, are the result of static institutions that vary across nations (but not within nations) to determine the balance of power between subnational and national level politicians. The static electoralist approach, along with the rational choice and elite decision models discussed above all emphasize the top-down micro-level causes of decentralization. While the interests and actions of national politicians are clearly important in determining decentralization, the uneven nature of local political autonomy in Mexico suggests that bottom-up pressures have also been important in decisions to reallocate control to the subnational governments. An approach that focuses solely on the interests and whims of the ruling elite misses a substantial piece of the explanation and does not explain subnational variation within countries. An interactive approach that combines the motives of subnational actors with those of national actors provides a more promising explanation of decentralization.

Stoner-Weiss (1997) provides a bottom-up dynamic institutional explanation of how electoral competition generates new incentives for elected politicians to increase their control over policy. She attributes the growing demands for local autonomy in the Russian regional governments to the introduction of competitive elections. Democratization of regional politics led to decentralization because the democratically elected leaders became accountable to the voters and therefore demanded new powers to meet the needs of the public. Stoner-Weiss asserts, "Multi-candidate, competitive elections in the Russian heartland created an impetus for increased regional power over policy. Not unreasonably, if local politicians were to be held accountable to their constituents, then they insisted on having more control over policy" (1997: 56–57). The idea that more competitive elections at the subnational level generate greater demands for local autonomy is also supported by evidence from Venezuela. A recent IDB report on decentralization in Venezuela (Kraemer, 1999) suggests that states ruled by opposition parties may be more likely to demand greater autonomy than states ruled by dominant parties.[3]

The institutional approach favored here provides theoretical flexibility, allowing for both top-down and bottom-up explanations. The dynamic institutional arguments that stress the changing nature of institutional arrangements and their effects on politics provide the most promising avenue for theoretical work on the changing nature of center-periphery relations within countries.

ELECTORAL COMPETITION AND DECENTRALIZATION IN MEXICO

Scholars have been quick to link the recent trend toward democratization in Latin America with the simultaneous move toward more decentralized policy making. Decentralization, however, has also coincided with neoliberal reform, new international pressures for decentralization, and elite interest in decentralization. Thus, to make a compelling case for a causal relationship between democratization and decentralization, it is necessary to specify the causal mechanisms that link the two processes. Complicating this task is the fact that both democracy and decentralization are very complex and thus difficult to measure. The first step toward elaborating a clear causal relationship is to disaggregate both of these multifaceted concepts and to analyze the relationship between key components of each. In order to do so, this analysis focuses on electoral competition and subnational fiscal autonomy, both key components of the broader processes of democratization and decentralization.

The Mexican political system is formally federal with three layers of government: the national, state, and municipal levels. Each state has its own constitution and an elected governor and legislature. Municipalities also elect an executive and a legislative council. While on paper Mexico has all of the formal institutions of a strong federal system, in reality it has functioned as a highly centralized regime in which power and resources have been tightly controlled by the president and national executive branch. The president has traditionally exerted informal powers to control governors. Governors have been appointed essentially by the national executive, through the president's control over the nomination process within the ruling party; and since the president also has been able to dismiss governors through his control of the Senate, the governors have served at the pleasure of the president.

The process of democratization in Mexico, which was characterized by increasing electoral competition in subnational elections that gradually percolated upwards from municipal to state and national elections, led to political decentralization, party system decentralization, and fiscal decentralization. Until the 1990s, most state governments demonstrated almost no independence from central authorities. Throughout the 1990s, however, some states began to exert substantial autonomy. Before 1989, state elections were relatively uncompetitive and the PRI ruled all thirty-one states. During the 1990s electoral competition began to emerge slowly in a number of states. The move toward increasingly competitive elections at the state level has breathed new life into the previously dormant federal institutions of the Mexican government. By combining the democratization hypothesis with the institutional and electoral explanations for decentralization, I argue that in the case of Mexico increasing electoral competition at the subnational level led to de facto political decentralization because the introduction of real democratic competition to subnational governments is in essence political decentralization in formerly dominant-party systems such as Mexico's. This political decentralization then generated incentives for subnational political leaders to push for fiscal decentralization.

Building on the insights of previous research, I argue that increasing electoral competition at the state level in Mexico has generated new incentives and opportunities for state-level politicians to develop autonomy from the central government. When the PRI dominated Mexican politics, PRI candidates were guaranteed victory. Since the governors of noncompetitive states owed their position to the national party leadership, who controlled nominations for the ruling party candidates, they had little incentive to struggle for autonomy from the central government. The only real constituency of local leaders in noncompetitive states was the national party leadership. Moreover, most of the governors of noncompetitive states came from the national bureaucracy and returned to the national bureaucracy once their term was over. Therefore, their interests were closely aligned with those of national politicians, and they were likely to follow the orders of party leaders.

In contrast, governors of electorally competitive states derive their power from their electoral appeal at the subnational level. Hence, they have strong incentives to gain control over the policy domains that concern the voters in their states. As electoral competition increases at the state level, leaders are expected to develop greater concern for the interests of the voters. Since the national party can no longer guarantee the election of their party members (in the case of members of the PRI), and officeholders can be held accountable by the voters for bad policy decisions, local leaders face incentives to gain control over greater policy domains and struggle for autonomy rather than simply take orders from the central government. Even though reelection is prohibited for all offices in Mexico, there are strong incentives for governors of competitive states to be accountable to voters. The vast majority of governors in Mexico remain in politics and often seek other elected offices. Those who seek political appointments in government bureaucracies after their gubernatorial terms must be in good standing with the party. Traditionally, the most important test for PRI governors was whether they were able to assure victory for the PRI in all elections in their state during their term. Assuring victory for the PRI may be difficult in competitive states. Therefore, there are clear incentives for a governor in a competitive state to remain attentive to the demands of the voters. Opposition governors also face incentives to be responsive to citizens in order to increase the potential of their party to win future elections. In order to meet the demands of the voters, local elected leaders will demand greater autonomy over fiscal policy, thus leading to fiscal decentralization. The following empirical analysis examines both revenue and expenditure decentralization, through an investigation of total public goods provision in the Mexican states as well as the capacity to generate revenue locally in each state.

The approach presented here is complementary to and consistent with the neoliberal hypothesis presented above. The Mexican states that are more democratic have tended to be those states that are most connected to the international economy. We could hypothesize that as local businesses begin to compete in the international market, they become more concerned with the efficient provision of public goods. As a result they sponsor opposition parties and spur increased electoral competition, which in turn generates incentives for elected politicians to demand greater control over areas that affect their constituents.

The focus on subnational electoral competition is similar to the institutional approach of Willis, Garman, and Haggard (1999) and Garman, Haggard, and Willis (2001) inasmuch as their model stresses candidate selection. Increased electoral competition tends to give local leaders more control over candidate selection and gives local constituents a viable veto option over nationally imposed candidates. Nevertheless, this analysis differs from their approach in a number of important ways. First, the theoretical logic of this model parallels more closely the dynamic logic of Stoner-Weiss (1997) than their relatively static logic. Second, it focuses on intranational variation in patterns of decentralization rather than cross-national variation. An examination of the heterogeneous pattern of decentralization within one country draws attention to the different interests and incentives of subnational politicians.

EMPIRICAL ANALYSIS

To test the competing explanations of decentralization, I employ an intracountry comparison of fiscal policy in the Mexican states. Subnational comparisons provide a number of methodological advantages over more traditional cross-country comparisons. First, focusing on variation among subnational units controls for many troublesome variables such as political culture and position in the global economy. Second, subnational comparisons allow for more precise and more consistent measurements of many variables. For example, because of the complexity of subnational electoral laws, it is difficult to test the influence of the timing of elections across nations. In Mexico each state has its own electoral calendar. Therefore, some states elect governors and mayors at the same time as national legislators, while others do not. A comparison across subnational units provides not only a much larger sample size, but also allows for a more refined measure of the timing of elections, thereby differentiating between those states that hold subnational elections at the same time as national elections and those that do not.[4]

In this section I use data from all of the thirty-one Mexican states over nine years in a cross-sectional time-series regression analysis to test the influence of electoral timing, an export-oriented economy, and electoral competition on patterns of local fiscal autonomy. The model allows me to test the opposing expectations of Willis, Garman, and Haggard (1999) and Turner (1998) regarding the relationship of concurrent local and national elections. It also allows me to test the importance of electoral competition versus electoral timing and an export-oriented economy in determining local fiscal autonomy. Since the electoral systems across the Mexican states are very similar, the model cannot test Garman, Haggard, and Willis's (2001) hypothesis regarding closed-list versus open-list PR.

I focus on state fiscal policy to test systematically the relationship between electoral competition and decentralization. For the dependent variables I use a measure of local public goods provision as an indicator of expenditure decentralization and a measure of local sources of independent income as an indicator of revenue decentralization. The budget data used in this section are published by the Mexican government (INEGI, 1991, 1994, 1998). The database includes local public goods expenditures, locally generated tax revenue, locally collected government fees (*derechos*), federal transfers (*participaciones*), and total income from each state from 1988 to 1996.

To test the relationship between electoral competition and local fiscal autonomy, I use a data set that contains both cross-sectional and time-series observations. A cross-sectional time-series data set provides substantial methodological advantages for testing the direction of causality in hypothesized relationships (Finkel, 1995). Unfortunately, however, such a data set also presents some statistical difficulties. Namely, cross-sectional time-series data sets tend to suffer from both heteroscedasticity and serial correlation (Beck and Katz, 1996). The model, therefore, is estimated using the GEE approach (Liang and Zeger, 1986) with Stata's correction procedure for first-order autocorrelation.

The first dependent variable measures expenditure decentralization using each state's per capita public goods expenditures (in constant 1990 pesos). When per capita federal transfers are controlled, this provides a good indicator of local public goods provision. The second dependent variable measures revenue decentralization using per capita revenue generated within the state (including taxes, fees, and products in constant 1990 pesos). The greater the per capita state income derived from local revenue sources, the greater the local fiscal autonomy. One of the most important means of developing greater control over public policy is to control greater sources of income. Without independent sources of income, local policy autonomy can be easily contained by the central government's control over budget transfers. Raising more revenue locally allows local politicians much greater autonomy over resources and ultimately over policy outputs. For local governments to perform effectively and ensure their autonomy, they must be able to raise revenues independent of the central government (Oates, 1993). The tax- and fee-raising capacity of local governments, therefore, is a key indicator of their autonomy (Weingast, 1995). While it may seem counterintuitive to talk about increasing taxes as an indicator of increased responsiveness to citizens' demands, it does make sense in the context of Mexican local government. Local governments historically have collected almost no revenue and therefore have had no possibility of developing policy autonomy. Thus, increasing local revenues is essential for developing greater policy autonomy and meeting the demands of citizens.

Independent variables are used to assess the impact of electoral competition, the timing of elections, and export production on local fiscal autonomy. Control variables for per capita federal transfers, total state GDP, state GDP per capita, urbanization, and state population are also included (INEGI, 1993: 52; Nacional Financiera, 1995). To measure electoral competition I replicate for the Mexican states the cross-national measure developed by Vanhanen (1990, 2000) using electoral data from state legislative elections (provided by the Centro de Estadística y Docu-

mentación Electoral at the Universidad Autónoma Metropolitana, Ix-
tapalapa). This measure is the amount of participation in the election
(turnout/total population) multiplied by the amount of competition
among the political parties (100 percent of votes of the largest party).
Participation and competition are two essential and uncontested elements of electoral democracy (Dahl, 1971). See Table 7.1 for the definition of the variables.

Drawing on the central hypothesis of Willis, Garman, and Haggard
(1999), the model includes an independent variable for the timing of
national and subnational elections. In Mexico national deputies are elected
every three years. Every six years the deputies are elected at the same
time as the president. Of the thirty-one states, eleven states elect governors and municipal presidents concurrent with national elections (Banamex, 1996: 636–37). Following the logic of Willis, Garman, and Haggard, it is expected that these states would be more autonomous than
states that do not have concurrent subnational and national elections.
The timing variable takes on a value of 1 for states that elect governors
and municipal presidents at the same time as the national deputies. The
variable takes on a value of 0 for the states that hold their gubernatorial and municipal elections at other times.

In order to test the expectations of the neoliberal hypothesis that
emphasizes the importance of an export-oriented economy for local autonomy, the model includes a variable measuring the importance of
export production in each state. This variable is the per capita wages and
salaries in the *maquila* export industry each year in each state (Nacional
Financiera, 1998: 498–99).[5] The logic of the neoliberal hypothesis suggests that states with strong export sectors will generate more revenue
locally instead of depending upon federal transfers in order to maintain
more autonomy for local public service provision. Thus, the variable for
export wages is expected to be positively related to locally generated
revenues.

The first model examines the impact of electoral competitiveness,
electoral sequencing, and export wages on per capita public goods expenditures, holding constant federal transfers. Vanhanen's Index is positive and statistically significant. Thus, the more competitive the state, the
greater the local public goods provision.

In contrast to the expectations of the static institutional approach to
decentralization, the timing of elections has no significant impact on

Table 7.1.   Definition of Variables

Variable	Definition
Public Goods Expenditures per capita	Total state expenditures/Total population
Locally Generated Revenue per capita	Total state income from taxes, *derechos*, and *productos*/Total state population
Vanhanen's Index	(Turnout/total population) × (100–%votes of largest party in state legislative races)
Electoral Timing	= 1 for concurrent local and federal elections = 0 for nonconcurrent local and federal elections
Export Wages per capita	Salaries and wages in the *maquila* sector/ Total state population
Federal Transfers per capita	Federal *participaciones*/Total state population
GDP	State gross domestic product
GDP per capita	State gross domestic product/Total state population
Urbanization	Urban population/Total state population
Population	Total state population

local public goods provision. Holding the level of electoral competitiveness constant, states that conduct their subnational elections at the same time as the national legislative elections provide no statistically different level of public goods than those states that hold their elections at other times. The coefficient for export wages is also insignificant. As expected, the per capita federal transfers are positive and significant. The controls for GDP and GDP per capita are both positive but just miss the 95 percent confidence level. The urbanization variable is negative and just misses standard levels of significance. The control for state population is not significant. Table 7.2 presents the results of the regression.

Table 7.2. Cross-Sectional Time-Series GEE Regression: The Impact of Electoral Competition on State Fiscal Policy

	Model 1: Dep. Var. = Public Goods Expenditures per capita	Model 2: Dep. Var. = Locally Generated Revenue per capita	Model 3: Dep. Var. = Federal Transfers per capita
Vanhanen's Index	13.857 (3.92)[b]	0.447 (2.92)[b]	0.871 (0.82)
Electoral Timing	5.372 (0.08)	−2.152 (0.45)	61.012 (1.84)
Export Wages per capita	0.129 (0.77)	0.020 (1.79)	0.007 (0.10)
Federal Transfers per capita	0.923 (4.53)[b]	0.030 (2.96)[b]	
GDP	0.000 (1.84)	0.000 (2.16)[a]	0.000 (0.26)
GDP per capita	0.022 (1.77)	0.002 (2.18)[a]	0.007 (1.45)
Urbanization	−518.230 (1.89)	−0.429 (0.02)	−59.976 (0.48)
Population	−0.078 (1.56)	−0.004 (1.34)	−0.016 (0.80)
Constant	300.864 (1.46)	−9.247 (0.70)	240.000 (2.64)[b]
Observations	279	279	279
Number of group (state)	31	31	31

Note: Data is corrected for first-order autocorrelation. Absolute value of z-statistics in parentheses.

[a] Significant at 5 percent level.

[b] Significant a 1 percent level.

The second model estimates the significance of the independent variables on per capita locally generated revenue. Again, Vanhanen's Index is positive and highly significant. The electoral timing dummy is insignificant. The export sector variable is positive and just misses standard levels of significance with p = 0.06. Thus, there is some evidence that states with strong export sectors raise more revenue locally and are less dependent on transfers from the federal government. Per capita federal transfers are positive and significant. GDP and GDP per capita are positive and significant. Urbanization and total population are insignificant.

The statistical data presented in models 1 and 2 seem to provide strong evidence that the level of electoral competition has a significant positive influence on local fiscal autonomy. Some may argue that this statistical relationship is a result of the fact that the PRI dominated the federal government and punished states that voted heavily for the opposition by denying them federal funds. If this were the case, then the higher percentage of local revenue in electorally competitive states might be merely a statistical artifact of the reduced federal transfers. The data presented here suggest that this is not the case because the statistical models hold federal transfers constant.

Model 3 further tests the contention that more competitive states are discriminated against in federal transfers. The model uses per capita federal transfers as the dependent variable. Electoral competition is insignificant in this equation. Moreover, when this same equation is estimated using the vote for the PRI instead of Vanhanen's Index, the PRI vote is also insignificant. Vanhanen's Index, though insignificant, is actually positive, suggesting that federal transfers may actually go up in more competitive states. This is consistent with evidence from Molinar and Weldon (1994) and Bruhn (1996: 157 and n. 35) that the federal government strategically transferred more federal funds to states that were opposition strongholds in order to buy off opponents and undermine opposition support.[6]

In summary, the data provide evidence that more electorally competitive states have greater fiscal independence from the central government and provide more public goods to their citizens. Additionally, there is some evidence to suggest that more export-oriented states have greater fiscal independence. The variable for concurrent subnational and national elections is not significant in any of the models. Hence, the data are consistent with the hypothesis that electoral competition creates incentives for elected politicians to acquire new influence over expanded policy-making arenas. The data also lend some support to the neoliberal hypothesis that suggests that states with more export-oriented economies will have more autonomy from the central government. Finally, the analysis suggests that electoral timing is not important in determining intracountry variation in local fiscal autonomy.

CONCLUSION

This chapter examines the influence of increasing electoral competition on local autonomy. Building on the institutional literature, it develops a dynamic institutional explanation of decentralization to shed new light on the relationship between democratization and decentralization. It tests static models that emphasize electoral rules against a dynamic model that emphasizes the changing incentives generated by a shifting political context. When examining the bottom-up dynamics of decentralization, the data suggest that in the case of Mexico increasing electoral competition is much more important for explaining relative local fiscal autonomy than the timing of elections. The strong results of the empirical analysis provide support for a model emphasizing the dynamics of institutional change rather than the static approaches that have dominated the institutional literature. The model also provides some evidence that an export-oriented economy creates incentives for local politicians to demand autonomy from the central government.

This analysis departs from the dominant studies of decentralization by focusing on intranational rather than cross-national variation. The findings highlight the importance of intranational variation and suggest the dangers involved in assuming that levels of local autonomy and democratization are constant across subnational units. The results of the empirical analysis also support the contention that the interests of subnational actors vary according to the political context they face. Future research should continue to focus on systematic analysis of subnational variation.

While it is too early to assess the consequences of decentralization in Mexico, the most likely outcome is increasing inequality among the states. There seems to be a virtuous circle in some states where economic growth and increasing political competition generate new demands for local autonomy. These states are then able to provide better public services, thus fueling further growth and higher quality democracy. Other states have fallen into a vicious circle of economic stagnation, authoritarian rule, and low quality public service provision.

NOTES

Material in this chapter appears in my *Electoral Competition and Institutional Change in Mexico* (Notre Dame, Ind.: University of Notre Dame Press, 2003), especially chapter 6.

1. Other prescriptive approaches emphasize the social benefits of decentralization. Decentralization is thought to strengthen democratic participation in government decision-making and increase the responsiveness of policy-makers to citizens (Rondinelli, 1981). Since local participation is widely believed to be necessary for successful development projects (e.g., Tendler, 1997), there is reason to believe that decentralization will contribute to economic development. Rondinelli (1981: 134) makes this argument explicit in his formulation that popular participation plus local leadership plus decentralization leads to development. Rondinelli also argues that decentralization cuts red tape and improves bureaucratic efficiency. Sabatier and Jenkins-Smith (1993) suggest that decentralization enhances policy learning because it creates opportunities for creative policy-making and provides a basis for comparison between policies. See the introductory chapter of this volume for further consideration of these points.

2. It should be noted that Garman, Haggard, and Willis (2001) categorize the Mexican electoral system as a closed-list PR system. They fail to mention that the majority of seats in the lower house are elected in single-member districts.

3. Kraemer finds that states governed by MAS decentralized faster than states governed by COPEI and AD (Kraemer, 1999: 22).

4. For more on the utility of the subnational comparative method, see Snyder (2001b).

5. The term *maquila* is used in Mexico to refer to the manufacturing sector comprised of foreign-owned factories that export the finished product.

6. While the empirical evidence of this chapter focuses on *participaciones,* Molinar and Weldon (1994) and Bruhn (1996) examine PRONASOL funding, which makes up a large proportion of the discretionary Ramo XXVI regional development investment financing.

PART III

Consequences for Economic Reform

CHAPTER 8

Decentralization, Democracy, and Market Reform

On the Difficulties of Killing Two Birds with One Stone

ERIK WIBBELS

Since the early 1980s, comparativists and political economists alike have been preoccupied with analyzing "dual transitions" toward free market economies and democratic politics across the developing world. This research has often focused on the contradictions between the two processes, including the political difficulties of implementing economic reform policies under democratically elected officials (Nelson, 1990), the constrained economic and political conditions for successful economic stabilization and adjustment (Haggard and Kaufman, 1995; Haggard and Webb, 1994), and the negative implications of economic reform for democracy (O'Donnell, 1994). As Montero and Samuels make clear in their introductory chapter, policies of fiscal, political, and administrative decentralization have often been cited and implemented as a means to overcome this conflict and advance simultaneously both transitions. It is widely assumed that by decentralizing, public policy making can be made both more democratic and more efficient (Weingast, 1995; Montinola, Qian, and Weingast, 1995). Nevertheless, it is becoming increasingly clear that decentralization can, and has in a number of nations, aggravated macro-economic problems (Ter-Minassian, 1996, 1997) and complicated economic reforms (Rodden and Rose-Ackerman, 1997; Gibson, 1997b; Remmer and Wibbels, 2000). Despite this evidence, little research has examined the potential for fundamental conflict between the economic and political logics of decentralization.[1]

The following analysis lays out the theoretical underpinnings of the generalized move toward economic and political decentralization in the developing world; examines the conditions under which to expect conflict between the dual exigencies of fiscal and political decentralization; explores the recent experience of Argentina as a crucial case that has faced, and attempted to overcome, this conflict; and briefly explores some of the implications of Argentina's experience for other large emerging market nations. Consistent with the introduction to this volume, I place significant emphasis on top-down, institutionalist and electoralist factors (and party systems in particular) in mediating the dilemmas of decentralization. Thus, while neoliberal reform clearly placed decentralization on former president Carlos Menem's agenda, it was through intergovernmental partisan relations that the political and economic logics of decentralization were filtered, ultimately shaping the intergovernmental system evident today in Argentina. In emphasizing these factors, the research attempts to achieve two things. First, the analysis questions the widespread notion that fiscal and political decentralization are complementary and focuses on the economic/democratic policy trade-offs that decentralization often generates. Second, it examines the effects of decentralization on intergovernmental relations rather than the more common emphasis on the impact of decentralization on service delivery (Cremer, Estache, and Seabright, 1995; Fox and Aranda, 1996; Dillinger, 1994).

The research focuses on Argentina for the simple reason that political and fiscal decentralization in the context of Argentina's deconcentrated public sector complicated many times over the nation's search for macroeconomic stability. In the 1980s and early 1990s national efforts to stabilize the economy were foiled in large part by democratically elected subnational politicians who pursued expansive fiscal policy (Sanguinetti and Tommasi, 1996; World Bank, 1996b; Remmer and Wibbels, 2000).

As the conflict between subnational economic policy and macroeconomic reform became increasingly evident, the Menem administration initiated a series of intergovernmental reforms that have helped constrain provincial purview vis-à-vis spending in many provinces (Gibson and Calvo, 2000), while simultaneously accentuating the conflict between the fiscal and political rationales for decentralization.

Despite central government discourse, which emphasized that decentralization was a means to move the dual transition forward, I argue that the attempt to eliminate the provincial fiscal threat in Argentina has been implemented at the expense of many of the theorized political advantages of decentralization. More specifically, the central government has devolved extensive expenditure responsibilities to provincial governments while tightening control over revenue sources. This process of fiscal "centralization via decentralization" has increased the political dependence of subnational governments on the center, in essence heightening the economic accountability of provincial officeholders to the central government while weakening their accountability to the citizens who elected them. This centralization of accountability does not presuppose that provincial governments were highly responsive to their electorates prior to the Menem administration's reforms, but it does make clear that fiscal decentralization and simultaneous political centralization are compatible. I argue that this reflects both a general trend in the developing world and the overwhelming concern of national governments and international donor communities with the macroeconomic, as opposed to democratic, aspects of decentralization. The implications for ongoing processes of decentralization and economic reform are extensive, suggesting the need for a more measured approach to additional decentralization, a reconsideration of the relationship between political and fiscal decentralization, and an increased focus on the decentralized politics of macroeconomic reform.

DECENTRALIZATION IN THEORY

The ongoing and extensive interest in decentralization in much of the developing world has its roots in the coincidence of historical conjunctures. First, a conservative, pro-market consensus developed with the widespread debunking of state-led development strategies in the wake of the debt crisis of the early 1980s. For many observers, decentralization is seen as a natural means to weaken market-constraining central governments (IDB, 1997; López-Murphy, 1995). Second, during the current "third wave" of democratization, the left in Latin America has viewed political decentralization as a way to increase the quality of democracy and bypass historically repressive central governments. At the same time, renewed commitment to the European Union (EU) has generated interest in the role of decentralized institutions in contexts where subnational governments have considerable power (von Hagen and Eichengreen, 1996). In the development of supranational EU institutions, researchers and policy makers have had to look elsewhere to the lessons learned from nations throughout the world in answering questions about which levels of government are best suited for various public sector functions.

As a policy proposal, however, decentralization has been unique to the extent that its champions have justified it as a tool in both of the transitions within the developing world, political and economic. Indeed, the economic and political arguments for decentralization have conveniently dovetailed. As outlined in the introduction to this volume, the literature on fiscal federalism has emphasized two benefits of decentralization. First, where fiscal responsibilities are devolved to local jurisdictions, local public sectors can more closely match the delivery of public goods with the preferences of local citizens (Oates, 1972, 1977). Second, local citizens unhappy with the taxing and spending policies of local governments can "vote with their feet," in effect moving to other jurisdictions that more closely approximate their ideal package of taxes and services (Tiebout, 1956). This mobility introduces a component of competition among local governments for tax bases that theoretically encourages policy experimentation and innovation. Together, proponents assume these two factors will ensure a smaller, more efficient public sector. The inflation-prone, deficit-inducing, employee-bloated central governments of the past are expected to give way to efficient, market-conforming local governments via concerted processes of fiscal decentralization.

The political arguments for decentralization converge nicely with the presumed economic benefits. First, decentralization is expected to democratize societies long repressed by antidemocratic central governments (Orlansky, 1998; Bird, Ebel, and Wallich, 1995).[2] While in the past distant central governments have freely ignored citizen input, local officials, by virtue of their close association with local conditions, are much more likely to take into account the concerns of local communities. Second, citizens are more likely to take part in local politics where they can more easily influence outcomes, and local officials, by virtue of proximity, can be held more accountable for their performance (Ostrom, Schroeder, and Wynne, 1993). The democratic vibrancy of local civil societies will therefore engage rejuvenated local governments in synergistic pressures for increased accountability that, in turn, will lead to better government.

It is on this point of accountability that the economic and political logics of decentralization come together. Both benefits accrue only under the assumption that decentralization will encourage the accountability of local politicians to their voters. Indeed, it is the supposition that accountability brings fiscal responsibility that motivates much of the support for the decentralization of government services. Because local citizens are presumed to be informed and active, local politicians are expected to be accountable to them. Accountability, in turn, ensures an efficient delivery of public services and a smaller and more democratically responsive government. It should not be surprising, therefore, that decentralization has been viewed by the international donor community, democratic theorists, and local activists alike as the natural means to kill two transition birds with one stone.

DECENTRALIZATION AND MACROECONOMICS

Nevertheless, some researchers have noted that the supposed virtues of decentralization can be constrained or even reversed under certain conditions (e.g. Prud'homme, 1995; Tendler, 1997; Broadway, Roberts, and Shaw, 1994). They suggest that where local democratic institutions are poorly developed, bureaucracies are weak, corruption is endemic, and/or citizens are apathetic, processes of decentralization can do more harm than good. Despite the generation of long lists of dangers associated with decentralization, however, there has been little coherent theorizing on the relationship between decentralization and economic reform. Unfortunately, most extant literature has ignored the political incentives faced by subnational politicians in decentralized contexts and thus has provided an incomplete account of the decentralization/marketization/democratization nexus.

The role of subnational political incentives is particularly significant with respect to macroeconomic stability and reform since subnational officials often have few incentives to manage decentralized spending in a macroeconomically "responsible" manner (Remmer and Wibbels, 2000;

Wibbels, 2001). This failure to recognize the macroeconomic implications of subnational economic policy results from the general facts that officials of subnational governments face few of the international incentives for economic reform,[3] and electoral considerations rarely encourage sound local fiscal policy, particularly where decentralized politics are dependent on patronage.[4] As a result, the fiscal incentives of decentralized governments will often run in the direction of overspending, thereby exacerbating structural obstacles to national stabilization in an international economic context that places a premium on macroeconomic stability.

Previous research has provided long lists of factors that might increase the costs of fiscal decentralization to macroeconomic policy and performance (Tanzi, 1995; Prud'homme, 1995). From these lists can be culled two necessary and jointly sufficient conditions for conflict between macroeconomic performance and decentralization: subnational governments must both control large proportions of public sector spending and face soft budget constraints. Though not particularly troublesome individually, the combination of both conditions encourages local elected officials to conduct subnational economic policy in a manner inconsistent with macroeconomic reform. Indeed, under these conditions the greater the level of fiscal decentralization, the greater the threat to national economic policy, *particularly* under ideal democratic circumstances.

Decentralized economic policies can have little macroeconomic impact if local governments have few fiscal resources. If a national government controls decisions over most of public sector taxing, spending, publicly-owned enterprises, public employment, and so forth, it makes little difference if subnational governments are largely autonomous in their own small fiscal sphere. The story is different when subnational governments control significant portions of the public sector. Where this is the case, the fiscal resources available to subnational governments limit the effect that any national stabilization policies might have on an economy as a whole; the paucity of the central government's fiscal resources all but preclude the success of the adjustments. Furthermore, subnational governments may even increase spending at just the time when national stabilization measures would require the opposite (IDB, 1994). Evidence exists that this has been the case in the United States (Peterson, 1995), Germany (Deeg, 1996), and Canada (J. S. Hunter, 1977).

Pro-cyclical policies are particularly likely in developing nations where the focus of decentralization policies has been on the delivery of social services by provincial and local governments (IDB, 1997; World

Bank, 1998). Thus, just as concerted reform policies at the national level have often led to economic decline, increased unemployment, and general social distress, the burden of increased pressure for employment generation, unemployment insurance, and other welfare policies has fallen on subnational governments. In the Argentine context, this potential for policy conflict can be clearly seen in the extensive, often violent, public protests over proposed provincial stabilization measures in 1995 at the same time that the national electorate was rewarding President Menem's orthodox economic reforms.[5]

Even where subnational governments control substantial portions of the public sector budget, however, decentralization may still not induce economic policy inconsistency across levels of government unless subnational policy-makers face soft budget constraints. Soft budget constraints are political and economic institutions that ensure that fiscally irresponsible local governments will be bailed out by higher governments (Rodden, 1999; Wildasin, 1997; Hausmann, 1998). Soft budget constraints have historically taken on a number of forms in various national contexts, including rediscounts of local debt by central banks, intergovernmental transfers that reward local budgetary disequilibria, the assumption of local debt by national governments, lack of controls on subnational borrowing autonomy, and even the issuance of script by some provincial governments. Individually or in combination, these mechanisms allow local governments to borrow and spend excessively, since they provide avenues to export the costs of local deficits to the nation as a whole. The ultimate result is an overgrazing of the common pool resources of monetary and fiscal policies.

Where democratic, decentralized, autonomous decision making coexists with subnational control of public spending and soft budget constraints, the economic and political logics of decentralization will conflict. The decentralization literature has long made an implicit, but fallacious, assumption that local enterprises, politicians, and citizens will not want their governments to spend more money than is prudent (Weingast, 1995; Shah, 1998). Yet, under the joint conditions stated above, the association between local government spending decisions and what would be fiscally "prudent" is lost. Because bailout mechanisms are more or less invisible to average citizens, those citizens associate the public goods and services they receive from local governments with local taxes paid when, in fact, they are being paid for in part by other jurisdictions. Suffering from "fiscal illusion," the citizens of local governments tend to make excessive demands on locally supplied public goods and services, and local politicians, particularly under ideal democratic conditions, will have every motivation to honor the demands of the local citizenry. In short, it becomes nearly impossible for electorates to hold their subnational officials accountable for their spending choices.

Despite the potential for fiscal decentralization to contribute to macroeconomic instability and delay reform policies, very little research has systematically explored the relationship between the two. As Tanzi makes clear, "the relation between decentralization and stabilization has not received the attention it deserves, especially in developing countries" (1995: 304). Under the conditions laid out above, the virtuous cycle between decentralization, democratization, and economic reform gives way to a significant dilemma for some nations: how can one decentralize fiscal and political decision making but maintain macroeconomic stability? Indeed, it is exactly this dilemma that has led to structural, chronic deficits and excessive borrowing in democratic nations such as Brazil throughout the 1990s, Argentina in the 1980s and first half of the 1990s, India during its recent phase of economic reform, China as it moves toward a market economy, and most recently Mexico in the late 1990s.[6]

The potential for a decentralization/democracy/macroeconomic trade-off has significant implications. First, it raises the distinct possibility that under some conditions, the current rush to decentralize will do more harm than good. Second, it has important policy significance for nations that find themselves, as Argentina has, confronting the dilemma between the dual exigencies of macroeconomic stability and decentralization in a global context that demands the former while preaching the virtues of the latter. Third, it has special importance for the federal nations of the developing world where state or provincial governments tend to have substantial political independence, control large portions of the public budget, and face intergovernmental institutions that often exacerbate economic collective action problems. Fourth, it points to the importance of focusing on the mechanisms such as political parties that are likely to be at the heart of intergovernmental conflicts over the competing rationales for decentralized governance. Finally and most significantly, it raises important questions about the complex relationships among democratic accountability, local governance, and national collective goods in contexts where the aggregation of citizen preferences are vastly complicated by decentralized institutions.

EVIDENCE FROM ARGENTINA

Argentina's experience with decentralization is particularly significant for a number of reasons. First, it is a nation that has struggled with the decentralization/economic stability dilemma. As is well documented, it experienced tremendous macroeconomic difficulties beginning in the early 1980s and continuing through the early 1990s, when President Menem's Convertibility Plan imposed price stability and a relatively stable macroeconomic environment. Less widely known is the mounting evidence that the economic policies of democratically elected decentralized governments, and provincial governments in particular, were important ingredients in Argentina's hyperinflationary economy and the stop-and-go reform policies that failed to bring about stability in the 1980s (Sanguinetti and Tommasi, 1996; Gibson, 1997b; World Bank, 1996b). Both before and after the tremendous revenue increases associated with the wave of economic growth in the early 1990s and the recent process of decentralization, the finances of provincial governments have often been characterized by excessive deficits and indebtedness. These imbalances continued to be the rule through most of the 1990s, despite one of the world's most concerted economic stabilization plans at the national level. Second, beginning in the early 1980s under authoritarian rule and accelerating rapidly in 1991 under President Menem, Argentina underwent extensive decentralization of many key fiscal responsibilities, including education, health care, and public security. As a result, subnational governments are responsible for the delivery of social services, while the national government is focused largely on macroeconomic policy, private sector promotion, and security (Zapata, 1999). Finally, in response to the macroeconomic threat posed by provincial overspending, the Menem administration initiated a series of reforms to help constrain provincial finances that were at least somewhat successful in hardening soft budget constraints (Dillinger and Webb, 1998). Using his position atop the Peronist Party, Menem was able to constrain some of the prerogatives of subnational politicians. In short, the Argentine experience is one in which the two conditions for conflict between decentralization and macroeconomic stability were met and where attempts have been made to address that conflict. The irony is that in beginning to overcome the decentralization dilemma, the Argentine national government usurped much of the autonomy of the provinces, the very same governments whose decentralized decision making, theory tells us, should provide democratic and economic payoffs.

Below, I briefly outline the historic roots of the decentralization conundrum in Argentina. Having established the concurrence of the two factors outlined above, I examine the series of intergovernmental policy reforms aimed at encouraging prudent subnational fiscal policy, deregulation, and privatization. A discussion of the implications of the Argentine experience follows.

The Roots of the Decentralization/Macroeconomy/ Democracy Trade-off

Beginning with the transition to democracy in 1983, the intergovernmental fiscal and political relations that would ultimately make provincial finances and governments such a crucial feature of Argentina's macroeconomic instability and generate considerable conflict between decentralization and economic reform began to take shape. Indeed, very quickly each of the conditions for the decentralization/macroeconomic conflict asserted themselves.

Table 8.1.   Fiscal Decentralization in Argentina, 1987 and 1997

	Nation		Provinces	
Spending (%)	1987	1997	1987	1997
Total Spending	60.2	46.9	33.1	43.5
Total Social Spending	54.1	50.6	39.0	41.7
Education and Culture	37.5	22.2	60.4	75.6
Health	19.4	14.6	66.7	69.1
Housing	10.0	0.6	90.0	99.4
Social Assistance	61.5	27.4	26.9	50.4
Economic Services	81.1	35.9	17.2	53.6

Source: Secretaría de Programación Económica y Regional.
Note: Percentages for the given years do not add up to 100 in some cases because municipal spending is not included in the table.

Even by standards of the late 1990s, Argentina at its transition to democracy in 1983 was a relatively decentralized nation. Table 8.1 shows the evolution of the subnational government share of total public sector expenditures and as a percentage of important government services, including education and health care, between 1987 and 1997. Using two measures of fiscal decentralization for eighteen countries between 1974 and 1986, the World Bank (1988) indicates that by the mid-1980s Argentina was already among the most decentralized nations in the developing world.[7] With provincial governments spending around 40 percent of total public sector expenditures, the potential for economic policy divergence between levels of government to have considerable impact on the macroeconomic condition of the nation as a whole was present.

It might be argued that provincial governments in Argentina do not really "control" their decentralized fiscal policies but that the centralization of power in the Argentine president, the federal government's capacity to remove provincial governments, and the unified structure of the two largest national parties effectively curtail the autonomy of provincial decision-makers.[8] These features of Argentina's federal structure have led some researchers to imply that Argentina's federation is a weak one whereby the political independence of local politicians is usurped by the national government (Weingast, 1995; Elazar, 1987). There are strong reasons to doubt the validity of these claims. First, while by some standards Argentina's party system may be centralized, it has also been characterized as both internally heterogenous and catchall in nature (Levitsky, 1998, 1999). Levitsky (1999), in particular, has noted that recent programmatic shifts of the ruling Peronist Party at the national level have not been accompanied by similar changes at the provincial and local levels. This is evidenced in the prevalence of internal opposition to various Menem initiatives among *Partido Justicialista* (PJ) governors in the 1990s and Menem's incapacity to impose his candidates on provincial and municipal party lists.[9] Third, while some provincial governments suffered intervention, in almost no cases has the national government's party made electoral gains in subsequent elections. In other words, intervention has had its political costs for the national government, and those costs have limited its usefulness as a weapon against the independence of provincial governments. Fourth, recent research is making it increasingly clear that the "hyper-presidential" character of the Argentine political system has been overstated by many observers. Provincial interests have left a marked impact on reform policies as diverse as privatization (Llanos, 1998) and social security (Palermo and Novaro, 1996: 488). Thus, despite the relative centralization of the Argentine political system, decentralized spending by provincial government did represent a threat to macroeconomic management.

The threat these decision-makers represented to the macroeconomy was realized because of the tremendously soft budget constraints that provincial governments enjoyed. Provincial governments had almost unrestrained access to a number of means of deficit financing, including provincially owned banks that made loans to provincial governments at below market rates, a mechanism whereby provincial debt with provincial banks was rediscounted by the Argentine central bank,[10] and the lack of regulations on the source or scope of provincial debt.[11] Furthermore, a number of provincial governments issued *bonos* (bonds) as payment to suppliers or public employees.[12] Having all of the characteristics of money, these *bonos* effectively appropriated the right of seignorage historically vested solely with the central government. In a troubled economic environment, each of these mechanisms contributed to extensive quasi-fiscal deficits, expansive monetary policy, and increased public indebtedness (Morduchowicz, 1996; Zentner, 1999).

The cumulative effects of the incentives for provincial governments to live well beyond their budgets were profound. By the end of 1988, aggregate provincial deficits were over 23 million pesos, accounting for more than half of the total public sector deficit.[13] By the end of the following year, when the nation's economic crisis helped bring about early elections and the utter defeat of President Raúl Alfonsín's Radical Party, provincial deficits had ballooned even further to 51.4 million pesos, turning a central government budget *surplus* of 39 million pesos into a total governmental deficit of 12.4 million. Furthermore, the various mechanisms for transferring provincial government debt to the Central Bank contributed significantly to the inflationary environment of the late 1980s.

As a result, provincial governments contributed in no small part to one of the worst cases of macroeconomic meltdown in recent history. Despite a series of macroeconomic stabilization measures throughout the 1980s, the Alfonsín administration was politically unwilling and unable to initiate the provincial economic adjustments necessary to complement periodic national attempts to bring about macroeconomic stability.[14] Most important in this respect was Alfonsín's weak position in the provinces where his Radical Party controlled few governorships. The result was that by 1989, inflation ran at 2314 percent, unemployment tripled its 1980 rate, the public sector debt ballooned by (U.S.) $58.4 billion, and the economy contracted by 10 percent over the course of the decade.[15] This data is not to suggest that decentralized governments were solely responsible for Argentina's economic problems in the 1980s. Extensive research places blame on the nature of Alfonsín's heterodox adjustment policies (Kaufman, 1990; Dornbusch and Edwards, 1991) and social opposition to various stabilization programs (Acuña, 1994). Nevertheless, provincial fiscal policies contributed significantly to the complexity and intransigence of the problems. Indeed, the inability of a weak Radical president to discipline a federal system dominated by *Peronista* governors was a crucial determinant of significant bailouts of provincial governments throughout the Alfonsín administration.[16] As a World Bank study summarized, "Despite its fundamental importance to macroeconomic policy formulation and implementation, provincial public finance has not received the attention that its importance in national fiscal policy requires" (1990: vii). Unfortunately for Argentina, this same dynamic has characterized President Fernando de la Rua's coalition government since its beginnings. Faced with overwhelming Peronist dominance in the provinces, the administration was hard-pressed to constrain provincial deficits, which exploded and thus added to the escalating financial crisis of 2001.[17]

The Decentralization Dilemma and Policy Trade-offs

The success of Carlos Menem's free market reforms have been widely cited in the literature (World Bank, 1990; Smith, Acuña, and Gamarra, 1994). After a brief period of profound struggle with the nation's economic situation, the administration embraced the policy proposals embodied in the "Washington Consensus." Though the stabilization package included extensive privatization, price and trade liberalization, the imposition of a currency board, and profound budget cuts, central among the reforms were the further decentralization of key public services to provincial governments and the reform of intergovernmental relations to encourage sustainable provincial fiscal policies.[18] Indeed, what is significant about both of these reforms is how the process of decentralization has been managed by the central government in order to encourage economic "rationality" at the provincial level. By closely tying fiscal transfers from the center to economic reform policies at the provincial level, the Menem administration was able to overcome at least some of the contradictions between Argentina's decentralized public sector and economic stability. The cost, however, was a significant emasculation of the decentralization process itself, whereby dependent provincial governments are even more responsive to the central government at the expense of local accountability. This change has, in essence, removed the possibility that decentralization in Argentina will provide the democratic benefits that its enthusiasts have promised.

It is worth noting that this argument does not presuppose that provincial governments were particularly responsive prior to the Menem administration's intergovernmental reforms. In a context of tremendously soft budget constraints, accountability for provincial fiscal policy was all but impossible. Moreover, provincial politics have long been characterized to varying degrees by clientelism and corruption (Novaro, 1994) that defy theoretical rationales for advancing policies of decentralization. Those rationales universally assume a high level of subnational political responsiveness to decentralized electorates. What was problematic about Menem's intergovernmental reforms is that while a few have served to increase provincial accountability to their citizens, on balance they have rather significantly shrunk the parameters within which provincial politicians have policy choices as opposed to central dictates. In other words, the democratic potential of provincial governments has been going in the direction opposite that suggested by decentralization theory despite significant expenditure devolution from national to provincial governments.

During the early years of Menem's administration, it became clear that the success and sustainability of the economic stabilization and reform project depended on carrying fiscal reform to the provincial level. Even as the Convertibility Plan established price stability, privatization was carried out with vigor, and the federal government experienced budget surpluses, provincial finances remained a thorn in the side of the reform process (World Bank, 1998). The evolution of provincial finances through the 1980s and 1990s can be seen in Table 8.2. Despite a short-term improvement in 1991 and 1992 that accompanied increased provincial-level revenues and federal transfers to the provinces, expenditures expanded more rapidly than revenues, and substantial subnational deficits reasserted themselves by 1993. The situation further declined in 1995 under the impact of the "tequila effect" associated with Mexico's devaluation in

Table 8.2.   Provincial Fiscal Performance in Argentina, 1983–96

Year	Provincial Deficit as % of Expenditures	Provincial Deficit as % of National Deficit
1983	−3.56	.
1984	15.21	91.30
1985	7.17	140.02
1986	6.97	160.57
1987	15.89	169.36
1988	22.77	32.21
1989	11.88	23.38
1990	21.03	36.14
1991	11.77	19.79
1992	4.08	8.88
1993	11.15	16.39
1994	11.90	17.34
1995	16.71	21.27
1996	14.96	16.22

Source: Ministry of Economy.

late 1994. Throughout this period, the Menem administration slowly increased pressure on the provinces to rationalize their budgets, control rapidly increasing wage bills, and privatize provincially owned enterprises, particularly the banks. Some of these reforms were quite innocuous vis-à-vis the autonomy of provincial decision-makers; while encouraging subnational fiscal discipline, the reforms did not significantly decrease the choices of local politicians in responding to their electorates. Key in this regard was the elimination of rediscounting of provincial debt that accompanied the Cavallo Plan in 1991. In essence, this reform eliminated the monetization of provincial debt, as provincial politicians could no longer simply incur debt and export its costs to the national government. By ensuring that the cost of provincially incurred debt would be borne by its citizens, the reform tightened the relationship between the costs and benefits of provincial spending policies and thereby made provincial politicians more accountable for their fiscal policies. These reforms did bear some economic fruits for the central government; in the second half of the 1990s overspending did not reach the epic levels experienced during the crisis-riddled 1980s (Dillinger and Webb, 1998; World Bank, 1999). Nevertheless, recent bailouts of select provincial governments, widespread wage delays, and a total provincial debt of $30 billion (and growing) suggest that provincial budget constraints are far from hard.[19]

Moreover, other reforms went well beyond simply hardening budget constraints to remove significant decision-making discretion from decentralized politicians. The intergovernmental initiatives of the Menem administration aimed at limiting provincial fiscal purview can be placed in four general categories: first, the centralization of revenue sources in the central government; second, the movement from automatic, non-earmarked to earmarked fiscal transfers to the provinces; third, the decentralization of high fixed-cost expenditures to the provinces; and fourth, the highly politicized use of presidential slush funds and provincial bailouts.

In each case, Menem took advantage of his popularity, his role as PJ party head, his formal constitutional powers, and informal cajoling to divide individual provinces or groups thereof against each other. In doing so, he precluded coherent, unified resistance from the provinces. As Steven Solnick has made clear, "[W]hile collective action among all provinces can deter the central government from predation, collective action among a *subset* of regions can produce an outcome in which the federal government consistently exploits one set of regions to appease a united veto block" (1998: 4). Because Menem could count on a large majority of provincial governors to accept the initiatives of their party head, opposition governors (including a few mavericks in his own party) could do little but opt out of intergovernmental agreements, a strategy which always hurt those provinces in the long run (Gibson, 1997b).[20]

Key among the central government's initiatives to remove decision-making authority from provincial offices was a consistent centralization of public sector revenue sources, in essence preventing provincial governments from conducting their own revenue policy (Morduchowicz, 1996). The concentration of revenue sources happened in two ways: first, political pressure was placed on provincial governments to give up their chief revenue-generating taxes; and second, each reform of the tax system favored the central government at the expense of its provincial counterparts. With respect to the first tactic, a series of fiscal pacts signed between the Menem administration and each province, including the

"Federal Pact" (1992, *Ley 24.130*), the "Federal Pact for Employment, Production and Growth" (1993, *Decreto 1807/93*), and their subsequent modifications, placed profound conditions on provincial governments.[21] The agreements required substantial restructuring of provincial economies, the privatization of provincial banks, and various other reforms, the most important of which for current purposes was the demand that provinces eliminate certain taxes, including the gross receipts tax, the chief source of revenue in most provinces. Its loss implied a significantly proscribed capacity to conduct independent fiscal policy at a time when provincial governments were struggling to deliver the services decentralized in the early 1990s.

A related fact is that almost every national tax reform during the Menem administration implied a loss of revenues for the provinces vis-à-vis the national government. One analysis suggests that seven out of eight major tax reforms initiated between 1989 and 1993 benefited the nation by shrinking the provincial portion of shared taxes (Spisso, 1995). These reforms were followed by changes to the value-added and corporate income taxes that increased the revenue shares of the nation relative to the provinces. By 1994 these reforms implied a loss of 28 percent of shared revenues for the provinces, and the original revenue-sharing formula codified in 1988 that established a 57/43 percent provincial/ national split for shared taxes had been turned on its head, with the nation receiving 57.5 percent of shared taxes (CECE, 1995: 8–9). By 1997 this implied a revenue loss of nearly $5 billion a year for the provinces. It is worth reemphasizing that this centralization of revenues took place during the same period that the provinces assumed health care, education, and many social service expenditures from the central government, and despite the widely held assumption that the level of government expenditure responsibilities should correspond to its revenue-raising capacity (World Bank, 1998). The combination of proscribed taxing capacity and the centralization of revenues led to a situation in which provincial governments became increasingly dependent on the national government, and provincial public sectors had few independent weapons to counter short-term revenue shortfalls or expenditure requirements. Not surprisingly, the federal government used this dependence to place restrictions on how provincial governments spent.

The tendency to restrict provincial expenditures is the second major change in intergovernmental policy that curtailed provincial autonomy; it can be seen most clearly in the move toward federal matching grants from the unconditioned, automatic transfers foreseen in the 1988 law governing intergovernmental finances.[22] The fiscal federalism literature has long suggested that unconditioned, automatic transfers are preferable to other types of grants because they allow decentralized decision-makers to respond to local needs as flexibly as possible (Oates, 1972; Filindra, 1999). Conditioned or nonautomatic ad hoc grants, by contrast, allow national governments to impose their preferences on lower-tier governments and distort local priorities. Clearly, when decentralized spending decisions are imposed by central governments, the democratic advantages of decentralization are stunted. Table 8.3 clearly shows the shift from unconditioned to conditioned grants since 1990. Although the 16.4 percent shift may not seem particularly large, the change can be understood to represent the degree to which the central government increased its control of provincial spending decisions. This shift was achieved in various ways, including agreements that settled long-standing intergovernmental debt questions while placing conditions on provincial spending; the fiscal pacts, which established that any revenues above certain floors could not be used to increase provincial public sector wages; and federal aid and grants, which were conditioned on changes in provincial expenditure policies. Together, these reforms represented a clear shift away from the democratic principles that underpin policies of decentralization.

The third major policy aimed at curtailing provincial fiscal autonomy consisted of decentralizing to provincial governments the delivery of services that are high in fixed costs. To the extent that provincial budgets become characterized by high fixed costs, they are inflexible and provide little room for politicians to respond to citizen demands. The most significant reform in this regard was the decentralization of secondary education and health care to provincial governments in 1991.[23] The high fixed costs of these services are largely associated with wages. Both education and health care are labor intensive, and workers in these sectors are represented by highly organized public sector unions across the nation. As a result, the decentralization of these services implied a decentralization of the most significant remaining political conflicts with public sector unions. These conflicts have been exacerbated by the fact that the decentralization of responsibilities was not matched by an increased provincial percentage of shared taxes. Instead, the central government retained the estimated costs of the delivery of services from existing *pro-*

Table 8.3.   Automatic, Unconditional Transfers vs. Conditioned and Nonautomatic Transfers as a Percentage of Total Transfers in Argentina, 1989–97

	(1) Automatic and Unconditional	(2) Conditioned	(3) Nonautomatic	((2+3)/total) Not Decentralization Friendly
1989	76.6	12.0	11.4	23.4
1990	75.7	17.8	6.5	24.3
1991	*80.9*	*15.2*	*4.0*	*19.2*
1992	71.9	26.3	1.9	28.2
1993	70.3	26.6	3.1	29.7
1994	68.7	27.6	3.7	31.3
1995	68.7	27.5	3.8	31.3
1996	65.3	31.4	3.3	34.7
1997	64.4	32.6	3.0	35.6

Source: For 1989–94, data taken from Rezk (1997). Data for 1995–97 calculated by the author on the basis of CFI (1998) data.
Note: The italicized row is that in which transfers were the most decentralization-friendly.

vincial shares of national taxes and insisted that the provinces use these funds to deliver the newly decentralized services. As a result, the wage burden for provincial governments rose after decentralization went into effect. Between 1991, the year prior to the actual decentralization of services, and 1993, the year after decentralization, the provincial wage bill increased by an average of 6 percent of net revenues for the provinces despite the fact that revenues increased by 72 percent during this period. Indeed, in interviews with provincial politicians and bureaucrats, the stickiness of provincial budgets and the difficulty of lowering wage burdens, in particular, were the most frequently mentioned obstacles to economic reforms and the efficient delivery of public services.

The fourth and final policy change that limited provincial autonomy was the politicized and nonobjective nature of intergovernmental fiscal relations that the Menem administration fostered to further its policy aims. Ad hoc transfers, irregular bailouts of provincial governments, and intergovernmental deal cutting were all used to impose conditions on provincial governments that contradict the notion that decentralized policy-makers should be able to respond to their electorates. The most obvious of the national government's tools in this respect was the highly politicized use of discretionary, non-earmarked presidential transfers known as ATNs (National Treasury Transfers).[24] In many cases, these transfers were used as simple rewards to the president's political allies. Since 1990 over 40 percent of total transfers went to Menem's home province despite the fact that it represented less than 1 percent of the nation's population. Where provinces were controlled by opposition parties, transfers were sent directly to municipalities governed by the PJ, despite the fact that the law governing ATNs states clearly that the funds must be awarded to provincial governments.[25] In other cases, transfers were conditioned on provincial implementation of nationally identified policy reforms. This happened, for instance, in the province of Tucumán, where the delivery of ATNs was conditioned on the privatization of the province's water system.[26]

The national government complemented the highly politicized use of ATNs with other informal measures that had a common tendency to restrict provincial government decision-making autonomy. The federal government politicized and conditioned aid to fiscally troubled provinces. The assumption of troubled provincial pension funds and subsidized loans almost exclusively benefited Peronist and Peronist-aligned provincial governments over which Menem's administration had the most leverage.[27] In nearly every case, the bailouts were conditioned on various structural reforms of provincial public sectors, including privatizations, targets for various kinds of spending, refusals to assume additional debt, and even ceilings on the number of public sector employees.[28] A related measure was to cut national government spending in the provinces. By selectively cutting central government public works and other investment projects in the provinces, the national administration could spare or compound the problems of pinched provincial budgets. In 1999, for instance, in response to the general economic slowdown associated with the Asian and Russian financial crises, the national government's budget proposal included spending cuts of $280 million in provincial public works.[29] In a clear warning to the provinces, the minister of agriculture explained that "the budget cut called for by President Carlos Menem is an eloquent signal to the provinces of the efforts that the national government will make to attain an effective containment of public spending."[30] Given the clear use of national budget cuts as a political tool to encourage provincial spending cuts, it should not be surprising that the two provinces with the largest cuts (Córdoba and Rio Negro) also happened to be governed by the opposition *Unión Cívica Radical* (UCR).

These are but a few significant examples of the ad hoc and politicized nature of intergovernmental relations in Argentina whereby the central government placed pressure on the decision making of provincial governments. Most recently, "complementary accords" between national and select provincial governments have been discovered that served as secret payments to ensure provincial support for the reforms outlined above during the Menem administration.[31] As one long-term observer and participant in intergovernmental fiscal relations made clear, "Relations between the provinces were better during the 1980s when meetings were more regular and institutionalized. Now, everything is very personalized and depends on individual relationships."[32] What is remarkable about the politicization of national/provincial interactions is that intergovernmental fiscal relations have supposedly been institutionalized, standardized, and depoliticized by the *Ley de Coparticipación* (Coparticipation Law) of 1988, which instituted automatic and supposedly transparent transfers from the central to provincial governments. Yet, despite the supposed advantages of automatic transfers, the central government increasingly used informal mechanisms to condition the actual delivery of funds. The result was a progressive centralization of actual decision making over increasingly decentralized spending.

All told, the results of these reforms, both formal and informal, have been significant. National government pressure resulted in various provincial reforms: in only three cases do provincial banks remain in public hands.[33] Public works including water and electricity are being transferred into private hands throughout the provinces. By 1997, provincial deficits as a whole had shrunk from $3.6 billion in 1995 to $1.2 billion, a 66 percent decrease in only two years.[34] In short, the provinces' status as a macroeconomic liability was, in part, mitigated. Yet, it needs to be emphasized that this was achieved partly at the expense of provincial political freedom of choice. Few of the provincial reforms identified above were achieved with the mandate or even acquiescence of provincial citizens. Indeed, throughout 1995, 1996, and again in 1999, widespread social upheaval accompanied central government–inspired economic reforms in the provinces.[35] Despite violent protests in more than half of the provinces, extensive reforms have been carried out that according to many observers have severely hampered the capacity of provincial governments to effectively deliver the services decentralized to them in the early 1990s. As one official in the central government's *Subsecretaria de Relaciones Fiscales y Economicas con las Provincias* (Subsecretary of Fiscal and Economic Relations with the Provinces) explained, "the social costs of provincial reforms have been huge."[36] The fact that reforms were carried out despite such costs provides further evidence that the capacity and flexibility of provincial decision-makers has been severely compromised by these reforms. Indeed, extensive interviews suggest that with very few exceptions, provincial representatives felt helpless in the face of profound and sustained pressure from the Menem administration for wide-ranging reforms of provincial public sectors.[37]

The very different experience of the de la Rua administration further underscores how important intergovernmental partisan relations are to managing the decentralization dilemma in conditions where transparent intergovernmental fiscal and political institutions do not exist. While Menem could rely on copartisans governing in a strong majority of provinces, de la Rua, as a Radical president, faced a majority of opposition governors. Despite a stated interest in reforming the coparticipation law, the de la Rua administration was unable to touch the issue in the face of provincial intransigence. Moreover, as the national economy continued in a deep recession, provincial governments once again began to accumulate significant deficits. In an effort to continue meeting International Monetary Fund targets, the central government became increasingly desperate to ensure the commitment of provincial governments to fiscal discipline, going so far as to declare "fiscal war" on the provinces. Absent the Menem administration's intergovernmental partisan tools, however, negotiations dragged on and exacerbated Argentina's ongoing economic crisis. Thus, while the provinces negotiated away much of their long-term influence during the Menem administration, their unwillingness to initiate new rounds of centrally inspired economic reforms have brought the conflicting logics of centralization to the fore in Argentina once again.[38] Without a doubt, provincial intransigence and fiscal irresponsibility were prominent factors in the ultimate breakdown of de la Rua's macroeconomic policy in late 2001.

THE EFFECT OF "CENTRALIZATION VIA DECENTRALIZATION"

As a cost of the Menem administration's increased short-term sustainability of the nation's macroeconomic reforms, decentralized institutions and decision-makers were seriously weakened. Argentina's decentralization/economic stability dilemma simply was decided in favor of the former at the expense of the latter. Provincial reforms helped impose a modicum of rationality on the spending patterns of Argentina's provincial governments. Data from 1996, 1997, and 1998 suggest that while the total public sector remained in deficit, the provinces as a whole initiated budget cutting, privatizations, and the like to a degree that their budgets approached balance. That 1999 saw a return to fairly large deficits, however, only goes to show how transient and context-dependent many of those provincial reforms were.[39] Absent a powerful party leader with a strong majority in the provinces, the balance of power has again begun to tip toward the provinces. As Montero and Samuels point out in their introductory chapter, decentralization and recentralization are *processes*. Yet, while debt service remains a significant problem for many provincial governments, the elimination of Central Bank rediscounts of provincial debt and the privatization of all but three provincially owned banks have greatly reduced provincial government access to additional indebtedness in the future. Many governments have also transferred deficit-laden provincial pension funds to the national government.

There are, however, reasons to believe that while all of the incentives that induced disruptive provincial economic policies in the 1980s and 1990s have not been eliminated, Menem's reforms of the 1990s have constrained the long-term capacity provincial governments had to threaten the nation's macroeconomic stability. First, the series of provincial privatizations initiated at the behest of the central government are not readily reversible. Second, as long as the national government remains closely attuned to the global incentives for macroeconomic stability, there are few reasons to believe that the mechanisms that historically have supplied soft budget constraints for provincial governments will return. Thus, while provincial deficits have again reasserted themselves, this is as much a function of a seriously weakened Argentine economy as it is of soft budget constraints. Third and finally, provincial governments have in many cases negotiated away many of their bargaining strengths vis-à-vis the federal government; in return for short-term economic relief, they have abdicated their control of the public enterprises and policies of greatest interest to the center. That the provinces have been reluctant to undergo another round of austerity under de la Rua does not change that fact, though it does underscore that the centralizing trend initiated under the Menem administration reached its zenith during the ill-fated de la Rua government.

More significant for broader theoretical debates on decentralization is the fact that many of these reforms, while contributing to the sustainability of Argentina's economic reforms overall, have served to limit the supposed economic and political advantages of decentralization. Ironically, in proscribing the economic behavior of provincial governments these reforms have limited the political maneuverability of subnational governments and lessened their accountability to their local constituencies. By tightening budget constraints, a few of these reforms can be interpreted as improving the tie between politicians and voters, but taken as a whole, the reforms severely proscribed the policy choices available to provincial governments. The hardening of provincial budget constraints was important, but in many cases, they were hardened at the expense of the independent decision making of provincial authorities. Ever larger portions of provincial tax shares are being earmarked and withheld under conditions in which bankrupt (or nearly so) provincial governments have little choice but to negotiate away their own decision-making powers for short-term budgetary relief. In large measure, these hard budget constraints were imposed by a central government that held significant bargaining power over provincial governments suffering recurrent fiscal crises.

Thus, while Argentina is at least statistically more fiscally decentralized than ever, the significance of that decentralization is muted. Indeed, what has occurred is a centralization of decision making via the decentralization of increasingly conditionalized spending. There is no greater evidence of this than the painful and significant cuts in provincially provided health care and education: the very same services decentralized over recent decades at the behest of a national government that used various mechanisms to control the purse strings to achieve its macroeconomic aims. This is not the kind of decentralization that proponents, at least theoretically, have envisioned. To the extent that ever larger shares of provincial tax shares were withheld by the central government for reasons ranging from debt service to urban development, the autonomy and hence accountability of provincial governments to provincial citizens was severely compromised.

This is not to suggest that there were not benefits to the intergovernmental reforms of the Menem years. For a government as deeply tied to macroeconomic stability as Menem's, shrinking the policy space of subnational governments was a central feature of the nation's economic reform process. For a nation weary of hyperinflation and economic instability, that is no small reward. It does, however, suggest that the complementarity of decentralization, as traditionally theorized, and economic marketization is questionable under certain general conditions. Indeed, Argentina's experience suggests that the two, at times, present an unfortunate trade-off whereby more of one necessarily means less of the other.

The Argentine experience also suggests that the timing and nature of the decentralization process may have significant implications for the democratization/decentralization/market reform trade-off. It is becoming increasingly clear that in many countries that have initiated policies of decentralization, the primary goal driving the process has been the improvement of central government finances, not the enhancement of local accountability of service delivery. This was clearly the case with respect to Argentina's decentralization of education and health care in the early 1990s.[40] Given the importance of macroeconomic stability and IFI focus on the same, the current process of decentralization is likely to be hollow in nature as national governments increase pressure on subnational governments to spend in a manner consistent with national macroeconomic goals.

This sharp division between the spending goals of subnational and national governments is a related by-product of an ongoing decentralization process. As in Argentina, many national governments are increasingly focused on social security, defense, and debt service spending, while subnational governments are responsible for the delivery of basic social and economic services (Morduchowicz, 1996). As a result, one of the unforeseen products of decentralization is likely to be that subnational and national governments cannot identify with the responsibilities of each other. This is clearly the case in Argentina, where interviews suggest that the national Ministry of Economy is overwhelmingly preoccupied with the interest rates of bond issues and provincial budget cuts, while provincial politicians are overwhelmed with constituent demands for improved education and health care services. The divergence between these sets of priorities suggests that it may become even more difficult for decentralizing nations to achieve consensus on the competing demands of budgetary equilibrium and service delivery. It also underscores the importance of intergovernmental institutions such as party systems as mechanisms for coordinating and negotiating competing priorities.

PARTY SYSTEMS, DECENTRALIZATION, AND ARGENTINA IN COMPARATIVE PERSPECTIVE

Given the general characteristics likely to generate conflict between political and fiscal decentralization, it is unsurprising that Argentina's experience is not unique in the developing world. In nations as diverse as Brazil and Russia, processes of decentralization and intergovernmental fiscal institutions that foster subnational economic mismanagement have combined to undermine market-oriented reforms and generate problems of macroeconomic instability. In these and other cases, the role of intergovernmental partisan relations has been central to the negotiation (and at times exacerbation) of the decentralization dilemma outlined above.

The most obvious referent for Argentina is Brazil. During the 1980s and 1990s, Brazil struggled through stop-and-go periods of failed economic reform. The roots of these failed reforms were in no small measure the strength of state politicians relatively unconcerned with macroeconomic management (Dillinger and Webb, 1998) and with Brazil's extensive fiscal decentralization (Shah, 1991a; Bomfim and Shah, 1994). Both factors were institutionalized by the 1988 constitution, which decentralized significant fiscal resources to subnational governments while being rather vague on their responsibilities. In an electoral context that encouraged the dependence of federal legislatures on governors and local politicians (Samuels, 2003), recurrent bailouts of state debt by both the federal government and state-owned banks became the norm (Souza, 1997; Bomfim and Shah, 1994). Indeed, the key role of state debt and federal/state conflict in sparking Brazil's most recent economic crisis has been widely covered in the mainstream media.

Despite President Fernando Enrique Cardoso's commitment to macroeconomic stability, he has lacked one key ingredient when compared with Menem in Argentina: significant partisan leverage over governors. While Menem could rely on his position as head of the PJ to influence the majority of provinces governed by his party, Cardoso governed in an electoral system that fostered party system fragmentation and weak party discipline (Mainwaring, 1999). As a result, his party controlled few state governments and the lack of party discipline minimized his influence even within his own minority party. If the Argentine provinces had few incentives to restrain spending, the Brazilian states had even fewer, since the one politician with overarching concern for macroeconomic health has been significantly weaker than Menem. In many ways, Cardoso's political position vis-à-vis decentralized governments is similar to that of de la Rua, who had little leverage in the provinces. In both nations, however, the decentralization dilemma remains and tips to and fro with electoral outcomes.

CONCLUSION

In addition to contributing to our understanding of the costs and benefits of decentralization policies, democratization, and economic reform, a number of more general conclusions can be drawn from Argentina's experience. First, it suggests how vastly complicated fiscal decentralization can be. To date, most literature on the subject has emphasized technocratic solutions to intergovernmental problems by focusing on reforms of intergovernmental institutions, the creation of provincial planning and budget systems, and the development of decentralized financial action plans ("getting the rules right," as Montero and Samuels note in their introductory chapter). Such recommendations ignore the complicated political relationship among local politicians, local electorates, and the national government, particularly with respect to budgetary issues. The long-held maxim that local electorates will hold local governments accountable for overspending and overhiring is surely questionable under certain conditions. Where this is the case, fiscal decentralization becomes even more complicated as diverse levels of democratically elected governments may be asked to execute conflicting policies by their respective electorates. Since 1989 this appears to have been the case in Argentina, where voters in national elections have consistently voted in favor of macroeconomic stability, while in provincial elections they have voted for traditional, patronage-based politicians and roundly protested sound provincial reforms. To date, little research has explored the prospect for intransitive policy preferences across levels of government, though it is entirely plausible that citizens will exact different demands from different levels of government. As current policies of decentralization take hold, this will likely emerge as a crucial area of research in coming years. This research, consistent with Montero and Samuels' introductory chapter, clearly suggests that one of the most important areas to look for answers as to how these intergovernmental conflicts are negotiated is the party system.

Second, it is clear that decentralization can have a negative impact on macroeconomic stability and reform. The literature on economic adjustment has long ignored the role of subnational governments and institutions in the conditioning of free market reforms, focusing instead on the national and international levels of analysis. As Argentina's case makes clear, ignoring the role of subnational politics and economics in national economic adjustments has considerable costs. Particularly where decentralized governments control substantial portions of the public sector budget, there is considerable room for subnational politics to complicate fiscal and monetary policies. Insulated from the vagaries of international economic pressures and responding to local political demands, there are few reasons to expect subnational decision-makers to go along with national stabilization and adjustment policies absent strong partisan loyalties across levels of government. As Argentina's case suggests, the recent wave of market reform and decentralization is likely to lead to pressures for an acutely "centralizing decentralization," as central governments committed to macroeconomic stability attempt to curtail the political autonomy of subnational governments at the same time that they delegate expenditure responsibilities. How this dynamic plays out, of course, will depend a great deal on party system and electoral institutions.

Finally, this analysis of the Argentine situation suggests the significance of research on the distinct nature of decentralization in federal systems. To date, much of the international lending community and researchers of decentralization (both political and economic) have failed to account for major differences between federal and unitary systems. As outlined above, the conditions that drove the logics of decentralization and macroeconomic stability to conflict so plainly in Argentina are most likely to exist in federal systems. The Argentine case suggests that the design of federalism is both subject to change and has considerable influence on the economic motives of subnational governments. It also suggests, however, that balancing the goals of decentralized democratic accountability and macroeconomic stability is extremely difficult. While systematic research has been scarce, preliminary evidence exists that decentralized spending by state governments in the federations of Brazil, India, Pakistan, Nigeria, Russia, and Mexico have all contributed, at times substantially so, to macroeconomic problems. This raises a series of crucial questions for future research: Do federal institutions encourage structural economic difficulties? What sets of federal arrangements are most conducive to macroeconomic stability and/or decentralization? Under what conditions, if any at all, can decentralization contribute successfully to both democratization and economic reform in a federal context? Given the size and importance of the federal nations throughout the developing world, the answers to these questions are of general importance for the sustainability of democracy and economic stability.

NOTES

This research was supported by grants from the National Science Foundation (SBR-9809211) and the Latin American Institute of the University of New Mexico's NAFTA/MERCOSUR Program. I thank the editors and the anonymous reviewers for their comments on earlier drafts.

1. For a strong exception, see Treisman (1999).

2. This assumption is also widely shared in the social movements literature. See Escobar and Alvarez (1992), Eckstein (1989), and Morris and Mueller (1992).

3. This results from the simple fact that market pressures are less prevalent at decentralized levels of government in developing nations, where local officials rarely have access to freely functioning capital markets.

4. On the likelihood that patronage-based politics will be more prevalent at decentralized levels of government, see Prud'homme (1995) and Falleti (1999).

5. On the scope of provincial protests, see *Latin American Weekly Report,* June 15, 1995, p. 260; July 6, 1995, p. 323; October 5, 1995, p. 456; October 19, 1995, p. 1; May 13, 1997, p. 217.

6. On the Brazilian case, see Shah (1994) and Souza (1997). On Argentina, see Remmer and Wibbels (2000), Sanguinetti and Tommasi (1996), and World Bank (1996b). On India, see World Bank (1996c). On China, see Huang (1996). On Mexico, see Ter-Minassian (1997).

7. The two measures of fiscal decentralization were the share of state and local governments in total government spending and the extent to which subnational governments were self-financing.

8. Article 75 of the Argentine Constitution was rewritten in 1994 and now requires legislative approval for intervention in provincial governments. See Hernández (1997: 42–44).

9. On the importance of provincial politics in determining provincial candidates, see Eaton (1998) and Levitsky (1999). Own party opposition to Menem policies has taken place most recently and consistently in Santa Cruz where the PJ governor Néstor Kirchner has insistently resisted President Menem's efforts to impose provincial economic adjustment in response to the Asian financial crisis. More recently, Kirchner actively criticized the PJ presidential campaign of Eduardo Duhalde. See *La Nación,* "Kirchner renegó de su apoyo a Duhalde y criticó la campaña," August 28, 1999. This division was confirmed in an interview with Sr. Raul Romero, Director de Gestión y Economía, Casa de Santa Cruz.

10. Note that this was a simple means for provincial governments to export their debt to the national government.

11. In theory, international borrowing by provincial governments is constrained by the necessity to receive approval from the national Chamber of Deputies. For all intents and purposes, however, this has not been a serious obstacle. Furthermore, unlike most U.S. states, Argentina's provinces do not have state laws requiring balanced budgets. See Sanguinetti and Tommasi (1996).

12. The provinces that have resorted to printing provincial script in the past include Buenos Aires, Salta, Jujuy, Catamarca, Tucumán, and La Rioja. See *La Gaceta,* "Hubo sesión, pero se paga con cheques diferidos," September 8, 1998, p. 1; *Ambito Financero,* "Hoy pagan a estatales con cheques diferidos," September 15, 1998, p. 9. This occurred most recently in Buenos Aires, where the provincial government issued the *patacón* to pay public employees and suppliers. See *Wall Street Journal,* "An Argentine Province, Fresh Out of Cash, Pushes an Alternative," August 21, 2001.

13. International Monetary Fund, *Government Finance Statistics Yearbook* (1997).

14. On Argentina's series of stabilization plans in the 1980s, see Smith, Acuña, and Gamarra (1994).

15. Data from Canitrot (1994) and IMF, *International Financial Statistics* (1997).

16. From 1983 through 1987, the Alfonsín administration controlled fewer than one-third of all provincial governorships. After the elections of 1987, the *Unión Civica Radical* (UCR) controlled few than 15 percent.

17. See the *Wall Street Journal,* "Argentina, Land of Loose Fiscal Cannons," March 2, 2001.

18. The centrality of the nation's macroeconomic project in the national government's effort to reform intergovernmental political and fiscal relations was confirmed in an interview with Juan Antonio Zapata (May 11, 1999), National

Subsecretary of Provincial Affairs from 1991 to 1994 and the chief negotiator for the nation in the two major reforms known as the Fiscal Pacts.

19. For details on the de la Rua adminstration's plan for provincial bailouts, see *La Nación,* "1400 millones para las provincias," January 13, 2000, p. 4.

20. The most obvious example of this is Córdoba's refusal to sign the fiscal pacts, which are outlined below. As a result, the province chose to forego the negotiated minimum transfers to the provinces during the 1995 "tequila crisis." In an overwhelming fiscal crisis, the province signed the pact in early 1996.

21. For the actual language of these reforms, see Ministry of Economy (MECON) (1994: 103–23).

22. On the coparticipation law, see World Bank (1998).

23. *Ley de Transferencia de Servicios,* No. 24049. See MECON (1994: 98–102).

24. See CECE (1997). For more recent coverage of ATNs, see *La Nación,* "Critica la Alianza el uso de ATN," September 12, 1998, p. 6; *Clarin,* "Senado: una polémica millonaria," April 11, 1999, p. 11.

25. This issue was a point of criticism particularly among UCR partisans in Córdoba and Rio Negro, two provinces governed by the opposition. Interviews with Norberto R. Bergami, President of the Economic Commission of the Cámara de Diputados of the Province of Córdoba (March 22, 1999) and Ricardo Gutierez, provincial legislature, Province of Rio Negro (June 15, 1999).

26. See *La Gaceta,* "El gobierno pedirá ayuda a la Nación," September 3, 1998, p. 12; *La Gaceta,* "Encuentros y compromisos para el acuerdo," September 13, 1998, p. 15.

27. The one exception is Rio Negro, a UCR-governed province, which received both subsidized loans and a bailout of its pension fund. Consistent with the other cases, however, conditionality was placed on the province that implied a provincial acceptance of the nationally defined priorities regarding spending cuts and spending priorities. This point was confirmed in interviews with Lic. Nestor A. Rozados, Budget Subsecretary of the Province of Rio Negro (June 9, 1999), and Lic. Roberto Meschini, chief economic advisor to the PJ in Rio Negro (June 8 and 10, 1999).

28. See Sanguinetti (1999) on the BOTESO 10 bond issue, which the central government used to bail out select provinces.

29. See *Ambito Financiero,* "Nación gastará en Córdoba 100 millones menos el año próximo," September 16, 1998, p. 6; *La voz del interior,* "Fernández apura la ley de presupuesto," September 14, 1998, p. 12a; *Rio Negro,* "Recortarán obras en las provincias por la crisis," September 11, 1998, p. 29.

30. *Rio Negro,* "A ajustar las expectativas," September 11, 1998, p. 29.

31. *La Nación,* "Acuerdos secretos con las provincias," June 8, 2000, p. 4.

32. Interview with provincial fiscal bureaucrat (May 28, 1999).

33. Córdoba, Buenos Aires, and La Rioja are the only three provinces which have not privatized their provincially owned banks. See *La voz del interior,* "Pasó la época de privatizar," September 14, 1998, p. 8.

34. *Rio Negro,* "La Nación seguirá de cerca las cuentas provinciales," September 20, 1998, pp. 6–7.

35. On the most recent set of protests in Tucumán, Chaco, Neuquén, Corrientes, and Buenos Aires, see *La Nación,* "Otra jornada marcada por las protestas," August 20, 1999, p. 5.

36. Interview with an economist in the Subsecretary of Fiscal and Economic Relations with the Provinces, MECON.

37. In response to a question on what their province had done to counter national pressure for reform, all but four answered with some variant of "nothing." In two of the other four cases, there were general references to the federal nature of the constitution, though subsequent questions about the real nature of intergovernmental politics led to similar conclusions. Only at the provincial offices of Mendoza and Córdoba was it suggested that the national government had economic and political considerations in these provinces that could be used by their governments as negotiating chips.

38. The reforms sought by the de la Rua administration included a five-year freeze on provincial spending, an agreement to cap tax transfers from the center to the provinces, and a commitment to reduce provincial deficits.

39. Preliminary reports put the 1999 provincial deficit at $3.7 billion. See *La Nación,* "1400 millones para las provincias," January 13, 2000.

40. Debate of the decentralization law in Congress reflected a profound recognition of this point by opposition representatives. See *Diario de Sessiones,* November 28, 1991.

CHAPTER 9

Political Incentives and Intergovernmental Fiscal Relations

Argentina, Brazil, and Mexico Compared

STEPHAN HAGGARD & STEVEN B. WEBB

The early analysis of fiscal federalism focused on the static efficiency gains from decentralization (Tiebout, 1956). Recent work by Barry Weingast and his collaborators has emphasized the *incentive effects* of federalism: how intergovernmental fiscal relations affect the behavior of different levels of government (Weingast, 1995; Montinola, Qian, and Weingast, 1995; Jin, Qian, and Weingast, 1999). This line of argument suggests that under an important but restrictive set of conditions, decentralization can provide powerful incentives for good policy. However, an important limitation to the incentive-based approach is that it assumes a "good" intergovernmental fiscal contract and focuses its attention on the policy and economic outcomes that flow from it (see the chapters by Wibbels and by Beer in this volume for more on this point).

Federal contracts that result in changes in centralization or decentralization themselves result from highly politicized processes, and such bargains may result in poorly designed federal arrangements, which in turn generate a variety of undesirable outcomes, from severe macroeconomic imbalances and low growth to poor delivery of services, corruption, and inequity across jurisdictions (Tanzi, 1995; Prud'homme, 1995; Fukasaku and de Mello, 1997; Fornasari, Webb, and Zou, 1998). This chapter shows how *political* incentives affect, and cause problems in, the intergovernmental fiscal contracts and institutions of Latin America's three largest federations: Argentina,[1] Brazil, and Mexico.

The framework for the political analysis of fiscal federalism begins with the assumption that intergovernmental fiscal contracts result from bargains among politicians at different levels of government. These bargains occur along two axes. The "horizontal" politics of fiscal federalism concerns how resources are allocated across subnational governments and legislative districts.[2] The "vertical" politics of fiscal federalism, on which we focus here, concerns the powers assigned and resources allocated to different levels of government. A variety of problems may emerge in this vertical relationship, but we focus on two. The first problem, and the one that has commanded most attention from advocates of federalism, is excessive centralism. This occurs when the center commands a disproportionate share of aggregate government revenues and spending, exercises strong influence over the behavior of subnational units, and thus dampens the incentives for good policy and innovation that federalism is supposed to unleash. Recent developments in Latin America and the former Soviet republics have called attention to the second problem, which arises when the center is too weak. In these circumstances, the central government has inadequate resources and lacks the ability to check state and local governments, resulting in subnational looting of the center, fiscal crises, problems of moral hazard, and poor provision of services.[3]

Two closely related factors help explain a nation's proclivity toward one or the other of these two pathologies. The first is the extent of legislative and, in some systems, gubernatorial support that the president enjoys. Presidents with strong legislative support are more likely to be able to rewrite the intergovernmental fiscal rules in their favor, although in part by crafting horizontal bargains that redistribute resources at the margin to their co-partisans or needed coalition partners (see Wibbels, this volume). By contrast, presidents who lack such support—either because of enduring features of the party system, such as its fragmentation, or because of divided government—face stronger decentralizing pressures and greater problems in controlling governors and mayors. Second, the effects of both unified and divided government on presidents' capacity to alter intergovernmental relations also depend on the lines of accountability between politicians at different levels of the political system (Willis, Garman, and Haggard, 1999; Garman, Haggard, and Willis, 2001; Samuels, 2003). Where parties are disciplined and legislators are responsive to the president and national party leadership, both the political and fiscal systems run the risk of overcentralization of power. In contrast, if legislators depend on governors and mayors to advance their political careers, decentralization is more likely to be premature, excessive, and poorly designed. These two interrelated factors help explain a great deal about the dynamics of intergovernmental relations in federal systems and can help us understand how and why pathologies emerge in federal contracts.

In the first section we provide an overview of the way intergovernmental fiscal contracts have evolved over the last two decades in Argentina, Brazil, and Mexico. To do so, we disaggregate the intergovernmental fiscal bargain into four key components: (1) the allocation of taxing powers and associated revenue-sharing agreements; (2) the assignment of spending responsibilities; (3) the rules governing subnational borrowing, as well as the means for dealing with subnational debt crises; and (4) discretionary transfers. In the second section we outline the political factors relevant for understanding these developments. The subsequent sections provide more detailed analysis on each of the four components of the fiscal contract. Each section has two objectives: to highlight the political incentives for intergovernmental bargaining in each issue area and to explain the variations we see in the three major Latin American federations. Ultimately, this exploration should serve to illuminate the political roots of important problems in intergovernmental fiscal relations that tend to impede any potential efficiency gains from decentralization.

The Changing Fiscal Contract in Mexico, Argentina, and Brazil

Taxing powers and spending responsibilities could be allocated so that subnational governments spend only as much as they raise in taxes, represented by point A in Figure 9.1.

Figure 9.1. Subnational Finances

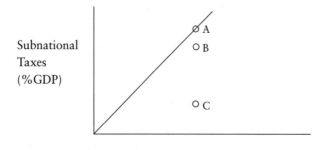

Subnational Spending (%GDP)

Some proponents of federalism suggest that such a system, with no intergovernmental fiscal transfers and no borrowing, provides the strongest incentives for subnational tax effort and, if credible, would eliminate problems of moral hazard. For efficiency as well as for political reasons, subnational spending in practice exceeds subnational taxing power,[4] as at points B or C. The vertical imbalance can be covered either through borrowing (temporarily) or transfers from the center. Transfers take many forms: revenue-sharing agreements between the central government and the states; transfers earmarked for particular purposes; bailouts to subnational governments; and discretionary transfers controlled by the president, bureaucracy, or legislature.

Figure 9.2 shows the movements of the three big Latin American federations in this space during the 1990s. The three states have quite different starting points, with Brazil more decentralized than Argentina and Mexico in both dimensions. With respect to taxing powers, the country that started out with the greatest dependence on the center for resources— Mexico—has also done the least to raise subnational revenue, implying an ongoing and substantial role for central-government transfers.

Argentina has politically negotiated revenue-sharing coefficients that are difficult to change because of the requirement that they be approved by the president, Congress, and all of the provinces. In Brazil, the hands of the central government are even more tightly bound by a politically negotiated formula written directly into the 1988 constitution.

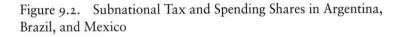

Figure 9.2.   Subnational Tax and Spending Shares in Argentina, Brazil, and Mexico

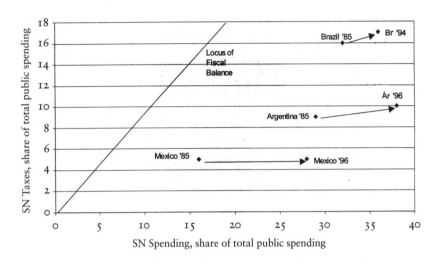

Source: IMF, *Government Financial Statistics;* World Bank estimates.

In contrast to the pattern with taxation, the share of public spending by subnational governments has converged. Decentralization by this measure has increased the most in Mexico, the country that was historically most centralized. Argentina has devolved enough tax authority to the provinces to cover a substantial part of their own spending at the margin and has limited unfunded mandates. In Brazil, the devolution of responsibilities has been the most chaotic, and the clear transfer of responsibilities has not matched the transfer of resources.

Regarding the rules governing subnational borrowing, Mexico historically has been the most conservative. In the 1990s, state and municipal debt was equivalent to approximately 2 percent of Mexico's GDP, compared to 5 percent of GDP in Argentina and above 20 percent in Brazil. Nonetheless, Mexico did not altogether escape subnational debt crises in the 1990s. Argentina had a history of debilitating subnational debt crises and bailouts in the 1980s. The national government imposed a relatively hard budget constraint after 1990, but faced a new round of subnational debt problems in 2000–2001 (see Wibbels, this volume).

Brazil up through the late 1990s is a textbook case of how to mismanage subnational borrowing: ex ante controls were blatantly evaded, the central government assumed virtually all state debt when crises hit, ceilings on debt service to the federal government were weak, capitalization of shortfalls in repayment continued, and serial renegotiations of bailout agreements routinely favored the states (Dillinger, 1997; Dillinger and Webb, 1998; Gómez, 2000).

The final element of the intergovernmental fiscal contract consists of discretionary transfers that are not associated either with revenue-sharing arrangements, earmarking for specific responsibilities, or bailouts.[5] For most of its history, the Mexican executive exercised wide-ranging discretion of this sort, but since the mid-1990s it has given up almost all discretionary transfers. The Argentine executive has some discretionary transfers at his disposal, but their scope is tightly circumscribed. In Brazil the executive controls virtually no cash transfers.

THE POLITICAL ECONOMY OF FISCAL FEDERALISM

The basic political structures of the three countries under consideration are discussed in more detail elsewhere in this volume. This section focuses on a few characteristics and political developments that are germane for our subsequent analysis, namely, the extent of legislative and gubernatorial support the president enjoys and the extent to which party politicians, particularly national-level legislators, are more or less accountable to subnational politicians. Our overall characterizations of the three political systems will not surprise any student of Latin American politics. Of the three countries, Mexico's political system has historically been the most centralized, although this changed rapidly over the 1990s (see Beer, this volume). Brazil and Argentina, by contrast, have relatively weaker central presidents and national legislatures and more powerful subnational governments (see Samuels on Brazil and Eaton and Wibbels on Argentina, this volume). These problems appear to be a more constant feature of the political landscape in Brazil than in Argentina, where the Menem government periodically enjoyed quite substantial legislative, party, and even gubernatorial support for reform initiatives, including those in the intergovernmental fiscal system.

In Mexico, the president and the Institutional Revolutionary Party (PRI) traditionally dominated the political system from the center. The system became much more competitive in the 1990s: Mexico witnessed, in quick succession, a highly competitive presidential and congressional election in 1988, followed by the election of the first non-PRI governors in 1989, the PRI's loss of its lower house majority in 1997, and its loss of the presidency and the Senate majority in 2000. We would expect these political changes to be accompanied by shifts in the vertical distribution of resources and powers and increasing limits on presidential discretion, particularly following the emergence of divided government after 1997.

Brazil's political system is in all respects more fragmented than Mexico's (Ames, 1995a, 1995b, 1998, 2001). The effective number of parties is higher and the president must construct a multiparty coalition to obtain a majority in both houses of the legislature, as well as deal with governors from a variety of parties. Furthermore, legislative coalitions shift, and politicians change party affiliations quite often (Mainwaring, 1999). These fissiparous tendencies in the political system were reflected in the constitutional convention of 1988. Sitting legislators, many of whom had strong ties to subnational governments, fundamentally rewrote the intergovernmental fiscal compact and delegated substantial resources to subnational governments but surprisingly few specific responsibilities.

Argentina sits between these two extremes, or more accurately, has oscillated between them. In the late Alfonsín period, the country experienced debilitating problems of divided government, during which provincial parties and leaders were able to blackmail the central government in a variety of ways. This situation was partly reversed during the Menem years when the president commanded broad legislative support for his initiatives, including ones that partly restored presidential power.

The powers of the president in each country are only partly determined by the strength of legislative and gubernatorial support. Even when such support is high and when legislative coalitions are cohesive, ruling parties may be subject to strong pulls from the subnational level. A number of features of the political system influence whether lines of authority and accountability within parties favor national or subnational politicians, such as control over campaign finance or the timing of elections. Table 9.1 summarizes two variables for Argentina, Brazil, and Mexico that reflect broader features of the degree of centralization in their political systems (Garman, Haggard, and Willis, 2001): control over nomination and the type of electoral system for the national legislature.[6]

Table 9.1.   Nomination Control and Electoral System in
Argentina, Brazil, and Mexico

	Nomination Control	Electoral System (Lower House)
Argentina	**Subnational** Both major parties use internal primaries for assembly elections at the provincial level.	**Closed List/Mixed Control** Provincial party leaders determine the rank order of the party list, but national party leaders can intervene in provincial party organizations or place the alternative national party list to a vote with the provincial list determined by rank and file.
Brazil	**Subnational** All parties hold municipal, state, and national conventions with each level nominating delegates to its superior convention. State conventions nominate candidates for congressional and Senate races, and national conventions nominate candidates only for presidential contests. Governors exert substantial influence in state conventions.	**Open List/Subnational Coalitions** Candidates employ personal vote strategies through making political alliances with subnational executives.
Mexico	**National** For PRI, control is historically highly centralized in party leadership and president. Party leadership also important in PRD and PAN, but with some use of conventions (PAN) and primaries (PRD) emerging.	**Closed List/SMD**

As the table suggests, Mexico's party system has been more centralized on these dimensions than either Argentina's or, in particular, Brazil's. The authority of the Mexican president long rested not on formal constitutional powers but on the hierarchical structure of the PRI and the dependence of politicians at lower levels of government on the president for nominations, finance, and ultimately career advancement. As true electoral competition has begun to emerge at all levels of government, the federal nature of the constitution has become more evident. How the system will operate in equilibrium remains to be seen. In Brazil the fragmentation of the party system is paralleled by internally weak parties that can not claim lasting allegiance even of elected leaders. National legislators depend heavily on state and municipal politicians, in part because legislators have ambitions to become governors and even state ministers or mayors (Ames, 1998; Samuels, 2003). Governors and state party leaders influence nominations and thus the careers of the national legislators. Argentina is again an intermediate case: provincial political leaders do have influence within the party organizations, but this influence is balanced by stronger party leadership and partisan discipline than is possible in Brazil.

TAX ASSIGNMENT AND REVENUE SHARING

As a first step in demonstrating the effects of these political arrangements, this section analyzes tax assignment and revenue-sharing transfers. What are the political concerns of politicians at different levels of government in this issue area? In the first instance, politicians in the central government want to retain adequate tax authority to cover their expenses. The total share of revenue passed to the states cannot be too large. The federal government will seek to retain some taxes that it can increase without having to share them in ways that subvert the conduct of fiscal policy. A second concern centers on the behavior of subnational governments. If subnational governments come to depend heavily on transfers, they will tend to avoid difficult political decisions about raising their own revenues.

Politicians in the central government are also concerned about ensuring that subnational governments treat the funding they receive from transfers with the same care and accountability that they treat resources raised from local taxpayers.[7] The key step in this regard is to set hard budget constraints on the amount of transfers to states, which also supports the center's concerns with respect to the control of borrowing. A final concern of politicians at the center is procedural: the political process should permit adjustment of revenue-sharing allocations to take account of changes in the geographic distribution of needs and fiscal capacity, and of the president's changing political needs as well.

State politicians are similarly concerned that they have adequate tax authority: that they can levy taxes and that the rates at the center leave adequate "tax room" to raise revenue without creating an excessive overall tax burden. When tax collection is ceded upward, states are also concerned that the central government will credibly distribute the revenue that the states view as theirs by right. State politicians, therefore, have an interest in ensuring that the agencies that actually "write the checks" are independent and implement the pact as negotiated, without influence from the president or Congress.

The final concerns at the state level are distributional. Politicians in poor states (low tax base per capita) wish to redistribute the nation's tax resources their way. Those in richer states, by contrast, typically seek formulae that closely reflect their existing tax base or population and limit the redistributive component to poorer states. *Ceteris paribus,* decision-making processes that favor poorer states, whether because of the composition of legislative coalitions or because of more enduring factors such as unequal congressional representation per capita, should result in more redistribution and greater equality in total revenues per capita.

The three Latin American federations vary quite noticeably in the distribution of taxing powers and the nature of revenue-sharing agreements. Table 9.2 provides an overview. The share of subnational spending covered by transfers is the lowest in Brazil, but the share of unconditional transfers is also highest there. In Mexico the reverse holds; subnational governments are still heavily dependent on transfers and more of those transfers have historically been conditional (although that has been changing). Argentina represents an intermediate case and one that has been subject to swings in both directions.

Mexico

The central government has historically dominated taxing and spending in Mexico to a greater extent than in either Argentina or Brazil. Rather than states collecting revenue they shared with the federal level, the federal level dominated the collection of revenue, which it then shared with the states. The key tool at the central government's disposal was oil revenue. The federal government's exclusive control over the taxation of

Table 9.2. Tax Assignment and Revenue Sharing in Argentina, Brazil, and Mexico

Variable	Argentina	Brazil	Mexico
Reallocation of tax bases	1930s. States gave up most existing taxes to the federal government in return for shares of revenue, defined in Ley de Coparticipación; revision requires unanimous approval of states, as well as of president and Congress. (States can unilaterally withdraw?)	Pre-1988, states had VAT on a limited base. 1988 constitution reduced federal tax base and expanded the base of state VATs.	1980 Fiscal Pact. States relinquish sales and business taxes to federal level. States retain option to withdraw from the pact each year.
Revenue sharing	1984–87. Ad hoc transfers after lapse of Copar law. 1988–present. New Copar Law; repeated delay of scheduled revision of allocation formula. 1992–93. Fiscal pacts reduce share of states in exchange for nominal floors.	1988 constitution reset the sharing formulas, increasing the shares that federal and state levels transferred to municipalities. Federal transfers to the states stayed roughly constant, as the formula changed somewhat to offset reallocations of the tax base.	1980 Fiscal Pact. In exchange for ceding almost all of their constitutional portion of tax base to the federal level, states get shares of most federal taxes and royalties. Revisions of formula continued up to 1990, making almost half of the transfer equal per capita.
All transfers as a share of subnational spending	Average 74% in 1985 to 41% in 1995, but varied: less than half in Buenos Aries province and almost all in low-population states	Average 37%, but wide variance: almost nothing in São Paulo; almost all in Amazon states (states outside the south get 85% of revenue sharing).	Average 75%; none more than 15% (except in Federal District).
Share of transfers from unconditional revenue sharing	72% in 1991; 57% in 1997 as special funds have grown	Over 90%, as set in 1988 constitution.	Prior to 1993, over 1/2; growth of earmarked transfers since then reduced relative importance of revenue sharing to about half in 1998 and less since then.

natural resources and the direct control of the oil industry through a state-owned enterprise produced huge revenue windfalls, from which most states did not benefit. In 1980 the government created a single consolidated National System of Fiscal Coordination (SNCF). The SNCF offered the opportunity for state governments to reap part of the benefits of the oil boom. However, this also meant that they would remain dependent on transfers from the central government. Thus, although by the late 1990s subnational governments in Mexico accounted for about a third of public spending—equal to 6 percent of GDP—they still collected less than 5 percent of all public revenues. Federal transfers could cover over 90 percent of state and local spending.[8] Unconditional transfers (i.e., those the central government *must* transfer) accounted for about half of these total transfers, while the remainder were earmarked and set in annual legislation. The share of unconditional revenue-sharing transfers in total transfers is low when compared to Argentina and Brazil, suggesting the ongoing dominance of central government.

Increased political competition in the 1990s generated mixed pressures on the system of transfers. On the one hand, the central government's interest in using the revenue-sharing system to help its co-partisans increased, particularly in the poorer states, where the PRI controlled a larger share of the subnational governments.[9] At the same time, changed economic and political circumstances also led some opposition leaders at the subnational level—including the mayor of the Federal District in 1998 and the governor of Nuevo León in 1999—to threaten to withdraw from the system. This threat had some credibility because state officials play an important role in the enforcement of federal taxes. If one state with a strong tax base stopped enforcing federal taxes and focused on its own taxes, then the same strategy would become more attractive to other states with strong bases, and the system could weaken to the point that a majority in Congress could favor wholesale revision.

At the end of 1999, non-PRI governors—by then a majority—began to demand a revision of the Fiscal Pact (see Beer, this volume). These demands filtered through Congress, where the PRI lost its outright majority in the lower house in 1997 and in the Senate in 2000. Congress put a program of ad hoc grants to states into the 2000 budget—with grants allocated by Congress rather than by formula—and doubled the size of the program in the 2001 budget. This congressional action put pressure on the executive branch for a comprehensive fiscal reform that would be more favorable to the states.

Argentina

Argentina exhibits a number of differences with Mexico in terms of taxing and revenue sharing. Subnational governments conduct a higher share of total public spending—almost 40 percent of all public sector spending or 10 percent of GDP—and raise 22 percent of public revenue. Provinces raised over 40 percent of their total revenues in the mid-1990s, up about 5 percentage points from 1991.[10] Also, the provincial share of federal revenues is theirs by law, and the federal government has little discretion in determining the amount or distribution of transferred funds.[11] Argentina has a higher share of total transfers in the form of unconditional revenue sharing than Mexico—nearly three-fifths of the total.

The transfer of tax bases from the provinces to the federal government and the establishment of a revenue-sharing arrangement (*coparticipaciones*) took place following the fiscal crises of the 1930s and gradually covered a wider number and broader pool of tax revenues over time (see Eaton, this volume; Dillinger and Webb, 1998).[12] Following the return of democracy in 1983, the new government was unable to pass a new Coparticipation Law, and the system began to rely on block transfers (*Aportes de Tesores Nacionales,* or ATNs). These transfers, in turn, created strong incentives for governors and legislators to hold their cooperation with the government hostage to still larger transfers. After the Peronist Party gained control of Congress and seventeen of twenty-two governorships, they forced the president to accept a new Coparticipation Law in 1988, which reflected the vertical and horizontal balances of power at the time. Any modification of this law requires not only congressional and presidential approval, but also approval by all the provincial legislatures. Consequently, it has proven impossible to revise the horizontal allocation, which was set according to political criteria. The law increased the provinces' aggregate share in national revenue, but it did not redress horizontal inequities or provide for adjustments as the size and economic status of provinces evolved.

In the midst of hyperinflation in 1989, the Peronist candidate Carlos Menem won the presidential election. In 1991 he exploited the crisis and strong support in both houses to initiate a wide-ranging stabilization program. The success of the stabilization generated a rapid and unexpected increase in provincial revenues, which facilitated new fiscal agreements to be reached in 1992–94. The agreements reduced the *share* of resources going to the provinces as a group and increased the responsibilities that went with the transfers. But no province was willing to accept any decrease of its share, and they all insisted on compensation in the form of a guarantee of no absolute reduction of transfers in nominal terms. The first agreement in 1992 (Pacto Fiscal I) diverted 15 percent of coparticipation funds to help pay for reform of the national social security system and shifted important responsibilities in both health and education to the provinces. A second fiscal pact in 1993 began the process of transferring the management of pensions from the provinces to the federal government (see Wibbels in this volume for details).

To reach the first pact, the president used other transfers as well as the reform itself to put together a coalition that spanned both houses: Buenos Aires province for its weight in the Chamber of Deputies and the low-population provinces for their weight in the Senate. A new *Fondo Conurbano* helped secure the support of legislators from Buenos Aires and partially offset the lower-than-average per capita funding that the province received with *coparticipaciones*. The small provinces received discretionary transfers that were high per capita. Because of their low population and high representation per capita, small provinces were inexpensive places to buy support in the Chamber of Deputies and especially the Senate (Gibson, 1997a).

The issue of revising the formula for allocating revenue-sharing arrangements arose again in 1999–2000. A program of debt rescheduling agreements, outlined in more detail below, was linked with another effective cut in the total pool of resources for coparticipation to the provinces, and yet another promise to revise the coparticipation formula in the near future. Again, part of the price for the deal was to guarantee a nominal floor on coparticipation funds, at the average of the 1998–99 level for 2000, rising by 1 percent for 2001–2, and then almost 3 percent per year thereafter. Like the deal in the early 1990s, this floor was expected to benefit the federal government (relative to the old rule) as the economy recovered. When the economic and fiscal recession worsened, however, it became increasingly costly to the federal level. The guarantee of the early 1990s was a safety net, whereas the guarantees in the 1999 and 2000 agreements put heavy pressure on federal government finances in 2001.

Argentina thus exhibits a back-and-forth pattern in the relative political influence of the two main levels of government. When government was divided in the late Alfonsín period, the provinces gained leverage and locked in both more resources and a fixed horizontal distribution. When the Peronists unified and won the presidency, the center gained leverage. Horizontal rationalization of the revenue-sharing formula was not possible because of the unanimity rule for the *ley de convenio,* a reflection of the continuing power of the provinces. When Radical president de la Rua took office in 1999, he faced a majority of opposition governors and then lost control of Congress when one party left his coalition. He had to bargain from a position of political weakness, for which he paid dearly during the financial debacle of late 2001. To extract any long-term bargain with respect to revenue sharing, the federal government exploited the short-term credit constraints of the provinces and promised debt relief in exchange for fiscal adjustment.[13]

Brazil

In Brazil, subnational governments undertake 42 percent of public spending, or 11 percent of GDP, roughly equal to the provincial share in Argentina. But they raise over 30 percent of public revenue, the highest of the three federations. Federal transfers account for only 30 percent of total state and local revenue, and almost three-fifths of this is unconditional revenue sharing. Brazil also differs in having the widest variation in the dependence of states on federal revenue sharing and other transfers. São Paulo receives essentially nothing from revenue sharing, while poorer and smaller states receive a majority of their income from the transfers, a few over 90 percent.

Brazil has always been highly decentralized and does not have a history of fiscal pacts under which states cede tax authority to the center in exchange for revenue sharing. Even under military rule, states continued to enjoy substantial fiscal independence. In fact, the military was responsible for the country's current system of revenue sharing, which ensures that states—particularly the poor states of the northeast—have a large and buoyant revenue source. In 1968, the states received the value-added tax (ICMS), the highest yielding non–social security tax in the country. In the large and wealthy states of the southeast, the ICMS is the principal source of state revenue and gives states an independent fiscal base.

For the smaller and poorer states of the northeast and interior, however, the ICMS does not yield anywhere near enough revenue to give them fiscal independence. In return for the ICMS, and because they were given little choice, the richer states agreed to strongly redistributive intergovernmental transfers. The formula shows the nature of the political bargain: 85 percent of the transfer fund is distributed to the states of the north, northeast, and center-west regions, and only 15 percent to the states of the south and southeast; the richest state, São Paulo, receives virtually nothing.[14]

The 1988 constitution also gave exceptionally favorable treatment to municipal governments. In addition to the assignment of several taxes, the municipalities also secured a fixed share of the federal income and industrial product taxes (22.5 percent, channeled through the *Fundo de Participão dos Municipios*). Twelve percent of this goes to state capitals, while the remainder is allocated to other *municipios* using a formula that favors less-populated areas. Moreover, state governments are also required by the constitution to share their ICMS revenues with the municipalities.

As Samuels demonstrates in this volume (chapter 3), the origins of this system cannot be traced to democratization alone: the pattern of favoring states and municipalities also began in the late military period as the government sought to build a political base that would survive the transition to democratic rule. Nonetheless, there can be little doubt that the nature of the electoral and party system was an important factor in this highly decentralized outcome. This system resulted both from the underrepresentation of the richer states in the convention that wrote the 1988 constitution, and more basically, from the increasing influence of municipal politicians in the electoral and career strategies of both governors and national legislators (Samuels, 2003).

The Political Economy of Tax Assignment and Revenue Sharing

All three countries have developed revenue-sharing systems that provide states with approximately enough resources to carry out their spending responsibilities, although Mexican states appear to be somewhat underfunded relative to their mandates and Brazilian states somewhat overfunded. The politics of revenue sharing have resulted in additional incentive problems that are not captured by the size of the aggregate vertical imbalance. The cases show, first, that while it is a mistake to have all taxes controlled by the center, incentive problems also arise if all taxes are shared. The transfer systems in all three countries leave many states and municipalities almost entirely dependent on federal money rather than local taxes; this is true in Mexico because of centralist tendencies that remained strong until quite recently, and in Argentina and Brazil because of payoffs to the smaller states (and in Brazil, to municipalities). As a result—and this is a second disability—the allocation of revenue-sharing transfers does not conform to any clear normative principle. Instead, revenue transfers are neither equal nor targeted to poor states but rather follow explicitly political principles of distribution. As a result, revenue-sharing arrangements are viewed as so onerous and unfair that states seek ways to opt out or subvert the federal fiscal system. Third, there are no adequate mechanisms to deal with fluctuations in the tax base for revenue sharing. State governments are too often credit-constrained and lack flexible tax-revenue bases of their own.

More importantly, the political nature of the institutions and procedures surrounding the allocation of taxing power and revenue sharing makes it extremely difficult to revise them, particularly in Argentina and Brazil. Mexico is a partial exception in that revenue sharing is defined in ordinary laws that can be changed to allow for evolution over time. But it may emerge that Mexican states have nearly as much leverage over the center as Brazilian ones, particularly with the emergence of "vertically divided" government (see Beer, this volume, for more on this argument).

SPENDING ASSIGNMENT: THE ALLOCATION OF POLICY RESPONSIBILITIES

The advantages of fiscal federalism reside in the appropriate assignment of spending decisions as well as taxing powers. Central governments are concerned that states fulfill the responsibilities associated with any tax authority and transfers. An ambiguous or poorly shared division of responsibilities can leave central government ministries responsible for the provision of a given service but with resources that are diminished by the amount of transfers. Central governments are also concerned with the performance of subnational governments in carrying out assigned duties. A common pattern is for incumbent governments to suffer political damage when the initiation of decentralization leads, at least in the short term, to a deterioration rather than improvement in the quality of services. To attenuate these short-term political costs, central governments typically seek to enforce the new vertical contract over the allocation of spending responsibilities during the transition by tying transfers to particular purposes and monitoring their use. Where the center is strong and enjoys discretion, this enforcement can be turned to political ends.

Subnational governments have a somewhat different set of concerns. First, they seek assurances that they will have adequate—or more than adequate—resources and authority to manage their policy responsibilities through a combination of their own taxes, unconditional revenue sharing, or earmarked transfers. States and municipalities will also seek to ensure that any earmarking of funds does not violate their liberty to tailor services to the needs and tastes of their citizens, which is a fundamental rationale for decentralization, and that they are not subjected to unfunded mandates or other central government decisions that limit the ability to manage costs, including wages and pensions.[15]

Table 9.3 summarizes important developments in the assignment of spending responsibilities over the last two decades in the three countries. Two differences across the cases stand out: the lower level of subnational government spending and the continued and increasing use of earmarked transfers in Mexico.

Mexico

In Mexico, there have been two main phases in the decentralization of spending responsibilities and associated transfers: 1988–93 and 1998–99. Given the hierarchical nature of the system, it was relatively easy during the first phase for the central government to shift responsibilities to the states. Health care was transferred to the state level beginning in the late 1980s, and basic education was transferred more quickly in 1993. As could be predicted, given the political subordination of the states, they did not fare well in this bargain. Federal employees in these sectors were shifted en masse to the state payrolls. In some states the education transfer did not cover all of the costs of the federal schools, and the states had to spend some of their *participaciones* or own-tax revenue. States that had their own schools and teachers before 1993 usually had to bring their salaries up to the federal pay scale, and the federal government gave a subsidy to cover this cost.

Table 9.3. Assignment of Spending Authority and Service Responsibility in Argentina, Brazil, and Mexico

Variable	Argentina		Brazil		Mexico	
Reallocation of spending	Decentralization of education and health care (1992) without substantial new transfers.		Constitution of 1988 established rights to public services but left unclear the assignment of key responsibilities for social services and transport. Repeated failure of executive attempts to clarify. Previous assignment of responsibility has been modified by ad hoc agreements.		Decentralization of health care (gradually since late 1980s) and education (1993).	
Sectoral earmarked transfers	Fondo Conurbano (for Buenos Aires). Fuel tax revenues shared via fixed formula to finance housing (FONAVI) and provincial road and infrastructure.		None. Sectoral infrastructure transferred along with ad hoc agreements to shift responsibility.		Ramo 26 and Ramo 33.	
	1985	1996	1985	1996	1985	1996
SN spending as a share of GDP	7%	10%	12%	11%	4%	6%
SN spending as a share of total public sector	29%	38%	32%	36%	16%	28%
Sector earmarked transfers as share of SN spending	0	small	0	0	25%	50%

Assignment of responsibilities to the municipalities has been some-what less clear in part because earmarked transfers were politicized dur-ing Carlos Salinas's administration. Earmarked transfers under the Solidaridad program were subject to substantial presidential discretion, and as one would predict in such a hierarchical system, they followed a distinct political logic (Molinar and Weldon, 1994; Díaz Cayeros and Courchene, 2000). First, allocations went not to the formal political structure of mayors and municipal councils and administrations, but rather to Solidarity committees, who were directly under the control of the president and bypassed the traditional party bosses. Second, the allo-cations showed a particular horizontal logic. The Ernesto Zedillo admin-istration, seeking to distance itself from the abuses of its predecessor and under greater congressional and local-level pressures, rationalized trans-fers to municipalities both by moving them through official channels and by dramatically reducing the president's discretion.

The second phase of decentralization of responsibilities, still ongo-ing, started in the fall of 1997, precisely when the PRI lost control of Congress. In return for the PAN's support of the budget, the opposition secured an expansion and rationalization of decentralization transfers (i.e., other than *participaciones*) under a new budget line, Ramo 33. For the states, Ramo 33 increased the predictability, if not the size, of edu-cation and health transfers.[16] But these items remained based on historical cost—teachers' salary bill, number of hospitals, and so forth—with only marginal adjustments for inflation and population growth. The cost-driven design reflected the influence of stakeholders at the center, such as the teachers' union, which negotiated wages directly with the federal ministry.

At the insistence of PAN representatives in Congress, Ramo 33 increased the resources going to municipalities. It also further depoliti-cized Solidaridad by setting formulas for the distribution of federal resources to the municipalities. At the same time, expenditure assign-ment loosened and small municipalities sometimes found themselves with more money than officials knew what to do with.

Argentina

Following its transition to democracy, Argentina's spending responsi-bilities were specified by custom and law rather than the constitution.

The federal government handled most secondary education and health responsibilities, and provinces paid for primary education, some health care, and provincial workers' pensions.

Both economic and political conditions allowed for a relatively clear adjustment of responsibilities over the 1990s. The hyperinflation of the late 1980s severely eroded the capacity of all levels of government to provide services. With the successful stabilization of the early 1990s, provincial income, especially from tax sharing, grew rapidly, and provinces had more resources than they needed to carry out their assigned duties. Menem maneuvered politically to shift secondary education and health care to the provincial level, sealing the deal with a guarantee of a nominal floor on future transfers.

Under the second fiscal pact, the central government offered to take over provincial pension funds as a way to control and reform what were effectively contingent liabilities of the federal government. Most provinces were reluctant to pay the political cost of moving employees to the less generous federal pension system, even though the actuarial value of their own systems was negative. But then the fiscal crisis of 1995 forced each province, one by one, to transfer their pensions (an example of necessity making a pragmatic solution politically feasible).

Although the assignment of responsibilities was relatively clear in Argentina, as in Mexico, the powers of the center and centralist tendencies in the organization of interest groups created problems for the provinces in the late 1990s. Prior to the 1999 presidential election, under pressure from the national teachers' union, the federal government passed a bill to raise teachers' salaries across the country. Political expediency here violated two principles of federalism: the raise was paid for by a special federal tax on a traditionally provincial tax base, and it created pressure on provincial governments to give similar raises to other employee groups, for which the federal government offered no assistance.

Brazil

In Brazil, the decentralizing 1988 constitution gave both the federal and state governments responsibility for education, health, and social protection (Dillinger and Webb, 1998). Such a laissez-faire approach could work efficiently in theory if voters had complete information and could effectively constrain the provision of services to the appropriate level of government. In fact, such shared responsibility generated costly redundancies and severe moral hazard problems. Social services enjoyed a constitutional guarantee as citizens' rights, which made the federal government the provider of last resort. Subnational governments could promise services but shirk on their delivery knowing that the federal government would have political incentives to step in.

Although the 1988 constitution was largely decentralizing in spirit, it also extended central control in areas such as personnel. It defined the rights of public sector employees at all three levels of government. Governments could neither dismiss redundant civil servants nor reduce salaries in nominal terms. Public employees were granted the right to retire after only thirty-five years of employment (fewer for women and teachers) and with a pension equal to their exit salary plus any subsequent increases granted to their previous position![17]

In Mexico and to some extent Argentina, the central government was able to force subnational governments to pay the costs of unfunded mandates. In Brazil, by contrast, the 1988 constitution left the federal government short of resources to provide services adequately and without fiscal room to earmark transfers to guarantee service provision. Subnational governments had no incentives to adjust costs, and subnational expenditure on salaries and wages escalated rapidly. Presidents José Sarney (1985–90) and Fernando Collor (1990–92) both tried to clarify the assignment problem—and to cut federal liabilities—by delegating responsibilities more clearly to states and municipalities. But state governors, who dominated their congressional delegations, blocked these efforts and retained revenue sharing without any conditions.

Having failed to decentralize federal functions formally, the federal government had to cut its own spending, especially in the stabilization of 1994, and started devolving the responsibility for certain expenditures via ad hoc agreements with individual subnational governments. State and municipal governments with adequate financial and management resources saw opportunities for improving services and taking the political credit. Examples include the suburban railways in São Paulo and Rio de Janeiro, formerly federal hospitals in Rio, and certain highways. The federal government also managed to shift some health care costs to subnational governments by reducing the amount of federal compensation payments. This random process left gaps and inequities, but it had the advantage of only passing responsibilities to governments that were interested and capable of assuming them.

The Political Economy of Spending Assignment

In the early phases of the decentralization process, states appear more likely to assume responsibilities if explicit links are made to fund transfers. This can take the form of formal earmarking (as in Mexico) or can be a condition attached to the reform of transfers (as in Argentina's guaranteed minimum of coparticipation transfers). Evidence from other countries, such as Canada, indicates that once citizens hold subnational governments accountable for services, such earmarking can be dropped, although neither Mexico nor Argentina has moved to this stage.

In Brazil, the political forces that dominated the 1988 constitutional convention decentralized revenues without a link to service responsibilities, but since then the political market for voter approval has devolved the responsibilities piecemeal through negotiations with individual states and municipalities. While less neat, the results for service delivery may be no worse than with the one-size-fits-all approach in the other two countries.

MANAGING SUBNATIONAL BORROWING AND DEBT

Subnational borrowing expands the ability of governments to finance public goods, infrastructure, and capital investments. But the problems of moral hazard associated with such borrowing are great, and in the 1990s, subnational debt crises forced central governments to bail out state or municipal governments and their lenders. Central governments are thus looking for institutions and procedures that can prevent moral hazard. The means to do this include prohibiting, limiting, or regulating access to international borrowing (ex ante controls) and a credible commitment to a no-bailout rule (ex post control). The credibility of this latter commitment hinges critically on limiting the ability of states, individually or collectively, to influence the bailout decision. As Table 9.4 shows, none of the three countries has been successful at this task, and particularly in Argentina and Brazil, the costs of bailouts have been very high.

Mexico

Mexico's constitution and the SNCF established important ex ante controls on subnational borrowing, including an absolute prohibition of foreign borrowing and the stipulation that borrowing be used only for productive purposes. However, the shortage of state-based revenue and the pressures arising from more competitive politics increased pressures for subnational borrowing. States exploited the federal government's concern to deliver politically important public services that had been decentralized. All states received bailouts in the wake of the 1995 financial crisis, and a few states have received bailouts since.

Moral hazard was generated in the first instance by the federal government's practice of acting as a trustee in servicing state debt that had been collateralized with *participaciones* (revenue sharing). The assumption of this role in 1980 created the perception that subnational borrowing carried an implicit guarantee. The ability to provide discretionary support to subnational governments compounded the problem and suggests the drawback of discretion:[18] sometimes, the federal government would pay the banks without deducting the amount from the *participaciones* of a financially strapped and politically friendly state.

To reverse this situation, the Zedillo administration established ex ante, market-based mechanisms that would prevent excessive subnational borrowing while conveying a credible signal that it would not bail out the parties involved in such borrowing. The new regulatory framework has four main components:

(1) The president relinquished his power over discretionary transfers to states, limiting his political largesse (and his successors') and thus also the capacity of states to blackmail him.
(2) The federal government gave up its role in securing debt with revenue-sharing payments, which left the states and their creditors to assume the risks for the collateralization of debt with *participaciones* through their own *fideicomiso* (trust) arrangements.
(3) Subnational debt was subjected to normal credit-exposure ceilings.
(4) Banks' capital-risk weighting of loans to subnational governments was linked to international ratings of the borrower governments' creditworthiness. The pricing of bank loans thus became a function of the underlying risk of the state government: financially stronger states would see the price of loans fall, while the weakest states are likely to be priced or rationed out of the private market.

Although the new structure appears to have limited excess borrowing to date, this is in part because the states have only just begun to get

Table 9.4. Subnational borrowing regimes in Mexico, Argentina, and Brazil

Borrowing constraints	Mexico Pre-1999	Mexico 2000–	Argentina Pre-1991	Argentina 1991–	Brazil Pre-1999
Central government controls subnational borrowing ex ante	Partial.	No	No	No; mainly requires reporting.	Yes, in principle; sophisticated rules but also significant loopholes.
Central government credibly commits to a no-bailout rule.	No. Official bailouts until 1995; and in practice until 1999.	Yes, in theory.	No	Yes. 1993 law prohibits bailouts.	No; cap on debt service allows interest capitalization. Federal government took over most state debt.
Federal guarantees	Official to 1996; de facto 1997–99.	None.	De facto through provincial banks.	None.	None official; but broad de facto.
Collateralization	Ministry of Finance arranges participations as collateral.	Private trusts; participations as collateral.	Not in practice.	Banco de la Nacion will contract to deduct debt service from Copar. Details negotiated with borrower.	Federal government has right to deduct debt service from revenue sharing; rarely practiced before 1999.
Regulators force creditors to accept the losses implied by any failure to service debt	No; federal bailouts.	Yes	No	Yes, but rare because debt service is deducted from transfers.	No
The central bank (and bank regulators) is autonomous and has a strong anti-inflation mandate	No	No	No	Strong autonomy and committed to fixed exchange rate.	Limited autonomy; discretionary monetary policy.

	Mexico 1985	Mexico 1991	Mexico 1996	Argentina 1987	Argentina 1991	Argentina 1996	Brazil 1987	Brazil 1991	Brazil 1996
Subnational debt (% GDP, estimates)	1%	1%	3%	6%	8%	6%	2%	6%	12%
Subnational deficits (% GDP, after transfers)	0.4%	0.3%	0.2%		1.5%	0.5%		2%	3%

international credit ratings and to negotiate the *fideicomiso* arrangements with the banks. Further tests will come when they resume active borrowing. These are positive steps, but the jury is still out.

Argentina

In Argentina, the politics of debt have been more complex. Bailouts of provincial banks accounted for at least half of the deficits contributing to the hyperinflation in the late 1980s. The capacity of the provinces to effectively blackmail the government stemmed from divided government, Peronist domination of overrepresented states, and Alfonsín's shrinking legislative coalition.

Hyperinflation eroded the real value of domestic debt and permitted a reconciliation of intergovernmental obligations. In the early 1990s, however, many of the provinces once again borrowed heavily from banks, including those owned by the provinces. The provinces also pledged their coparticipation transfers as a guarantee to private creditors. The federal government was a party to this arrangement, but in different ways than in Mexico. Rather than the executive controlling the transfers, the relatively independent Banco de la Nación performed the function of deducting the debt service from federal tax receipts, diminishing the prospect of bailouts.

The economic crisis of 1994–95 tested the ability of new institutions to impose a hard budget constraint. Provinces at first reacted to higher interest costs and reduced revenues by trying to borrow more. They then turned to arrears to suppliers and personnel, which the states paid off with bonds that could be converted to cash at a discount and used to pay taxes. These two kinds of forced lending accounted for more than half of the debt incurred in 1994–95. Provinces with debt-servicing difficulties suddenly found that Banco de la Nación was withholding over half of their *coparticipaciones* to pay creditors. Nonetheless, the states were ultimately forced to adjust. In some cases the federal treasury facilitated refinancing of provincial debt, but at market rates with no bailouts. Neither the federal government nor its agencies took over any provincial debt. In short, the central government largely maintained the credibility of its commitment to manage the moral hazard problem through ex post consequences, rather than ex ante constraints.

How did the federal government manage this feat? The stabilization plan of 1991 legislated hard budget constraints that forbade the federal government from assuming subnational debt. The collateral arrangements with the Banco de la Nación, outlined above, helped make the hard budget constraint credible. Tight, and above all statutory, limits on central bank credit to the public sector allowed the federal government to reject provincial pleas for more resources—many of which were also coming from opposition states—on the grounds that such transfers would endanger the gains from stabilization and the very survival of the Currency Board system. The plan also constrained the provinces' ability to borrow from their own banks by eliminating their access to the central bank rediscount facility and tightening bank regulation.[19]

In 1999 the federal government began to revise its strategy in the face of a persistent recession. The large states sought financing from multilateral banks for refinancing, but other provinces gained access to a new federal fund for debt refinancing. But debt relief required eliminating deficits, divestiture of any remaining banks and pension funds, and limits on personnel expenditure. As noted above, the refinancing also required agreement to long-term reductions in the share of the national tax collection distributed to provinces, but in exchange for immediate increases to the floor on transfers, which, as it turned out, the federal government could not afford. Perhaps the biggest lesson for intergovernmental fiscal relations emanating from the 2001 Argentine financial crisis is that the best rules for subnational debt will fail if the federal government does not itself have sound finances and a viable fiscal position.

Brazil

As in Argentina, Brazil suffered major macroeconomic imbalances as a result of excessive state deficits and subsequent mismanagement of debt. Since the transition to democracy, the government has been through no fewer than four rounds of subnational debt crises and rescheduling: in 1988, 1993, 1994–95, and 1998–99 (Dillinger, 1997; Ter-Minassian, 1997; Gómez, 2000). The state debt crises that occurred prior to the initiation of the stabilization program of 1994 established three precedents that adversely influenced subsequent debt agreements; all reflected the power of the states vis-à-vis the center. First, the federal government actually put the state debt on its books (mostly at the central bank) and then provided relief in the form of rescheduling. Second, through the combination of grace periods, rescheduling, and debt service caps, the agreements reduced the debt service burden of incumbent state administrations—

namely, those responsible for the debt—while leaving the fiscal consequences to their successors. Third, for heavily indebted states, especially the four largest, Congress intervened to grant them limits on debt service. These limits largely eliminated the cost of recent borrowing and allowed interest capitalization.

The repeated cycle of federal government refinancing of state debt, the absence of ex post consequences for those incurring the debt, and caps on debt service had precisely the perverse incentive effects that one would expect. The group of bankrupt states was too big and influential for the federal government to impose the costs on them directly, prior to 1999, and their debt had grown too large for any solution without substantial debt relief. In contrast to 1990s Argentina, the president's comparative lack of control of a legislative majority in combination with the political weight of the governors weakened the position of the federal government, and the terms for rescheduling were correspondingly generous.

Subnational debt as a share of GDP was at a level similar to Argentina's at the start of the 1990s but had more than doubled by 1997, despite the relatively successful stabilization program of 1994. Most of the debt was owed to the central government or to state banks, and until the debt-rescheduling agreements in 1998, much of it was not being serviced by the states and interest was capitalized. State debt and deficits accounted for fully one-third of the increase in domestic public debt from 1994 to 1997.

One important error was tactical: the federal government negotiated the state debt deals one at a time, with all results made public, thus allowing any deal struck to serve as the floor for the next deal. The political problems were of a more enduring sort. First, the president's party was a minority in Congress, and the president lacked the power to exert pressure on governors of his own party. The president also lacked the political and fiscal capacity to use side payments to get a satisfactory vertical distribution of control of state borrowing. The second problem was that the Senate, which strongly represented the interests of governors, controlled the rules for state borrowing and rescheduling (Gomez, 2000). The Senate also enjoyed a constitutionally defined influence over the Central Bank and used it to hinder Central Bank efforts to restrain commercial bank lending to the states.

The crises of the late 1990s and the corresponding dependence of the states on the federal government provided the executive some leverage.

The Ministry of Finance and the Central Bank set some ex ante limits on state borrowing, preventing state deficits except to unpaid service on outstanding debt (effectively requiring a primary surplus). The agreements of 1998 also allowed the federal government to withhold debt service from transfers, as in Argentina. Thus, when Minas Gerais refused to pay its debt service, the federal government stepped in to cover it but subsequently deducted the payments from Minas Gerais's transfers. The Law of Fiscal Responsibility, passed in May 2000, also calls for deductions of debt service from transfers (*participaciones*). If this new strategy works, the recent crisis may end up being of the same importance for Brazil as the 1994–95 crisis was for Argentina. Again, the jury is still out.

The Political Economy of Subnational Borrowing

None of the three countries was able to reach a regime for subnational borrowing that fully met the concerns of both the center and the states, with the potential exception of the new regime in Mexico. Particularly in Argentina prior to the 1990s and in Brazil, the states had the power to blackmail the center. All three countries have subsequently developed mechanisms to use tax-sharing transfers to collateralize subnational debt, and have shown that they can enforce repayment. But as in the past, these new regimes ultimately depend on the making of credible commitments, whether through institutions that remove federal discretion, such as independent central banks, or that limit subnational access to bailouts, an ongoing problem in Brazil. Since the political commitment to impose ex post consequences is weak and not credible for extreme cases, experience in these countries shows the need for complementary measures that regulate and monitor borrowing ex ante, to prevent the extreme cases from arising.

DISCRETIONARY TRANSFERS

We can deal more succinctly with the final set of intergovernmental fiscal issues concerning transfers over which the executive exercises direct discretionary control. Should they exist at all? Executives naturally favor having some discretion, to respond to contingencies such as natural disasters and for political and electoral purposes. Often, legislators and particularly governors and mayors seek to limit such discretion. But executives who enjoy strong and coherent legislative backing can secure support for such discretion if they are politically helpful. Similarly, state and municipal governments with strong links to the executive or ruling party might accept such arrangements as part of their supportive political machine.

Executives in all three countries have been forced, to differing degrees, to give up such discretion. In Mexico, the share of discretionary transfers in total transfers has declined most precipitously and is both consequence and perhaps cause of the decline of PRI and presidential dominance. Traditionally the president enjoyed a variety of funds he could distribute to state governments and, in the Carlos Salinas period (1988–94), to municipal Solidarity committees. He also exercised substantial control over federal investment. Strong statistical as well as anecdotal evidence demonstrates that the president used this money to reward supporters, deter and punish opponents, and give particular help to PRI governors facing opposition challenges (Díaz Cayeros and McClure, 2000). Zedillo began cutting discretionary transfers in the first half of his term and then lost them almost completely after the PRI lost control of Congress in 1997 (Díaz Cayeros, Magaloni, and Weingast, 1999).

In Argentina and Brazil, legislators and governors quickly placed limitations on discretionary transfers from the executive following the transition to democratic rule. In Argentina the Coparticipation Law of 1988 granted the president discretionary control of only one percent of the total transfer fund. Menem used these funds both to reward his home state and to sustain the legislative and provincial coalition that supported his adjustment policies, but the amounts were significant only in the context of small provincial finances. In Brazil, the executive has virtually no discretionary funds, which has clearly handicapped the president's efforts to impose fiscal discipline.

CONCLUSION

The three cases examined here illustrate a fundamental political dilemma of the decentralization process. The ideal equilibrium is a set of institutions that protects the interests of both the national and the subnational governments. Yet if the system is highly centralized at the outset, as was the case two decades ago in Mexico, Argentina, and even Brazil in some respects, then the forces for decentralization must be strong enough to break with the status quo. However, if they are strong enough to do so, it is highly possible that they will overshoot the ideal balance. The result will be excess decentralization along at least some dimensions, with a corresponding loss of central authority to coordinate and to monitor spending and borrowing.

As shown in Table 9.5, none of the federations has fully succeeded in striking a stable and positive balance between the national and the subnational governments. The risks differ somewhat across the cases, however. Mexico exhibits continuing centralist trends—although central power has weakened significantly in the second half of the 1990s—while in Brazil the opposite tends to be the case.

The outcomes we have pointed to are related to features of each country's political system—both enduring ones, such as lines of account-ability within parties, and temporary ones such as whether the president's party has control of Congress and of most governorships. Not surprisingly, decentralization was more radical where governors and mayors exercised more influence over national-level politicians or where the president lacked legislative support. To the extent that the former problem exists, only quite fundamental constitutional change or reform of political parties is likely to make a difference, and such changes are unlikely pre-cisely because of the balance of political power currently in place.

Our analysis also permits some conclusions about specific compo-nents of fiscal pacts, however, and these might well be more relevant to policy making. A major barrier to rationalizing the system of taxes and revenue sharing was the nature of horizontal politics: the inherent and often zero-sum conflict between the interests of richer and poorer states and of large and small ones. Reforms that would increase the efficiency of the tax system and increase incentives for desirable subnational fis-cal behavior often lead to redistribution and thus run up against difficult political constraints. More research is needed on how malapportionment and particular coalitions of state-level interests in the legislature affect the degree of redistribution, and on the conditions under which redis-tribution can follow a formula such as compensation for poverty or merely reflect political bargaining.

In terms of spending, unfunded mandates are a recurrent problem; the temptation of central government politicians is to dictate subnational

Table 9.5. Federal Outcomes: Mexico, Argentina, and Brazil Compared

Area and Concern	Mexico	Argentina	Brazil
Tax and Transfers			
Center			
Retains adequate tax authority	Yes	Yes	No
Some efficient taxes not shared	No	No	No
Feasible process to revise the revenue-sharing allocations	Yes	No	No
Hard budget constraints on transfers to states	No, until 1999	Yes	Yes
States			
Adequate own tax authority	No	Partial	Yes
At least fair share to poor states	Yes	No	Yes
No more than fair share from rich states	No	No	No
Avoid excess competition	Yes	Yes	No
Spending Authority and Service Responsibility			
Center			
States fulfill the responsibilities	Yes	Yes	No
Quality control	No	No	No
Transparency	No	No	Yes
States			
Resources adequate to meet responsibilities	No, until 2000	Yes	Yes
Control of costs, including wages and pensions	No	Yes	No, until 1999
No unfunded mandates	No	Yes	No
Accommodation to local needs and tastes	No	Yes	Yes

Subnational Borrowing and Debt Management

Center			
Prevention of monetary financing to states	Yes	Yes, since 1991	Yes, since 1994
Ex ante limits on state borrowing	Yes, partial	No, until 2001	Not effective until 1999
Limiting states' access to international financing	Yes	Yes	Not effective until 1999
Enforcing ex post consequences	Partial	Yes	No, until 1999
States			
Access to capital markets	Partial	Yes	Partial
Ability to pledge transfers as collateral	Yes	Yes	Yes
Discretionary Transfers			
Center			
Respond to natural disasters	Yes	Yes	Yes
Reward marginal members of key coalitions	Yes	Yes	No
States			
Limit discretionary transfers	No, until 2000	Yes	Yes, except bailouts

priorities. In addition to the desire of the president and (national) legislators to claim credit for actions that are costless to them, we found that the organization of interest groups contributed to such mandates. Where service providers such as doctors, nurses, and teachers are organized nationally, they usually have an interest in setting wages nationally, thus tying the hands of lower-level jurisdictions that make the payment.

Debt management involves a number of problems in making commitments credible. The central government must be able to commit firmly to a no-bailout rule and to make subnational governments and/or their creditors bear the consequences of any excess borrowing. All the Latin American federations have unfortunate histories in this regard. However, all three have recently introduced systems that combined ex ante controls with no-bailout rules. While one must wait to see whether these outcomes hold, it is striking that governments have arrived at potentially stable solutions in the debt area while they have had persistent difficulties in reaching stable, efficient, and fair regimes for taxation, revenue sharing, and spending. Perhaps this is because rules governing subnational debt can be written to improve the welfare of all parties, whereas reallocation of taxes and spending usually entails zero-sum conflicts.

Finally, more research is needed on the interaction among the component parts of the intergovernmental fiscal pact that we have outlined. For example, inadequate taxing power may be one reason why subnational governments face debt problems or end up facing the perverse incentives created by high dependence on transfers. Linking new spending powers with the capacity, and obligation, to tax remains crucially important if the promise of fiscal federalism is to be realized.

NOTES

1. In the case of Argentina our analysis does not continue through events at the end of 2001. At the time of writing the outcome remained most unclear.

2. Since subnational governments typically differ in their ability to tax, "neutral" systems with all transfers allocated equally per capita in practice result in large inequities in revenues per capita across states. In "redistributive" systems the design of intergovernmental fiscal relations strives to partially or even completely equalize per capita revenues.

3. Unfortunately, these two different disabilities may coexist within the same system. For example, the theory of fiscal federalism gives priority to the

appropriate assignment of spending responsibilities. The assignment of taxes and decisions about transfers should follow and accommodate this basic choice. A typical syndrome in newly democratizing federations, however, is for politicians to reap political gains from transferring spending and borrowing powers and resources to lower levels of government in advance of the transfer of taxing powers.

4. The optimal scale for collecting taxes and deterring evasion is usually greater than the optimal scale for making and implementing spending decisions. As a result, there are efficiency as well as equity reasons for central governments to collect more taxes than they spend and to transfer a portion of them back to lower levels of government.

5. In addition to those examined here, discretionary transfers can include block grants set by some per capita formula.

6. In some countries, nomination procedures vary according to political party, but in our analysis we have sought the central tendency across parties.

7. The center may also desire to keep the subnational units dependent fiscally by denying them tax bases or dependent politically by retaining full discretion over transfers, but these can be labeled inappropriate in the sense that they seek to reverse the decentralization process rather than to make it work. See Wibbels's chapter in this volume for a discussion of how this occurred in Argentina.

8. The high dependence on federal transfers at the end of the 1990s was relatively uniform across states, with transfers covering over 90 percent everywhere except the federal district.

9. For discussions of the formulas and their changes, see Bonifaz Chapoy (1992); Arellano Cardena (1996); Aguilar Villanueva (1996); Díaz Cayeros (1995).

10. The degree of provincial dependence on transfers varies widely. In large provinces transfers constitute about half of revenues; in small provinces, the transfers typically account for more than 75 percent of revenues, reaching 95 percent in La Rioja and Tierra del Fuego.

11. For the vast majority of transfers, the volume of funds subject to sharing is determined either as a fixed share of specified taxes or as a fixed amount in pesos.

12. The taxes subject to revenue sharing now include the federal income tax, value-added tax (VAT), and excise and asset taxes; in short, all the major federal domestic taxes other than social security and fuel. Before the transfer, several deductions are made from the provinces' share and transferred to the national social security system and to several funds for the provinces.

13. The provincial concession proved insufficient to close the federal fiscal gap. This was not the fault of the provinces but rather the fault of federal government for not creating the large fiscal safety net that it needed for itself

because the convertibility law ruled out other safety nets, such as devaluation and seigniorage.

14. Within each group of states, 95 percent of the funds are distributed among states on the basis of population and per capita income, with poorer states receiving proportionately more and the remainder being distributed on the basis of geographic area.

15. For example, if central governments negotiate wage settlements with teachers' unions, this becomes a constraint from the perspective of the subnational government.

16. Ramo 33 also contained a new, relatively small state infrastructure fund.

17. This policy was revised in late 1998.

18. This discretion was embedded in the annual budget through a special and often large line item controlled by the executive, especially within Ramo 23.

19. After the 1994–95 economic shock, most provinces had to recapitalize or privatize their banks, rather than being able to borrow from them. Eighteen of the provincial banks were privatized in 1994–96, and more have gone through the process since then (World Bank, 1998).

References

Abalos, José Antonio Abalos. 1994. "La Descentralización en Chile: Antecedentes Históricos y Reformas Actuales." *Serie Azul* 4. Instituto de Estudios Urbanos, Pontificia Universidad Católica de Chile.

Abers, Rebecca. 2000. *Inventing Local Democracy: Grassroots Politics in Brazil*. Boulder, Colo.: Lynne Rienner.

Abrucio, Fernando. 1998. *Os Barões da Federação: os Governadores e a Redemocratização Brasileira*. São Paulo: Departamento de Ciência Política da USP/Hucitec.

Abrucio, Fernando, and David Samuels. N.d. "Federalism and FHC." Unpublished manuscript, University of Minnesota.

Acuña, Carlos H. 1994. "Politics and Economics in the Argentina of the Nineties (Or, Why the Future No Longer Is What It Used to Be)." In *Democracy, Markets, and Structural Reform in Latin America*, ed. William C. Smith, Carlos H. Acuña, and Eduaro A. Gamarra. New Brunswick, N.J.: Transaction Publishers.

Affonso, Rui. 1996. "Os Municípios e os Desafios da Federação no Brasil." *São Paulo em Perspectiva* 10, no. 3: 3–10.

Afonso, José Roberto. 1995a. "Evolução das relações intergovernamentais no Brasil entre 1968/1988: transferências e endividamento." M.A. thesis, Universidade Federal do Rio de Janeiro, 22.

———. 1995b. "A Questão Tributária e o Financiamento dos Diferentes Níveis de Governo." In *Reforma Tributária e Federação*, ed. José Roberto R. Afonso and Pedro Luiz Barra Silva. São Paulo: FUNDAP/UNESP.

Afonso, J. R. R., and Nelson de Castro Serra. 1994. "Despesa Pública—Competências, Serviços Locais, Descentralização: O Papel dos Municípios." *Texto para Discussão* no. 23. Rio de Janeiro: CEPP.

Aguilar-Barajas, Ismael, and Nigel Spence. 1988. "Industrial Decentralization and Regional Policy, 1970–1986: The Conflicting Policy Response." In *The Mexican Economy*, ed. George Philip. London: Routledge.

Aguilar Villanueva, Luis F. 1996. "El federalismo mexicano: funcionamiento y tareas pendientes." In *¿Hacia un Nuevo Federalismo?* Mexico City: Fondo de Cultura Económica.

Almeida, Maria Hermínia Tavares de. 1994. "Redefinição de Competências entre Esferas de Governo na Prestação de Serviços Públicos na Área Social." Final Report, "Balanço e Perspectivas do Federalismo Fiscal no Brasil." São Paulo: IESP/FUNDAP.

Ames, Barry. 1987. *Political Survival: Politicians and Public Policy in Latin America*. Berkeley: University of California Press.

———. 1995a. "Electoral Rules, Constituency Pressures, and Pork Barrel: Bases of Voting in the Brazilian Congress." *Journal of Politics* 57 (May): 324–43.

———. 1995b. "Electoral Strategy under Open-List Proportional Representation." *American Journal of Political Science* 39 (May): 406–33.

———. 1998. "Toward a Theory of Legislative Parties in Brazil." Department of Political Science, University of Pittsburgh. Mimeo.

———. 1999. "Approaches to the Study of Institutions in Latin American Politics." *Latin American Research Review* 34, no. 1: 221–36.

———. 2001. *The Deadlock of Democracy in Brazil*. Ann Arbor: University of Michigan Press.

Archondo, R. 1997. *Trés Años de Participación Popular: Memoria de un Proceso*. La Paz, Bolivia: Secretaría Nacional de Participación Popular.

Ardaya, Ruben. 1991. *Sobre Municipalidad y Municipio*. La Paz, Bolivia: Instituto de Investigaciones y Desarrollo Municipal.

Arellano Cadena, Rogelio, ed. 1996. *México hacia un nuevo federalismo fiscal*. Mexico City: Fondo de Cultura Económica.

Arretche, Marta. 2000. *Estado Federativo e Políticas Sociais: Determinantes da Descentralização*. São Paulo: FAPESP/Editora Revan.

Arretche, Marta, and Vicente Rodríguez, eds. 1998. *Descentralização das Políticas Sociais no Estado de São Paulo*. São Paulo: FAPESP/IPEA/Edições Fundap.

Bahl, Roy, and Johannes Linn. 1986. "Public Expenditure Decentralization in Developing Countries." *Government Policy* 4 (November): 405–18.

———. 1992. *Urban Public Finance in Developing Countries*. New York: Oxford University Press.

———. 1994. "Fiscal Decentralization and Intergovernmental Transfers in Less Developed Countries." *Publius: The Journal of Federalism* 24: 1–19.

Banamex. 1996. *Mexico Social, 1994–1995 Estadísticas Seleccionadas*. Mexico City: Banco Nacional de Mexico, S.A.

Barbery Anaya, Roberto. 1997. "Una Revolución en la Democracia." In *El Pulso de la Democracia: Participación Ciudadana y Descentralización en Bolivia*, ed. Secretaría Nacional de Participación Popular. La Paz, Bolivia: Ministerio de Desarrollo Humano.

Beck, Nathaniel, and Jonathan N. Katz. 1996. "Nuisance vs. Substance: Specifying and Estimating Time-Series-Cross-Section Models." *Political Analysis* 6 (July): 1–37.

Bird, Richard M. 1993. "Threading the Fiscal Labyrinth: Some Issues in Fiscal Decentralization." *National Tax Journal* 46 (June): 207–27.

Bird, Richard M., and François Vaillancourt. 1998. "Fiscal Decentralization in Developing Countries: An Overview." In *Fiscal Decentralization in Developing Countries*, ed. Richard M. Bird and François Vaillancourt. New York: Cambridge University Press.

Bird, Richard M., Robert D. Ebel, and Christine I. Wallich, eds. 1995. *Decentralization of the Socialist State*. Washington, D.C.: World Bank.

Blakemore, Harold. 1954. "The Chilean Revolution of 1891 and Its Historiography." *Hispanic American Historical Review* 45, no. 3 (August): 393–421.

Boisier, Sergio. 1994. "Regionalización, descentralización y desarollo regional: Perspectivas político-administrativas en Chile." *Serie Ensayos* (ILPES-CEPAL, Santiago) 94, no. 23 (July).

Boisier, Sergio, and Gladys Zurita. 1993. "Gobierno regional y desarollo económico (El caso chileno)." *Serie Ensayos* (ILPES-CEPAL, Santiago) 93, no. 16 (May).

Bomfim, Antúlio, and Anwar Shah. 1994. "Macroeconomic Management and the Division of Powers in Brazil: Perspectives for the 1990s." *World Development* 22, no. 4: 535–42.

Bonifaz Chapoy, Beatriz. 1992. *Finanzas nacionales y finanzas estatales*. Mexico City: UNAM.

Boylan, Delia M. 1998. "Preemptive Strike: Central Bank Reform in Chile's Transition from Authoritarian Rule." *Comparative Politics* 30, no. 4 (July): 443–62.

Brasileiro, Ana Maria. 1973. *O Município como Sistema Político*. Rio de Janeiro: FGV.

Bresser Pereira, Luiz Carlos. 1993. "Economic Reforms and Economic Growth: Efficiency and Politics in Latin America." In *Economic Reforms in New Democracies: A Social-Democratic Approach*, ed. Luiz Carlos Bresser Pereira, José María Maravall, and Adam Przeworski. Cambridge: Cambridge University Press.

Breton, Albert. 1996. *Competitive Governments: An Economic Theory of Politics and Public Finance*. New York: Cambridge University Press.

Brewer-Carias, Alan. 1994. *Informe sobre la descentralización en Venezuela*. Caracas: Presidencia de la República.

Broadway, Robin, Sandra Roberts, and Anwar Shah. 1994. "The Reform of Fiscal Systems in Developing and Emerging Market Economies: A Federalism Perspective." World Bank Working Paper no. 1259.

Bruhn, Kathleen. 1996. "Social Spending and Political Support: The 'Lessons' of the National Solidarity Program in Mexico." *Comparative Politics* 28, no. 2: 151–78.

———. 1999. "PRD Local Governments in Michoacán: Implications for Mexico's Democratization Process." In *Subnational Politics and Democratization in Mexico*, ed. Wayne A. Cornelius, Todd A. Eisenstadt, and Jane Hindley. La Jolla: Center for U.S.-Mexican Studies, University of California, San Diego.

Burki, Shadid J., G. E. Perry, and W. R. Dillinger. 2000. *Beyond the Center: Decentralizing the State*. Washington, D.C.: World Bank.

Caballero, Francisco Rodriguez. 1996. "Understanding Resistance to Reform: Conflict and Agency in the Venezuela Experience." Harvard University, Department of Economics. Mimeo.

Cabrero Mendoza, Enrique. 1998. *Las Políticas Descentralizadoras en México (1983–1993): Logros y Desencantos*. Mexico City: Centro de Investigación y Docencias Económicas.

Cagnoni, José. 1979. *Las Regiones la Descentralización Territorial*. Montevideo: Fundación de Cultura Universitaria.

Camargo, Aspásia. 1993. "La Federación Sometida: Nacionalismo Desarrollista e Inestabilidad Democrática." In *Federalismos Latinoamericanos: México/Brasil/Argentina*, ed. Marcello Carmagnani. Mexico City: Fondo de Cultura Económica/El Colegio de México.

———. 1999. "Do federalismo oligárquico ao federalismo democrático." In *Repensando o Estado Novo*, ed. Dulce Pandolfi. Rio de Janeiro: Editora FGV.

Cammack, Paul. 1982. "Clientelism and Military Government in Brazil." In *Private Patronage and Public Power: Political Clientelism in the Modern State*, ed. Christopher Clapham. London: Frances Pinter.

Campbell, Tim. 1990. "Decentralization in Chile: A Country Report." Report prepared for a regional study by the World Bank, Washington, D.C.

Campbell, Tim, George Peterson, and J. Brakarz. 1991. *Decentralization to Local Government in LAC*. Washington, D.C.: World Bank.

Canessa, Julio. 1979. *La regionalización: Sus proyecciones y la nueva institucionalidad*. Santiago: CONARA.

Canitrot, Adolfo. 1994. "Crisis and Transformation of the Argentine State (1978–1992)." In *Democracy, Markets, and Structural Reform in Latin America: Argentina, Bolivia, Brazil, Chile, and Mexico*, ed. William C. Smith, Carlos H. Acuña, and Eduaro A. Gamarra. New Brunswick, N.J.: Transaction Publishers.

Cann, Kenneth. 1970. "Federal Revenue Sharing in Brazil: 1946–1966." *Bulletin for International Fiscal Documentation* 24, no. 1: 12–27

Carey, John M. 1996. *Term Limits and Legislative Representation*. New York: Cambridge University Press.

Castro, Maria Helena Guimarães de. 1987. "Equipamentos sociais, política partidária e governos locais no Estado de São Paulo (1968–1982)." M.A. thesis, UNICAMP.

Castro, Sergio de, and Juan Carlos Méndez. 1992. *El ladrillo: Bases de la política económica del gobierno militar chileno*. Santiago: Centro de Estudios Públicos.

Cavalcanti, Carlos Eduardo G., and Sérgio Prado. 1998. *Aspectos da Guerra Fiscal no Brasil*. Brasília: IPEA.

Cavarozzi, Marcelo. 1992. "Beyond Transitions to Democracy in Latin America." *Journal of Latin American Studies* (October): 665–84.

Centro de Estudios para el Cambio Estructural (CECE). 1995. "La Coparticipación de Impuestos durante 1994." *CECE Serie Estudios* (April). Buenos Aires: CECE.

———. 1997. "Aportes del Tesoro Nacional: Discrecionalidad en la relación financiera entre la Nación y las provincias." *CECE Serie Estudios* no. 21 (October). Buenos Aires: CECE.

Chile, Ministerio del Interior, Subsecretaría de Desarrollo Regional y Administrativo (SUBDERE). 1991. *La reforma municipal*. Santiago: SUBDERE.

———. 1992a. *Democracia Regional y Local* 5 (March).

———. 1992b. *Democracia Regional y Local* 4 (January–February).

Chile, Ministerio Secretaría General de Gobierno, Secretaría de Comunicación y Cultura (SECC). 1991. *Mensaje Presidencial: Discurso de S.E. el Presidente de la República Don Patricio Aylwin Azócar en el inicio de la legislatura ordinaria del Congreso Nacional*. Santiago: Ministerio Secretaría General de Gobierno.

Chile, Senado de la República. 1991a. *Minutes of the Comisiones Unidas de Gobierno Interior, Regionalización, Planificación y Desarollo Social del Senado y de Constitución, Legislación y Justicia de la Cámara de Diputados*. Valparaíso: Comisión de Gobierno Interior, Descentralización y Regionalización (July–August). Unofficial edited transcripts.

———. 1991b. *Minutes of the Comisiones Unidas de Gobierno Interior, Regionalización, Planificación y Desarollo Social del Senado y de Constitución, Legislación y Justicia de la Cámara de Diputados*. Valparaíso: Comisión de Gobierno Interior, Descentralización y Regionalización (July 10). Unofficial edited transcript.

———. 1991c. *Minutes of the Comisiones Unidas de Gobierno Interior, Regionalización, Planificación y Desarollo Social del Senado y de Constitución, Legislación y Justicia de la Cámara de Diputados*. Valparaíso: Comisión de Gobierno Interior, Descentralización y Regionalización (July 2). Unofficial edited transcript.

Cleaves, Peter S. 1969. *Developmental Processes in Chilean Local Government*. Berkeley: University of California Press.

Collier, Ruth Berins, and David Collier. 1991. *Shaping the Political Arena*. Princeton: Princeton University Press.

COPRE (Comisión Presidencial para la Reforma del Estado). 1986. *Documentos para la reforma del Estado*. Caracas: COPRE.

Consejo Federal de Inversiones (CFI). 1988. *Acerca de las relaciones Nación-Provincias*. Buenos Aires: CFI.

Coppedge, Michael. 1994. *Strong Parties and Lame Ducks: Presidential Partyarchy and Factionalism in Venezuela*. Stanford: Stanford University Press.

Corporación Tiempo 2000. 1992. "La discusión sobre el protocolo para eligir alcaldes: Algunas aclaraciones necesarias" and "Concertación de Partidos por la Democracia: Protocolo de acuerdos para la elección de alcaldes." *Bitacora Legislativa* 51 (June 29–July 3).

Correa R., Enrique. 1994. "Las funciones del municipio." In "Desafíos para el fortalecimiento municipal." *CPU Serie de Documentos de Trabajo (Corporación de Promoción Universitaria)* 38, no. 94 (December).

Costa, João Bosco Araújo da. 1996. "A Ressignificação do Local: o Imaginário Político Brasileiro pós-80." *São Paulo em Perspectiva* 10, no. 3: 113–18.

Costa, Vera L. C. 1998. "Descentralização da Educação no Brasil: As Reformas Recentes no Ensino Fundamental." Paper presented at the Latin American Studies Meeting, Chicago.

Cremer, Jacques, Antonio Estache, and Paul Seabright. 1995. "The Decentralization of Public Services: Lessons from the Theory of the Firm." In *Decentralizing Infrastructure: Advantages and Limitations*, ed. Antonio Estache. Washington, D.C.: World Bank.

Crisp, Brian. 1997. "Presidential Behavior in a System with Strong Parties: Venezuela, 1958–1995." In *Presidentialism and Democracy in Latin America*, ed. Scott Mainwaring and Matthew Soberg Shugart. New York: Cambridge University Press.

———. 1998. "Presidential Decree Authority in Venezuela." In *Executive Decree Authority*, ed. John M. Carey and Matthew Soberg Shugart. New York: Cambridge University Press.

———. 2000. *Democratic Institutional Design: The Powers and Incentives of Venezuelan Politicians and Interest Groups*. Stanford: Stanford University Press.

Crisp, Brian F., and Daniel H. Levine. 1998. "Democratizing the Democracy? Crisis and Reform in Venezuela." *Journal of Interamerican Studies and World Affairs* 40, no. 2 (Summer): 27–61.

Cumplido, Francisco. 1983. "La estructura institucional del modelo de descentralización." *Documento de Trabajo* 3, Centro de Estudios del Desarrollo (May).

Dahl, Robert A. 1971. *Polyarchy: Participation and Opposition.* New Haven: Yale University Press.

———. 1992. "The Problem of Civic Competence." *Journal of Democracy* 3, no. 4: 45–59.

Dahl, Robert A., and Edward R. Tufte. 1973. *Size and Democracy.* Stanford: Stanford University Press.

Deeg, Richard. 1996. "Economic Globalization and the Shifting Boundaries of German Federalism." *Publius* 26: 27–52.

De Posadas, Diego. 1988. *Dignidad y Regocijo, Arriba y Abajo: Alegato Histórico sobre la Descentralización, la Autonomía, y la Gente.* Montevideo: Editorial Barreiro.

Diamond, Larry. 1999. *Developing Democracy: Toward Consolidation.* Baltimore: Johns Hopkins University Press.

Díaz Cayeros, Alberto. 1995. *Desarrollo económico e inequidad regional: Hacia un nuevo pacto federal en México.* Mexico City: Miguel Ángel Porrúa.

———. 1999. "Do Federal Institutions Matter? Rules and Political Practices in Mexico." Paper presented at the conference on Federalism, Democracy, and Public Policy, Centro de Investigación y Docencia Económicas, Mexico City, June.

Díaz Cayeros, Alberto, and Thomas Courchene. 2000. "Transfers and the Nature of the Mexican Federation." In *Achievements and Challenges of Fiscal Decentralization, Lessons from Mexico,* ed. Marcelo Giugale and Steven Webb. Washington, D.C.: World Bank.

Díaz Cayeros, Alberto, Beatriz Magaloni, and Barry R. Weingast. 1999. "Democratization and the Economy in Mexico: Equilibrium (PRI) Hegemony and Its Demise." Stanford University. Mimeo.

———. 2000. "Federalism and Democratization in Mexico." Paper presented at the Annual Meeting of the American Political Science Association, Washington D.C., August 31–September 3.

Díaz Cayeros, Alberto, and Charles McLure, Jr. 2000. "Tax Assignment." In *Achievements and Challenges of Fiscal Decentralization, Lessons from Mexico,* ed. Marcelo Giugale and Steven Webb. Washington, D.C.: World Bank.

Dillinger, William. 1994. *Decentralization and Its Implications for Urban Service Delivery.* Urban Management Programme Series 16. Washington, D.C.: World Bank.

———. 1997. "The Brazilian Debt Crisis." Washington, D.C.: World Bank. Mimeo.

Dillinger, William, and Steven B. Webb. 1998. "Fiscal Management in Federal Democracies: Argentina and Brazil." Mimeo.

———. 1999. "Fiscal Management in Federal Democracies: Argentina and Brazil." *Policy Research Working Paper* 2121. Washington, D.C.: World Bank.

Dillinger, William, Guillermo Perry, and Steven B. Webb. 1999. "Macroeconomic Management in Decentralized Democracies: The Quest for Hard Budget Constraints in Latin America." Washington, D.C.: World Bank. Mimeo (June).

Doner, Richard F., and Eric Hershberg. 1996. "Flexible Production and Political Decentralization: Elective Affinities in the Pursuit of Competitiveness." Paper presented at the Annual Meeting of the American Political Science Association, San Francisco, Calif.

Dornbusch, Rudiger, and Sebastian Edwards, eds. 1991. *The Macroeconomics of Populism in Latin America.* Chicago: University of Chicago Press.

Dye, Thomas R. 1990. *American Federalism: Competition among Governments.* Lexington, Mass.: Lexington Books.

Eaton, Kent. 1998. "Fiscal Policy Making in the Argentine Legislature." Working Paper, Department of Political Science, Yale University.

———. 2001. "Political Obstacles to Decentralization: Evidence from Argentina and the Philippines." *Development and Change* 32, no. 1: 101–27.

———. 2002. *Politicians and Economic Reform in New Democracies.* University Park: Pennsylvania State University Press.

Eckstein, Susan, ed. 1989. *Power and Popular Protest: Latin American Social Movements.* Berkeley: University of California Press.

Elazar, Daniel J. 1987. *Exploring Federalism.* Tuscaloosa: University of Alabama Press.

Ellner, Steve. 1996. "Political Party Factionalism and Democracy in Venezuela." *Latin American Perspectives* 23, no. 3 (Summer): 87–109.

Escobar, Arturo, and Sonia E. Alvarez, eds. 1992. *The Making of Social Movements in Latin America: Identity, Strategy, and Democracy.* Boulder, Colo.: Westview.

Espinoza, José, and Mario Marcel. 1994. "Descentralización fiscal: El caso de Chile." *CEPAL Serie Política Fiscal* 57 (April).

Evans, Peter B., ed. 1997. *State-Society Synergy: Government and Social Capital in Development.* Berkeley: IAS/University of California at Berkeley.

Faig, Juan Francisco. 1999. "La Revolución de 1897 en el Desarrollo Político e Institucional de Nuestro Pais." In *La Revolución de 1897,* ed. Enrique Mena Segarra. Montevideo: Ediciones de la Plaza.

Falleti, Tulia G. 1999. "New Fiscal Federalism and the Political Dynamics of Decentralization in Latin America." Paper presented at the conference "International Institutions, Global Processes, Domestic Consequence." Duke University, Durham, N.C., April 9–11.

Fausto, Boris. 1987. "A Revolução de 1930." In *Brasil em Perspectiva,* 16th edition, ed. Carlos Guilherme Mota. São Paulo: Bertrand Brasil.

Ferreira, Wolfgran Junqueira. 1965. "Aspectos Negativos da Reforma Tributária." *Revista de Administração Municipal* 73: 414–23.

Figueiredo, R., and Bolivar Lamounier. 1996. *As Cidades que Dão Certo: Experiências Inovadoras na Administração Pública Brasileira.* Brasília: MH Comunicação.

Filindra, Alexandra. 1999. "Fiscal Federalism and the Politics of Inter-governmental Grants: Lesson from the European Union." Paper presented at the Annual Meeting of the American Political Science Association, Atlanta, Ga.

Finkel, Steven E. 1995. *Causal Analysis with Panel Data.* Thousand Oaks, Calif: Sage Publications.

Finot, Ivan. 1990. *Democratización del Estado y Descentralización.* La Paz, Bolivia: ILDIS.

Fitzgibbon, Russell. 1954. *Uruguay: Portrait of a Democracy.* New Brunswick, N.J.: Rutgers University Press.

Fornasari, Francesca, Steven B. Webb, and Heng-Fu Zou. 1998. "Decentralized Spending and Central Government Deficits: International Evidence." LCSPR/ DECRG World Bank, Washington, D.C. Mimeo.

Foweraker, Joe. 1993. *Popular Mobilization in Mexico: The Teacher's Movement, 1977–1987.* Cambridge: Cambridge University Press.

Fox, David J. 1992. "Decentralization, Debt, Democracy, and the Amazonian Frontierlands of Bolivia and Brazil." In *Decentralization in Latin America: An Evaluation,* ed. Arthur Morris and Stella Lowder. New York: Praeger.

Fox, Jonathan. 1994. "Latin America's Emerging Local Politics." *Journal of Democracy* 5 (April): 105–16.

———. 1996. "How Does Civil Society Thicken? The Political Construction of Social Capital in Rural Mexico." *World Development* 24, no. 6: 1089–1103.

Fox, Jonathan, and Josefina Aranda. 1996. "Decentralization and Rural Development in Mexico: Community Participation in Oaxaca's Municipal Funds Program." Monograph Series 42. Center for U.S.-Mexican Studies, University of California, San Diego.

Frias, Pedro. 1980. *El Federalismo Argentino: Introducción al Derecho Público Provincial.* Buenos Aires: Depalma.

Fuentealba, Rafael. 1991a. "El Senado estudiará cambios a sistema de gobierno regional." *La Epoca* (March 31).

———. 1991b. "El Parlamento debe decidir el futuro de la reforma municipal." *La Epoca* (March 30).

Fukasaku, Kiichiro, and Luiz R. de Mello. 1997. "Fiscal Decentralization and Macroeconomic Stability: The Experience of Large Developing and Transition Economies." Paper prepared for the 8th International Forum on Latin American Perspectives, the Inter-American Development Bank and the OECD Development Centre, Paris, France, November 20–21.

Fundación de Investigaciones Económicas Latinoamericanas (FIEL). 1993. *Hacia Una Nueva Organización del Federalismo Fiscal en la Argentina.* Buenos Aires: Ediciones Latinomericanas.

Garman, Christopher, Stephan Haggard, and Eliza Willis. 1996. "Decentralization in Latin America." Paper presented at the Annual Meeting of the American Political Science Association, San Francisco, Calif.

———. 2001. "Fiscal Decentralization: A Political Theory with Latin American Cases." *World Politics* 53, no. 2 (January): 205–36.

Garretón, Manuel Antonio. 1995. "Redemocratization in Chile." *Journal of Democracy* 6 (January): 146–58.

Garretón, Manuel Antonio, Marta Lagos, and Roberto Méndez. 1994. *Los chilenos y la democracia: La opinión pública 1991–1994, Informe 1993*. Santiago: Ediciones Participa.

Gibson, Edward L. 1997a. "Federalism and Electoral Coalitions: Making Market Reform Politically Viable in Argentina." Department of Political Science, Northwestern University, Evanston, Ill. Mimeo.

———. 1997b. "The Populist Road to Market Reform: Policy and Electoral Coalitions in Mexico and Argentina." *World Politics* 49, no. 3 (April): 339–71.

Gibson, Edward and Ernesto Calvo. 2000. "Federalism and Low-Maintenance Constituencies: Territorial Dimensions of Economic Reform in Argentina." *Studies in Comparative International Development* 35: 32–55.

Gil, Federico G. 1966. *The Political System of Chile*. Boston: Houghton Mifflin Company.

Gillespie, Charles. 1991. *Negotiating Democracy: Politicians and Generals in Uruguay*. Cambridge: Cambridge University Press.

Gómez, Eduardo. 2000. "Brazil: A Political Economy of Sub-national Debt Control and Financial Regulation." Paper prepared for the conference "The Political Economy of Reform in Latin America." David Rockefeller Center for Latin American Studies, Harvard University, Cambridge, Mass.

González, Luis. 1991. *Political Structures and Democracy in Uruguay*. Notre Dame, Ind.: University of Notre Dame Press.

González Block, Miguel Angel. 1991. "Economic Crisis and the Decentralization of Health Services in Mexico." In *Social Responses to Mexico's Economic Crisis of the 1980's*, ed. Mercedes González de la Rocha and Agustín Escobar Latapí. San Diego: Center for U.S.-Mexican Studies, University of California at San Diego.

Grindle, Merilee. 1996. *Challenging the State: Crisis and Innovation in Latin America and Africa*. Cambridge: Cambridge University Press.

———. 2000. *Audacious Reforms: Institutional Invention and Democracy in Latin America*. Baltimore: Johns Hopkins University Press.

Gwynne, Robert N. 1992. "Industrial Decentralization in Mexico in Global Perspective." In *Decentralization in Latin America: An Evaluation*, ed. Arthur Morris and Stella Lowder. New York: Praeger.

Haggard, Stephan, and Robert R. Kaufman. 1995. *The Political Economy of Democratic Transitions*. Princeton: Princeton University Press.

Haggard, Stephan, and Steven Webb, eds. 1994. *Voting for Reform: Democracy, Political Liberalization, and Economic Adjustment.* New York: Oxford University Press/World Bank.

Hagopian, Frances. 1996. *Traditional Politics and Regime Change in Brazil.* Cambridge: Cambridge University Press.

Hausmann, Ricardo. 1998. "Fiscal Institutions for Decentralising Democracies: Which Way to Go?" In *Democracy, Decentralisation and Deficits in Latin America*, ed. Kiichiro Fukasaku and Ricardo Hausmann. Paris: IDB/OECD.

Hernández, Antonio María. 1997. *Federalismo, autonomía municipal y ciudad de Buenos Aires en la reforma constitucional de 1994.* Buenos Aires: Depalma.

Horn, Murray J., and Kenneth A. Shepsle. 1989. "Commentary on 'Administrative Arrangements and the Political Control of Agencies': Administrative Process and Organizational Form as Legislative Responses to Agency Costs." *Virginia Law Review* 75 (March): 499–508.

Huang, Yasheng. 1996. *Inflation and Investment Controls in China.* New York: Cambridge University Press.

Hunter, J. S. 1977. *Federalism and Fiscal Balance: A Comparative Study.* Canberra: Australian National University Press.

Hunter, Wendy. 1997. *Eroding Military Influence in Brazil: Politicians against Soldiers.* Chapel Hill: University of North Carolina Press.

Instituto Brasileiro de Administração Municipal (IBAM). 1976. *Relações Intergovernamentais União-Município.* Rio de Janeiro: IBAM.

Instituto Brasileiro de Geografia e Estatística (IBGE). 1998. "Dados Tabulados dos Censos de 1996, Resultados Definitivos da Contagem da População 1996." Computer archives from the IBGE website, www.ibge.gov.br. Accessed on October 29, 1998.

INEGI. 1986. *Finanzas Públicas Estatales y Municipales de México, 1975–1984.* Aguascalientes: Instituto Nacional de Estadística, Geografía e Informática.

———. 1991. *Finanzas Públicas Estatales y Municipales de México, 1979–1988.* Aguascalientes, Mexico: Instituto Nacional de Estadística, Geografía e Informática.

———. 1992. *XI Censo de Poblacion y Vivienda, 1990.* Aguascalientes, Mexico: Instituto Nacional de Estadística, Geografía e Informática.

———. 1994. *Finanzas Públicas Estatales y Municipales de México, 1989–1992.* Aguascalientes, Mexico: Instituto Nacional de Estadística, Geografía e Informática.

———. 1996. *Sistema de Cuentas Nacionales de Mexico: Producto Interno Bruto por Entidad Federativa, 1993.* Aguascalientes, Mexico: Instituto Nacional de Estadística, Geografía e Informática.

———. 1998. *Finanzas Públicas Estatales y Municipales de México, 1992–1996.* Aguascalientes, Mexico: Instituto Nacional de Estadística, Geografía e Informática.

IDB (Inter-American Development Bank). 1994. *Economic and Social Progress in Latin America, 1994 Report. Special Report: Fiscal Decentralization.* October. Washington, D.C.: IDB/Johns Hopkins University Press.

———. 1997. *Economic and Social Progress in Latin America, 1997 Report. Latin America after a Decade of Reforms.* September. Washington, D.C.: IDB/Johns Hopkins University Press.

Intergovernmental Decentralization Fund (FIDES). 1996. *Fides: Una experiencia positiva.* Caracas: Fides.

Jacob, Raúl. 1983. *El Uruguay de Terra: 1931–1938.* Montevideo: Ediciones de la Banda Oriental.

Jin, Hehui, Yingyi Qian, and Barry R. Weingast. 1999. "Regional Decentralization and Fiscal Incentives: Federalism, Chinese Style." March. Working Paper, Hoover Institution, Stanford University.

Jones, Mark. 1997. "Evaluating Argentina's Presidential Democracy: 1983–1995." In *Presidentialism and Democracy in Latin America,* ed. Scott Mainwaring and Matthew Shugart. New York: Cambridge University Press.

———. 2001. "Carreras políticas y disciplínas partidárias en la Cámara de Diputados Argentina." *PostData* (Buenos Aires) 7 (May): 189–230.

Jones, Mark, et al. 2001. "Keeping a Seat in Congress: Provincial Party Bosses and the Survival of Argentine Legislators." Paper presented at the Annual Meeting of the American Political Science Association, San Francisco, Calif.

Karl, Terry Lynn. 1986. "Imposing Consent? Electoralism vs. Democratization in El Salvador." In *Elections in Latin America,* ed. Paul Drake and Eduardo Silva. San Diego: University of California Press.

Katzenstein, Peter J. 1985. *Small States in World Markets: Industrial Policy in Europe.* Ithaca, N.Y.: Cornell University Press.

Kaufman, Robert R. 1990. "Stabilization and Adjustment in Argentina, Brazil, and Mexico." In *Economic Crisis and Policy Choice: The Politics of Adjustment in the Third World,* ed. Joan M. Nelson. Princeton: Princeton University Press.

Kornblith, Miriam. 1996. "Crisis y transformación del sistema político venezolano." In *El sistema político venezolano: Crisis y transformaciones,* ed. Angel Alvarez. Caracas: Universidad Central de Venezuela.

Kornblith, Miriam, and Daniel H. Levine. 1995. "Venezuela: The Life and Times of the Party System." In *Building Democratic Institutions: Party Systems in Latin America,* ed. Scott Mainwaring and Timothy R. Scully. Stanford: Stanford University Press.

Kraemer, Moritz. 1999. "One Decade of Decentralization: An Assessment of the Venezuelan Experiment." Inter-American Development Bank, Washington, D.C.

Langston, Joy. 1995. "Sobrevivir y prosperar: una búsqueda de las causas de las facciones políticas intrarrégimen en México." *Política y Gobierno* 2, no. 2: 243–77.

Larangeira, Sônia M. G. 1996. "Gestão pública e participação: a experiência do orçamento participativo em Porto Alegre." *São Paulo em Perspectiva* 10, no. 3: 129–37.

Levitsky, Steven. 1998. "Institutionalization and Peronism: The Concept, the Case and the Case for Unpacking the Concept." *Party Politics* 4: 77–92.

———. 1999. "From Laborism to Liberalism: Institutionalization and Labor-Based Party Adaptation in Argentina (1983–1997)." Ph.D. diss. University of California at Berkeley.

Liang, Kung-Yee, and Scott L. Zeger. 1986. "Longitudinal Data Analysis Using Generalized Linear Models." *Biometrika* 73: 13–22.

Lindahl, Goran. 1962. *Uruguay's New Path*. Stockholm: Library and Institute of Ibero-American Studies.

Linz, Juan J., and Alfred Stepan. 1992. "Political Identities and Electoral Sequences: Spain, the Soviet Union, and Yugoslavia." *Daedalus* 121, no. 2: 123–40.

———. 1996. *Problems of Democratic Transition and Consolidation: Southern Europe, South America, and Post-Communist Europe*. Baltimore: Johns Hopkins University Press.

Lipset, Seymour Martin, ed. 1995. *The Encyclopedia of Democracy*. Washington, D.C.: Congressional Quarterly.

Litvack, Jennie, Junaid Ahmad, and Richard Bird. 2000. "Rethinking Decentralization at the World Bank." Washington, D.C.: World Bank. Mimeo.

Llanos, Mariana. 1998. "El presidente, el Congresso y la política de privatizaciones en la Argentina (1989–1997)." *Desarrollo Económico* 151: 743–70.

López-Maya, Margarita. 1997. "The Rise of Causa R in Venezuela." In *The New Politics of Inequality in Latin America: Rethinking Participation and Representation*, ed. Douglas Chalmers, Carlos Vilas, Katherine Hite, Scott B. Martin, Kerianne Piester, and Monique Segarra. New York: Oxford University Press.

López-Murphy, Ricardo, ed. 1995. *Fiscal Decentralization in Latin America*. Washington, D.C.: Inter-American Development Bank.

Love, Joseph L. 1993. "Federalismo y Regionalismo en Brasil, 1889–1937." In *Federalismos Latinoamericanos: México/Brasil/Argentina*, ed. Marcello Carmagnani. Mexico City: Fondo de Cultura Económica/El Colegio de México.

Mahar, Dennis J. 1971. "The Failures of Revenue Sharing in Brazil and Some Recent Developments." *Bulletin for International Fiscal Documentation* 225, no. 3: 71–79.

Mahar, Dennis, and William Dillinger. 1983. "Financing State and Local Government in Brazil: Recent Trends and Issues." World Bank Staff Working Papers no. 612.

Mainwaring, Scott. 1999. *Rethinking Party Systems in the Third Wave of Democratization: The Case of Brazil.* Stanford: Stanford University Press.

Manor, James. 1995. "Democratic Decentralization in Africa and Asia." *Institute of Development Studies Bulletin* 26, no. 2: 81–88.

———. 1999. *The Political Economy of Democratic Decentralization.* Washington, D.C.: World Bank.

Marcel, Mario. 1994. "Decentralization and Development: The Chilean Experience." In *En Route to Modern Growth: Essays in Honor of Carlos Díaz-Alejandro,* ed. Gustav Ranis. Washington, D.C.: Johns Hopkins University Press.

Martelli, Giorgio, ed. 1994. *Manual para la gestión regional.* Santiago: Fundación Friedrich Ebert, Centro de Estudios Socioeconómicos Para el Desarollo (CED), and Instituto para el Nuevo Chile.

———. 1998. "Asociación Chilena de Municipalidades: Historia, Hechos, Desafíos y Reflexiones." Fundación Friedrich Ebert working paper.

———. N.d. "Algunas propuestas para un municipio democrático y eficaz." Centro de Estudios Municipales. Mimeo.

Martins, Daniel. 1978. *El Municipio Contemporaneo: Los Gobiernos Locales de Occidente y del Uruguay.* Montevideo: Fundación de Cultura Universitaria.

Martner, Gonzalo D. 1993. *Descentralización y modernización del Estado en la transición.* Santiago: LOM Ediciones.

McCoy, Jennifer, and William C. Smith. 1995. "Democratic Disequilibrium in Venezuela." *Journal of Interamerican Studies and World Affairs* 37, no. 2 (Summer): 113–79.

McCubbins, Mathew D., Roger G. Noll, and Barry R. Weingast. 1987. "Administrative Procedures as Instruments of Political Control." *Journal of Law, Economics and Organization* 3, no. 2 (Fall): 243–77.

———. 1989. "Structure and Process, Politics and Policy: Administrative Arrangements and the Political Control of Agencies." *Virginia Law Review* 75: 431–82.

Medeiros, Antônio C. 1986. *Politics and Intergovernmental Relations in Brazil, 1964–1982.* London: Garland.

Mello, Diogo Lordello de. 1955. "Panorama da Administração Municipal Brasileira." *Cadernos de Administração Pública* 26, Fundação Getúlio Vargas. Rio de Janeiro.

———. 1965. *Problemas Institucionais do Município.* Rio de Janeiro: Instituto Brasileiro de Administração Municipal.

———. 1971. *O Município na Organização Nacional.* Rio de Janeiro: Instituto Brasileiro de Administração Municipal.

Mill, John Stuart. 1958. *Considerations on Representative Government.* New York: Liberal Arts Press.

Ministry of Economy (MECON). 1994. *Cambios estructurales en la relación Nación Provincias.* Buenos Aires: Ministry of Economy.

Moe, Terry M. 1990. "Political Institutions: The Neglected Side of the Story." *Journal of Law, Economics and Organization* 6 (December): 213–53.

Molina, José Enrique. 1991. *El sistema electoral venezolano y sus consecuencias políticas.* Caracas: Vadell Hermanos.

———. 2000. "Comportamiento electoral en Venezuela: Cambio y continuidad." Paper presented at the 22nd Congress of the Latin American Studies Association, Miami, Fla., March 16–18.

Molina, José E., and Carmen Pérez. 1998. "Evolution of the Party System in Venezuela, 1946–1993." *Journal of Interamerican Studies and World Affairs* 40, no. 2 (Summer): 1–26.

Molina, Sergio, and Iván Arias. 1996. *De la Nación Clandestina a la Participación Popular.* La Paz, Bolivia: CEDOIN (Centro de Documentación e Información).

Molina Monasterios, Fernando. 1997. *Historia de la Participación Popular.* La Paz, Bolivia: Secretaría Nacional de Participación Popular.

Molina Saucedo, Carlos Hugo. 1990. *La Descentralización Imposible y la Alternativa Municipal.* Santa Cruz, Bolivia: Editorial Cabildo.

———. 1997. "Participación Popular y Descentralización: Instrumentos Para el Desarrollo." In *El Pulso de la Democracia: Participación Ciudadana y Descentralización en Bolivia,* ed. Secretaría Nacional de Participación Popular. La Paz, Bolivia: Ministerio de Desarrollo Humano.

Molinar Horcasitas, Juan, and Jeff Weldon. 1994. "Electoral Determinants and Consequences of National Solidarity." In *Transforming State-Society Relations in Mexico: The National Solidarity Strategy,* ed. Wayne Cornelius, Ann Craig, and Jonathan Fox. La Jolla: Center for U.S.-Mexican Studies, University of California, San Diego.

Montero, Alfred P. 1998. "Assessing the Third Wave Democracies." *Journal of Interamerican Studies and World Affairs* 40, no. 2 (Summer): 117–34.

———. 2000. "Devolving Democracy? Political Decentralization and the New Brazilian Federalism." In *Democratic Brazil: Actors, Institutions, and Processes,* ed. Peter R. Kingstone and Timothy J. Power. Pittsburgh: University of Pittsburgh Press.

———. 2001. "Decentralizing Democracy: Spain and Brazil in Comparative Perspective." *Comparative Politics* 33, no. 2 (January): 149–69.

———. 2002. *Shifting States in Global Markets: Subnational Industrial Policy in Contemporary Brazil and Spain.* University Park: Pennsylvania State University Press.

Montinola, Gabriella, Yingyi Qian, and Barry R. Weingast. 1995. "Federalism, Chinese Style: The Politics Basis for Economic Success in China." *World Politics* 48, no. 1 (October): 50–81.

Morduchowicz, Alejandro. 1996. "Las relaciones fiscales nación-provincias en la última década-soluciones temporarias a problemas permanentes." *Informe de Coyuntura:* 19–38.

Morris, Aldon D., and Carol McClurg Mueller. 1992. *Frontiers in Social Movement Theory.* New Haven: Yale University Press.

Morris, Arthur. 1992. "Decentralization: The Context." In *Decentralization in Latin America: An Evaluation,* ed. Arthur Morris and Stella Lowder. New York: Praeger.

Munck, Gerardo. 1994. "Democratic Stability and Its Limits: An Analysis of Chile's 1993 Elections." *Journal of Interamerican Studies and World Affairs* 36, no. 2 (Summer): 1–35.

Murillo, María Victoria. 1999. "Recovering Political Dynamics: Teachers' Unions and the Decentralization of Education in Argentina and Mexico." *Journal of Interamerican Studies and World Affairs* 41, no. 1 (Spring): 31–57.

Musgrave, Richard A. 1983. "Who Should Tax, Where, and What?" In *Tax Assignment in Federal Countries,* ed. Charles McLure. Canberra: Center for Research on Federal Financial Relations, Australian National University.

Nacional Financiera. 1993. "En busca del pacto perdido: la fallida búsqueda del consenso en la Venezuela de los 80 y los 90." In *Venezuela la Democracia Bajo Presión,* ed. Andrés Serbin et al. Caracas: Editorial Nueva Sociedad.

———. 1995. *La Economía Mexicana en Cifras, 1995, 14a Edición.* Mexico City: Nacional Financiera, S.N.C.

———. 1998. *La Economía Mexicana en Cifras, 1998, 15a Edición.* Mexico City: Nacional Financiera. S.N.C.

Naím, Moisés. 2001. "The Real Story behind Venezuela's Woes." *Journal of Democracy* 12, no. 2 (April): 17–31.

Navarro, Juan Carlos. 1995. "In Search of the Lost Pact: Consensus Lost in the 1980s and 1990s." In *Venezuelan Democracy under Stress,* ed. Jennifer McCoy, Andrés Serbin, William C. Smith, and Andrés Stambouli. New Brunswick, N.J.: Transaction Publishers.

Nelson, Joan, ed. 1990. *Economic Crisis and Policy Choice: The Politics of Adjustment in Developing Countries.* Princeton: Princeton University Press.

Nickson, R. Andrew. 1995. *Local Government in Latin America.* Boulder, Colo.: Lynne Rienner.

Nogueira, Júlio Cesar de A. 1995. "O Financiamento Público e Descentralização Fiscal no Brasil." *Texto para Discussão* no. 34. Rio de Janeiro: CEPP.

Nohlen, Dieter, ed. 1991. *Descentralizacíon Política y Consolidacíon Democrática: Europa y América del Sur.* Caracas: Nueva Sociedad.

Novaro, Markos. 1994. *Pilotas de tormentas: Crisis de representación y persona-lización de la política en Argentina (1989–1993)*. Buenos Aires: Letra Buena.

Nunes, Edison. 1995. "Conclusión." In *Municípios y Servícios Públicos: Gobi-ernos Locales en Ciudades Intermédias de América Latina*, ed. Alfredo Rodríguez and Fabio Velásquez. Santiago: Ediciones Sur.

———. 1996. "Instituições, Política e Economia: A Economia Política do Desen-volvimento Brasileiro." Unpublished paper, Rio de Janeiro.

Nunes Leal, Victor. 1976. *Coronelismo, Enxada e Voto: o Município e o Regime Representativo no Brasil*. São Paulo: Editora Alfa-Omega.

———. 1977. *Coronelismo: The Municipality and Representative Government in Brazil*. Trans. June Henfrey. London: Cambridge University Press.

Nuñez Miñana, Horacio and Alberto Porto. 1982. "Coparticipación Federal de Impuestos: Distribución Primaria." *Jornadas de Finanzas Públicas* 15: 1–73.

———. 1983. "Coparticipación Federal de Impuestos: Distribución Secundaria." *Jornadas de Finanzas Públicas* 16: 1–56.

Nylen, William R. 2000. "The Making of a Loyal Opposition: The Workers' Party (PT) and the Consolidation of Democracy in Brazil." In *Democratic Brazil: Actors, Institutions, and Processes*, ed. Peter Kingstone and Timo-thy J. Power. Pittsburgh: University of Pittsburgh Press.

Oates, Wallace E. 1972. *Fiscal Federalism*. New York: Harcourt, Brace, Jo-vanovich.

———. 1993. "Fiscal Decentralization and Economic Development." *National Tax Journal* 46: 237–43.

———, ed. 1977. *The Political Economy of Fiscal Federalism*. Lexington, Mass.: D. C. Heath and Company.

O'Donnell, Guillermo. 1994. "Delegative Democracy." *Journal of Democracy* 5: 55–69.

Oliveira, Fabrício Augusto de. 1995. *Autoritarismo e Crise Fiscal no Brasil (1964–84)*. São Paulo: Hucitec, 62.

Oliveira, Francisco de. 1995. "A Crise da Federação: Da Oligarquia á Globali-zação." In *A Federação em Perspectiva: Ensaios Selecionados*, ed. Rui de Britto. São Paulo: Fundação do Desenvolvimento Administrativo.

O'Neill, Kathleen. 2000. "Tugging at the Purse Strings: Fiscal Decentralization and State Discretion." Paper presented at the Annual Meeting of the Latin American Studies Association, Miami, Fla.

Oporto Castro, Henry. 1996. "Descentralización en Bolivia: Esperanzas y Frus-traciones." *Nueva Sociedad* 105 (January–February): 46–54.

Organisation for Economic Cooperation and Development (OECD). 1998. *De-centralization and Local Infrastructure in Mexico: A New Policy for Devel-opment*. London: OECD.

Orlansky, Dora. 1998. "Las políticas de descentralización." *Desarrollo Econó-mico* 151: 827–43.

Ostrom, Elinor, L. Schroeder, and S. Wynne. 1993. *Institutional Incentives and Sustainable Development*. Boulder, Colo.: Westview Press.

Palermo, Vicente, and Marcos Novaro. 1996. *Política y poder en el gobierno de Menem*. Buenos Aires: FLACSO.

Partido Nacional. 1989. *Documentos Sobre el Proyecto de Descentralización y Acondicionamiento Territorial del Partido Nacional*. Montevideo.

Pascal, Andrés. 1968. *Relaciones de poder en una localidad rural*. Santiago: ICIRA.

Peterson, Paul. 1995. *The Price of Federalism*. Washington, D.C.: Brookings Institution.

Pírez, Pedro. 1986. *Coparticipación federal y descentralización del estado*. Buenos Aires: Centro Editor de America Latina.

Power, Timothy J., and J. Timmons Roberts. 2000. "A New Brazil? The Changing Sociodemographic Context of Brazilian Democracy." In *Democratic Brazil: Actors, Institutions, and Processes*, ed. Peter Kingstone and Timothy J. Power. Pittsburgh: University of Pittsburgh Press.

Prud'homme, Rémy. 1995. "The Dangers of Decentralization." *The World Bank Research Observer* 10, no. 2 (August): 201–20.

Putnam, Robert D. 1993. *Making Democracy Work: Civic Traditions in Modern Italy*. Princeton: Princeton University Press.

Quintana Bigolotti, Mario. 1992. *El Proceso de Descentralización de la Intendencia Municipal de Montevideo*. Montevideo: Asociación de Administradores Gubernamentales.

Rabkin, Rhoda. 1992–1993. "The Aylwin Government and 'Tutelary' Democracy: A Concept in Search of a Case?" *Journal of Inter-American Studies and World Affairs* 34 (Winter): 119–94.

Raczynski, Dagmar, and Claudia Serrano. 1987. "Administración y gestión local: La experiencia de algunos municipios en Santiago." *Colección Estudios CIEPLAN* 22 (December).

Rehren, Alfredo José. 1986. "Municipal Government in an Authoritarian Regime: The Case of Chile: 1974–1984." Ph.D. diss., University of Texas at Austin.

Remmer, Karen L., and Erik Wibbels. 2000. "The Subnational Politics of Economic Adjustment: Provincial Politics and Fiscal Performance in Argentina." *Comparative Political Studies* 33, no. 4 (May): 419–51.

Rezende, Fernando. 1995. "Federalismo Fiscal no Brasil." *Revista de Economia Política* 15, no. 3: 5–17.

Rezk, Ernesto. 1997. "Experiences of Decentralization and Inter-Governmental Fiscal Relations in Latin America." *Jornada de Finanzas Públicas* 30: (10): 1–26.

———. 1998. "Argentina: Fiscal Federalism and Decentralization." In *Fiscal Decentralization in Developing Countries*, ed. Richard M. Bird and François Vaillancourt. New York: Cambridge University Press.

Riker, William. 1964. *Federalism: Origin, Operation, and Significance.* Boston: Little Brown.

Rilla, José. 1985. "La Política Impositiva: Asedio y Bloqueo del Battlismo." In *El Primer Batllismo,* ed. Jorge Balbis. Montevideo: Ediciones de la Banda Oriental.

Rock, David. 1985. *Argentina, 1516–1982: From Spanish Colonization to the Falklands War.* Berkeley: University of California Press.

———. 1987. *Argentina: 1516–1987: From Spanish Colonization to Alfonsín.* Berkeley: University of California Press.

Rodden, Jonathan. 1999. "Soft Budget Constraints and Deficits in Decentralized Fiscal Systems." Paper presented at the Annual Meeting of the American Political Science Association, Atlanta, Ga.

Rodden, Jonathan, and Susan Rose-Ackerman. 1997. "Does Federalism Preserve Markets?" *Virginia Law Review* 83: 1521–72.

Rodríguez, Victoria E. 1993. "The Politics of Decentralisation in Mexico: From *Municipio Libre* to *Solidaridad.*" *The Bulletin of Latin American Research* 12, no. 2: 133–45.

———. 1997. *Decentralization in Mexico: From Reforma Municipal to Solidaridad to Nuevo Federalismo.* Boulder, Colo.: Westview Press.

Rodríguez, Victoria E., and Peter M. Ward. 1992. *Policy-making, Politics, and Urban Governance in Chihuahua: The Experience of Recent Panista Governments.* Austin: Lyndon B. Johnson School of Public Affairs, University of Texas at Austin.

———. 1994. *Political Change in Baja California: Democracy in the Making?* Monograph Series 40. Center for U.S.-Mexican Studies, University of California at San Diego.

———, eds. 1995. *Opposition Government in Mexico.* Albuquerque: University of New Mexico Press.

Romero, Aníbal. 1997. "Rearranging the Deck Chairs on the Titanic: The Agony of Democracy in Venezuela." *Latin American Research Review* 32, no. 1: 7–36.

Rondinelli, Dennis. 1981. "Government Decentralization in Comparative Perspective: Theory and Practice in Developing Countries." *International Review of Administrative Science* 47.

———. 1989. "Decentralizing Public Services in Developing Countries: Issues and Opportunities." *Journal of Social, Political, and Economic Studies* 14, no. 1 (Spring): 77–98.

Rondinelli, Dennis, John Nellis, and G. S. Cheema. 1984. "Decentralization in Developing Countries: A Review of Recent Experience." World Bank Staff Working Papers no. 581.

Rosenfeld, Alex, Alfredo Rodríguez, and Vicente Espinoza. 1989. "La situación de los gobiernos locales en Chile." In *Descentralización y democracia: Gobi-*

ernos locales en América Latina, ed. Jordi Borja, Fernando Calderón, María Grossi, and Susana Peñalva. Santiago: CLACSO, SUR, CEUMT-Barcelona.

Sabatier, Paul A. and Hank C. Jenkins-Smith. 1993. *Policy Change and Learning: An Advocacy Coalition Approach.* Boulder, Colo.: Westview Press.

Saffirio Suárez, Eduardo. 1995. "El sistema de partidos y la sociedad civil en la redemocratización chilena." In *Sociedad civil y partidos políticos: Elementos de análisis.* Caracas: Fundación Konrad Adenaur and Organización Demócrata Cristiana de América.

Saiegh, Sebastian, and Mariano Tommasi. 1998. "Argentina's Federal Fiscal Institutions." Buenos Aires: Centro de Estudios para el Desarrollo Institucional. Unpublished paper.

Samuels, David J. 2000a. "Concurrent Elections, Discordant Results: Presidentialism, Federalism, and Governance in Brazil." *Comparative Politics* 33, no. 1 (October): 1–20.

———. 2000b. "The Gubernatorial Coattails Effect: Federalism and Congressional Elections in Brazil." *Journal of Politics* 62, no. 1 (February): 240–53.

———. 2003. *Ambition, Federalism, and Legislative Politics in Brazil.* New York: Cambridge University Press.

Samuels, David, and Fernado Luiz Abrucio. 1997. "The New Politics of the Governors: Subnational Politics and the Brazilian Transition to Democracy." Paper presented at the Annual Meeting of the International Political Science Association, Seoul, Korea.

Sanguinetti, Juan. 1994. "Intergovernmental Transfers and Public Sector Expenditures: A Game Theoretic Approach." *Estudios de Economía* 21, no. 2: 179–212.

———. 1999. "Restricción de Presupuesto Blanda en los niveles Subnacionales de Gobierno: el Caso los Salvatajes en el caso Argentina." Paper presented at the Fourth International Conference on Fiscal Federalism, Universidad Nacional de La Plata. La Plata, Argentina, November 26.

Sanguinetti, Pablo, and Mariano Tommasi. 1996. "Los Determinantes Económicos e Institucionales de los Déficits en los Presopuestos Provinciales." Working Paper, Inter-American Development Bank.

Santos, Milton. 1994. *A Urbanização Brasileira.* São Paulo: Editora Hucitec.

Santos, Wanderley G. dos. 1971. "Governadores-Políticos, Governadores-Técnicos, Governadores-Militares." *Dados: Revista de Ciências Socias* 8: 123–28.

Sarles, Margaret J. 1982. "Maintaining Political Control through Parties: The Brazilian Strategy." *Comparative Politics* 15 (October): 41–71.

Sawers, Larry. 1996. *The Other Argentina: The Interior and National Development.* Boulder, Colo.: Westview Press.

Schlesinger, Joseph. 1966. *Ambition and Politics: Political Careers in the United States.* Chicago: Rand McNally.

Schmitter, Phillippe. 1973. "The 'Portugalization' of Brazil?" In *Authoritarian Brazil: Origins, Policies, Future*, ed. Alfred Stepan. New Haven: Yale University Press.

Schönwälder, Gerd. 1997. "New Democratic Spaces at the Grassroots? Popular Participation in Latin American Local Governments." *Development and Change* 28, no. 4: 753–70.

Schuurman, Frans J. 1998. "The Decentralisation Discourse: Post-Fordist Paradigm or Neo-Liberal Cul-de-Sac?" In *Globalisation, Competitiveness, and Human Security*, ed. Cristobal Kay. London: Frank Cass.

Scully, Timothy R. 1995. "Reconstituting Party Politics in Chile." In *Building Democratic Institutions: Party Systems in Latin America*, ed. Scott Mainwaring and Timothy R. Scully. Stanford: Stanford University Press.

Scully, Timothy, and J. Samuel Valenzuela. 1993. "From Democracy to Democracy: Continuities and Changes of Electoral Choices and the Party System in Chile." Working Paper no. 199, Helen Kellogg Institute for International Studies, University of Notre Dame (July).

Shah, Anwar. 1991a. *The New Fiscal Federalism in Brazil*. Washington, D.C.: World Bank.

———. 1991b. "The New Fiscal Federalism in Brazil." *World Bank Discussion Papers* 124.

———. 1994. *The Reform of Inter-governmental Fiscal Relations in Developing and Emerging Market Economies*. Washington, D.C.: The World Bank.

———. 1998. "Fiscal Federalism and Macroeconomic Governance: For Better or for Worse?" World Bank Working Paper. Washington, D.C.: The World Bank.

Sherwood, Frank P. 1967. *Institutionalizing the Grass Roots in Brazil: A Study in Comparative Local Government*. San Francisco: Chandler Publishing Company.

Shoup, Carl. 1965. *The Tax System of Brazil*. Rio de Janeiro: Fundaçao Getulio Vargas.

Siavelis, Peter M. 1997. "Executive-Legislative Relations in Post-Pinochet Chile: A Preliminary Assessment." In *Presidentialism and Democracy in Latin America*, ed. Scott Mainwaring and Matthew Soberg Shugart. New York: Cambridge University Press.

———. 2000. *President and Congress in Postauthoritarian Chile*. University Park: Pennsylvania State University Press.

Silva, Guilherme L., and Basilia M. B. Aguirre. 1992. "Crise político-econômica: as raízes do impasse." *Estudos Avançados* 14: 79–94.

Silva, Zilda Pereira da. 1996. "O município e a descentralização da saúde." *São Paulo em Perspectiva* 10, no. 3: 81–87.

Skidmore, Thomas, E. 1967. *Politics in Brazil, 1930–64: An Experiment in Democracy*. Oxford: Oxford University Press.

Skidmore, Thomas, and Peter Smith. 1997. *Modern Latin America*. 4th edition. New York: Oxford University Press.

Smith, Peter. 1979. *Labyrinths of Power: Political Recruitment in Twentieth-Century Mexico*. Princeton: Princeton University Press.

Smith, William C., Carlos H. Acuña, and Eduaro A. Gamarra, eds. 1994. *Democracy, Markets, and Structural Reform in Latin America*. New Brunswick, N.J.: Transaction Publishers.

Snyder, Richard. 1999. "After Neoliberalism: The Politics of Reregulation in Mexico." *World Politics* 51, no. 2 (January): 173–204.

———. 2001a. *Politics after Neoliberalism: Reregulation in Mexico*. New York: Cambridge University Press.

———. 2001b. "Scaling Down: The Subnational Comparative Method." *Studies in Comparative International Development* 36, no. 1 (Spring): 93–110.

Sola, Lourdes. 1987. "O Golpe de 1937 e o Estado Novo." In *Brasil em Perspectiva*, 16th edition, ed. Carlos G. Mota. São Paulo: Bertrand Brasil.

Solnick, Steven. 1998. "Hanging Separately? Cooperation, Cooptation, and Cheating in Developing Federations." Paper presented at the Annual Meeting of the American Political Science Association, Boston, September.

SourceMex, various. "SourceMex—Economic and Political News on Mexico." Latin America Database, Latin American Institute, University of New Mexico, http://ladb.unm.edu.

Souza, Celina. 1996a. "Reinventando o Poder Local: Limites e Possibilidades do Federalismo e da Descentralização." *São Paulo em Perspectiva* 10, no. 3: 103–12.

———. 1996b. "Redemocratization and Decentralization in Brazil: The Strength of the Member States." *Development and Change* 27, no. 3: 529–55.

———. 1997. *Constitutional Engineering in Brazil: The Politics of Federalism and Decentralization*. New York: St. Martin's Press.

———. 1998. "Intermediação de Interesses Regionais no Brasil: o Impacto do Federalismo e da Descentralização." *Dados—Revista de Ciências Sociais* 41, no. 3: 569–92.

Spisso, Rodolfo. 1995. "La ley de coparticipación tribuutaria y el principio de lealtad federal." *Derecho Tributario* 5: 241–48.

Stansfield, David E. 1992. "Decentralization in Mexico: The Political Context." In *Decentralization in Latin America: An Evaluation*, ed. Arthur Morris and Stella Lowder. New York: Praeger.

Stein, Ernesto. 1999. "La descentralización fiscal y el tamaño del gobierno en América Latina." In *Democracia, Descentralización, y Deficit Presupuestarios en América Latina*, ed. Kiichiro Fukasaku and Ricardo Hausmann. Washington, D.C.: Inter-American Development Bank.

Stepan, Alfred. 1978. *The State and Society: Peru in Comparative Perspective*. Princeton: Princeton University Press.

———. 1988. *Rethinking Military Politics: Brazil and the Southern Cone.* Princeton: Princeton University Press.

———. 2000. "Brazil's Decentralized Federalism: Bringing Government Closer to the Citizens?" *Daedalus* 129, no. 2 (Spring): 145–69.

Stoner-Weiss, Kathryn. 1997. *Local Heroes: The Political Economy of Russian Regional Governance.* Princeton: Princeton University Press.

Tanzi, Vito. 1995. "Fiscal Federalism and Decentralization: A Review of Some Efficiency and Macroeconomic Aspects." *Annual Bank Conference on Development Economics 1994.* Washington, D.C.: International Monetary Fund.

Tendler, Judith. 1997. *Good Government in the Tropics.* Baltimore: Johns Hopkins University Press.

Ter-Minassian, Teresa. 1996. "Decentralization and Macroeconomic Management." International Monetary Fund Working Paper 97/155.

———. 1997. "Brazil." In *Fiscal Federalism in Theory and Practice: A Collection of Essays,* ed. Teresa Ter-Minassian. Washington, D.C.: International Monetary Fund.

Ter-Minassian, Teresa, and Jon Craig. 1997. "Control of Subnational Government Borrowing." In *Fiscal Federalism in Theory and Practice: A Collection of Essays,* ed. Teresa Ter-Minassian. Washington, D.C.: International Monetary Fund.

Tiebout, Charles M. 1956. "A Pure Theory of Local Government Expenditure." *Journal of Political Economy* 64: 416–24.

Tommasi, Mariano, and Pablo Spiller. 2000. *Las fuentes institucionales del desarrollo argentino.* Buenos Aires: Editorial Universitaria de Buenos Aires.

Topik, Steven. 1987. *The Political Economy of the Brazilian State: 1889–1930.* Austin: University of Texas Press.

Tourreilles, Ramiro. 1999. "La Revolución de 1897." In *La Revolución de 1897,* ed. Enrique Mena Segarra. Montevideo: Ediciones de la Plaza.

Treisman, Daniel. 1999. "Political Decentralization and Economic Reform: A Game-Theoretic Analysis." *American Journal of Political Science* 43, no. 2: 488–517.

Trejo, Guillermo, and Claudio Jones. 1998. "Political Dilemmas of Welfare Reform: Poverty and Inequality in Mexico." In *Mexico under Zedillo,* ed. Susan Kaufman Purcell and Luis Rubio. Boulder, Colo.: Lynne Rienner Publishers.

TSE (Tribunal Superior Eleitoral). 2000. "Resultados das Eleições Municipais de 2000." Computer files, www.tse.gov.br. Brasília: TSE.

Turner, Brian. 1998. "The Impact of Decentralization on Political Parties: Political Careers and Party-Building at the Sub-national Level." Paper presented at the Annual Meeting of the Latin American Studies Association, Chicago, Ill.

Urenda Díaz, Juan Carlos. 1998. *La Descentralización Deficiente.* La Paz, Bolivia: Imprenta Landivar S.R.L.

Valenzuela, Arturo. 1977. *Political Brokers in Chile: Local Government in a Centralized Polity.* Durham, N.C.: Duke University Press.

———. 1999. "Chile: Origins and Consolidation of a Latin American Democracy." In *Democracy in Developing Countries: Latin America,* ed. Larry Diamond, Juan Linz, and Seymour Lipset. Boulder, Colo.: Lynne Rienner Publishers.

Valenzuela, J. Samuel. 1992. "Democratic Consolidation in Post-Transitional Settings: Notion, Process, and Facilitating Conditions." In *Issues in Democratic Consolidation: The New South American Democracies in Comparative Perspective,* ed. Scott Mainwaring, Guillermo O'Donnell, and J. Samuel Valenzuela. Notre Dame, Ind.: University of Notre Dame Press.

Van Cott, Donna Lee. 2000. *The Friendly Liquidation of the Past: The Politics of Diversity in Latin America.* Pittsburgh: University of Pittsburgh Press.

Vanger, Milton. 1963. *José Battle y Ordonez of Uruguay: The Creator of His Times.* Cambridge: Harvard University Press.

Vanhanen, Tatu. 1990. *The Process of Democratization: A Comparative Study of 147 States, 1980–88.* New York: Crane Russak.

———. 2000. "A New Dataset for Measuring Democracy, 1810–1998." *Journal of Peace Research* 37: 251–65.

Varas Alfonso, Paulino, and Salvador Mohor Abuauad. 1992. *Reforma regional, provincial y municipal.* Santiago: Editorial Jurídica de Chile.

Varsano, Ricardo. 1997. "A Evolução do Sistema Tributário Brasileiro ao Longo do Século: Anotações e Reflexões para Futuras Reformas." *Pesquisa e Planejamento Econômico* 27, no. 1: 1–46.

Velasco Baraona, Belisario. 1994. "Los Gobiernos Regionales y la Descentralización Administrativa." *El Mercurio* (August 7).

Véliz, Claudio. 1980. *The Centralist Tradition of Latin America.* Princeton: Princeton University Press.

von Hagen, Jürgen, and Barry Eichengreen. 1996. "Federalism, Fiscal Restraints, and European Monetary Union." *American Economic Review* 86: 134–38.

Ward, Peter M., and Victoria E. Rodríguez. 1999. "New Federalism, Intra-Governmental Relations and Co-governance in Mexico." *Journal of Latin American Studies* 31: 673–710.

Weingast, Barry A. 1995. "The Economic Role of Political Institutions: Market-Preserving Federalism and Economic Development." *Journal of Law, Economics, and Organization* 11, no. 1: 1–31.

Wiarda, Howard. 1986. "Social Change, Political Development, and the Latin American Tradition." In *Promise of Development: Theories of Change in*

Latin America, ed. Peter F. Klarén and Thomas J. Bossert. Boulder, Colo.: Westview Press.

Wibbels, Erik. 2001. "Federal Politics and Market Reform in the Developing World." *Studies in Comparative International Development* 36, no. 2 (Summer): 27–53.

Wildasin, David E., ed. 1997. *Fiscal Aspects of Evolving Federations.* New York: Cambridge University Press.

Willis, Eliza J. 1996. "Influencing Industrial Location through Regional and Local Development in Federal States: Some Lessons." *International Review of Administrative Science* 62: 401–11.

Willis, Eliza, Christopher Garman, and Stephan Haggard. 1999. "The Politics of Decentralization in Latin America." *Latin American Research Review* 34, no. 1: 7–56.

Wirth, John D. 1970. *The Politics of Brazilian Development.* Stanford: Stanford University Press.

Wong-Gonzalez, Pablo. 1992. "International Integration and Locational Change in Mexico's Car Industry: Regional Concentration and Deconcentration." In *Decentralization in Latin America: An Evaluation*, ed. Arthur Morris and Stella Lowder. New York: Praeger.

World Bank. 1988. *World Development Report.* New York: Oxford University Press.

———. 1990. *Argentina: Provincial Government Finances.* Washington, D.C.: World Bank.

———. 1996a. *Argentina: The Convertibility Plan: Assessment and Potential Prospects.* Washington, D.C.: World Bank.

———. 1996b. *Argentina: Provincial Finances Study.* Washington, D.C.: World Bank.

———. 1996c. *India: Five Years of Stabilization and Reform and the Challenges Ahead.* Washington, D.C.: World Bank.

———. 1997. *World Development Report: The State in a Changing World.* Washington, D.C.: World Bank/Oxford University Press.

———. 1998. *Argentina: The Fiscal Dimension of the Convertibility Plan.* Washington, D.C.: World Bank.

———. 1999. *Beyond the Center: Decentralizing the State.* Washington, D.C.: World Bank.

———. 2001. *Argentina: Provincial Finances Update.* Washington, D.C.: World Bank.

Xavier, Rafael. 1950. *Campanha Municipalista.* Rio de Janeiro: Serviço Gráfico do IBGE.

Yáñez, José, and Leonardo Letelier. 1995. "Chile." In *Fiscal Decentralization in Latin America*, ed. Ricardo López Murphy. Washington, D.C.: Inter-American Development Bank.

Yashar, Deborah J. 1999. "Democracy, Indigenous Movements, and the Postliberal Challenge in Latin America." *World Politics* 52 (October): 76–104.

Zapata, Juan Antonio. 1999. *Argentina: el BID y los gobiernos subnacionales.* Washington, D.C.: Inter-American Development Bank.

Zegada, María Teresa. 1998. *La Representación Territorial de los Partidos Políticos en Bolivia.* La Paz, Bolivia: ILDIS (Instituto Latinoamericao de Investigaciones Sociales).

Zentner, Alejandro. 1999. "Algunas cuestiones macroeconomicas del federalismo fiscal en la argentina." Paper presented at the Fourth International Conference on Fiscal Federalism, Universidad Nacional de La Plata. La Plata, Argentina, November 26.

Contributors

CAROLINE C. BEER received her Ph.D. from the University of New Mexico in 2000 and is assistant professor of political science at the University of Vermont. Her research focuses on decentralization and electoral politics in Mexico. She is the author of *Electoral Competition and Institutional Change in Mexico* (University of Notre Dame Press, 2002). Her articles have appeared in *Comparative Politics, Latin American Research Review,* and the *American Political Science Review.*

GARY BLAND received his Ph.D. from the Johns Hopkins University School of Advanced International Studies in 1997. He is currently Senior Public Policy and Governance Specialist at the Research Triangle Institute in Washington, D.C. He has served as a decentralization advisor and a Democracy Fellow at the Center for Democracy and Governance of the U.S. Agency for International Development. He specializes in comparative politics and democracy in Latin America, with a particular focus in recent years on decentralization and subnational institutional development. He has written on democratization in Latin America and has published numerous policy papers with USAID and the World Bank. His book manuscript, "Decentralizing to Democratize: The Search for Good Local Governance in Chile and Venezuela," is currently under review.

KENT EATON received his Ph.D in political science from Yale University in 1998 and is currently assistant professor in the department of politics and the Woodrow Wilson School of

Public and International Affairs at Princeton University. His research concentrates on federalism and the politics of economic reform in Latin America and East Asia. He is currently conducting comparative historical research on the design of subnational institutions in South America. He is the author of *Politicians and Economic Reform in New Democracies* (Pennsylvania State University Press, 2002). His research has appeared in *Comparative Politics, Latin American Research Review, Journal of Asian Studies, Journal of Latin American Studies,* and *Development and Change.*

STEPHAN HAGGARD received his Ph.D. in political science from the University of California, Berkeley, in 1983. He is professor at the Graduate School of International Relations and Pacific Studies at the University of California, San Diego, and the Larry and Sally Krause Professor of Korean Studies. His interests are international and comparative political economy, with particular emphasis on the developing countries of East Asia and Latin America. His publications include *Pathways from the Periphery: The Political Economy of Growth in the Newly Industrializing Countries* (Cornell University Press, 1990); *The Political Economy of Democratic Transitions,* with Robert Kaufman (Princeton University Press, 1995), which received the Luebbert Prize of the American Political Science Association for the best book in comparative politics; and *The Political Economy of the Asian Financial Crisis* (Institute for International Economics, 2000). He is currently working on a project with Robert Kaufman on social contracts in East Asia, Latin America, and Central Europe.

ALFRED P. MONTERO received his Ph.D in political science from Columbia University in 1997 and is associate professor of political science at Carleton College. His research focuses on the political economy of decentralization in Latin America and Europe. He is the author of *Shifting States in Global Markets: Subnational Industrial Policy in Contemporary Brazil and Spain* (Pennsylvania State University Press, 2002). He has also published his work in *Latin American Politics and Society, Comparative Politics, Studies in Comparative International Development, Publius: The Journal of Federalism,* and the *Journal of Interamerican Studies and World Affairs.*

KATHLEEN M. O'NEILL received her Ph.D. in government from Harvard University in 1999 and is assistant professor of government at Cornell University. Her research interests lie within the field of comparative politics, in particular, political economy of reform, political parties, and the relationship between political institutions and political and economic outcomes. She has written extensively on decentralization, focusing on the Andean region of Latin America. In her dissertation, "Decentralization in the Andes: Power to the People or Party Politics?" she develops and tests a theory linking decentralization reforms to the electoral incentives of political parties in Bolivia, Peru, Ecuador, Colombia, and Venezuela.

MICHAEL PENFOLD-BECERRA received his Ph.D. in political science from Columbia University in 1999. He was a Fulbright Scholar between 1996 and 1997 and wrote his dissertation on electoral incentives and decentralization outcomes in Colombia and Venezuela. He has taught at the Advanced Institute for Administrative Studies (IESA) in Caracas, Los Andes University in Bogotá, and Columbia College in New York. He is currently the executive director of Venezuela's National Council for Investment Promotion (CONAPRI). His most recent publication is *El Costo Venezuela: Opciones de Política para Mejorar la Competitividad* (Caracas: CAF-CONAPRI, 2002).

DAVID J. SAMUELS received his Ph.D. in political science from the University of California, San Diego, in 1998 and is associate professor of political science at the University of Minnesota. He specializes in the comparative study of political institutions, with particular emphasis on Brazilian politics, electoral systems, political parties, legislatures, and federalism. He is the author of *Ambition, Federalism, and Legislative Politics in Brazil* (Cambridge University Press, 2003). His work has appeared in *Comparative Political Studies, Comparative Politics, Journal of Politics, British Journal of Political Science, Party Politics, Publius: The Journal of Federalism, Journal of Democracy,* and *Legislative Studies Quarterly.*

STEVEN B. WEBB received his Ph.D. in economics from the University of Chicago in 1978 and is a lead economist for the Latin America and Caribbean region at the World Bank, Washington, D.C. He currently does research and operational work on the issues of fiscal decentralization, taxes, political economy of policy reform, and public expenditure management. His publications include *Voting for Reform: The Politics of Adjustment in New Democracies*, coedited with Stephan Haggard (Oxford University Press/World Bank, 1994); *Decentralization and Accountability of the Public Sector in the Caribbean*, coedited with Javed Burki, Guillermo Perry, et al. (World Bank, 2000); and *Achievements and Challenges in Decentralization: Lessons from Mexico*, coedited with Marcelo Giugale (World Bank, 2000).

ERIK WIBBELS received his Ph.D in political science from the University of New Mexico in 2000 and is assistant professor of political science at the University of Washington. His research interests include market transitions in Latin America and comparative federalism. His articles have appeared in *International Organization, Studies in Comparative International Development, American Journal of Political Science, Comparative Political Studies,* and *American Political Science Review.*

Index